Rhetoric as Currency

Number Four:
Presidential Rhetoric Series
Martin J. Medhurst, General Editor

In association with
The Center for Presidential Studies
George Bush School of Government
and Public Service

Davis W. Houck

Rhetoric as Currency

*Hoover, Roosevelt,
and the
Great Depression*

Texas A&M University Press

College Station

Davis Houck, "Reading the Body in the Text: FDR's 1932
Speech to the Democratic National Convention," *The Southern
Communication Journal* 63 (1997), 20–36. Reprinted with the
permission of the Southern States Communication Association.

"Rhetoric as Currency: Herbert Hoover and the 1929 Stock
Market Crash," *Rhetoric and Public Affairs* 3, no. 2 (2000).
Reprinted with the permission of
Michigan State University Press.

Lyrics from "Blood Brothers" by Bruce Springsteen,
copyright 1995 by Bruce Springsteen (ASCAP),
reprinted with permission.

Lyrics from "Reason to Believe" by Bruce Springsteen,
copyright 1982 by Bruce Springsteen (ASCAP),
reprinted with permission.

The paper used in this book meets the minimum requirements
of the American National Standard for Permanence of Paper
for Printed Library Materials,
Z39.48-1984.
Binding materials have been chosen for durability.

Library of Congress Cataloging-in Publication Data

Houck, Davis W.
Rhetoric as currency: Hoover, Roosevelt, and the
Great Depression/Davis W. Houck.—1st ed.
p. cm.—(Presidential rhetoric series ; no. 4)
Includes bibliographical references and index.
ISBN 1-58544-109-0
1. Communication in politics—United States.
2. United States—Economic conditions—1918–1945.
3. United States—Economic policy.
4. Depressions—1929—United States.
I. Title. II. Series.
JA85.2.U6 H68 2001
330.973'0916—dc21
00-010486

To Roy Engle:

"We played king of the mountain out on the end
 The world came chargin' up the hill, and we were
        women and men . . .
 But the stars are burnin' bright like some mystery
        uncovered
 I'll keep movin' through the dark with you in my
        heart
 My blood brother."

—Bruce Springsteen, "Blood Brothers"

Contents

Preface

The beginnings of this book date well before my formative years in graduate school, back to those heady days now known as "The Reagan Revolution." Contrary to what my professor of microeconomics was teaching, I discovered that the "economy" wasn't a carefully delineated and circumscribed series of assumptions. Nor was it a mathematically precise and elegantly drawn diagram on a blackboard. Rather, it was a story. It was a drama with heroes and villains. And it was moved by how we were moved.

This book represents another part of that story, told from the vantage points principally of Herbert Hoover and Franklin D. Roosevelt. It was intended originally to be a study of the Roosevelt administration's famous first 100 days. I wanted to see firsthand just how the heroic FDR saved capitalism in three short months. Even a lousy storyteller couldn't mess this one up. And then along came Herbert Hoover, the grim-faced villain of countless renderings of America's Great Depression. In what was supposed to be merely "background" reading, it became clear that Roosevelt's story couldn't be told without Hoover. Or, perhaps the better word is "shouldn't." To make sense of those first 100 days, Hoover must be in the foreground, seated next to FDR just like that infamous Inauguration Day ride of March 4, 1933. Popular memory has inscribed FDR's inaugural aphorism— "the only thing we have to fear is fear itself"—into the lexicon of the American story. It was sentiment lifted right out of the Hoover years.

Hoover and Roosevelt both understood that the Great Depression was "Great" largely because of a collective state of mind. The "story" had lost its way, and thus had millions of Americans. Legislatively sponsored macroeconomic policy was only a partial solution to a much more profound problem. That was the problem of belief. It was also a macroeconomic problem. And because it was a question of collective belief it was also a rhetorical problem. This is a book about those rhetorical problems and their attempted rhetorical solutions.

I suppose that it's appropriate in a book ostensibly about money to note some of the debts that I've incurred in writing this book—and to repay them, at least textually. Dick Gregg advised the dissertation, where this book initially got its legs. The highest praise that I can give him is that he enabled me to write the dissertation that I wanted to write—warts and all. Marty Medhurst helped me to excise many of those warts; more importantly, his constant encouragement and enthusiasm for the project sustained me in many a dark hour. The words that follow have cardboard around them only because of his many and kind intercessions.

It isn't just dirty laundry that a spouse has to put up with. An academic spouse has also to put up with "dirty" prose, which of course, her husband sees as unblemished. My spouse, Kay Picart, has the innate gift of transforming the ugly into the beautiful. For helping me to see and experience that in these pages and in many other places, she has my undying admiration and affection.

Several other people read and commented upon earlier drafts. To Andy Furman, Dennis Gouran, Jack Spielvogel, Steve Browne, Amos Kiewe, Ray Fleming, Bill Leuchtenburg, and David Henry, my sincere thanks. The flaws that remain are due solely to my own hardheadedness. Thanks are also in order to the staffs of the Herbert Hoover Presidential Library and the Hoover Institution on War, Revolution and Peace. Their efforts and expertise frequently helped to unearth important pieces in the evidentiary puzzle. The Franklin D. Roosevelt Presidential Library proved helpful, largely in spite of its staff.

The talented staff at Texas A&M University Press has been great to work with. My acquiring editor was instrumental in getting the manuscript reviewed in a timely fashion, and her advocacy on behalf of the project will not be soon forgotten. Nor will our sushi dinner. For the care in copyediting the manuscript and catching my many "barbarisms and solecisms," my thanks to my in-house editor and her staff.

And last, just a brief note to my dear friend and "blood brother," Roy Engle, to whom this book is dedicated. Our conversations enliven me, our past makes the present more vibrant, and your love and example sustain me. Always.

Davis W. Houck
Tallahassee

Rhetoric
as Currency

Chapter One

Introduction

For I think it is manifest to all that foreknowledge of future events is not vouchsafed to our human nature, but that we are so far removed from this prescience that Homer, who has been conceded the highest reputation for wisdom, has pictured even the gods as at times debating among themselves about the future—not that he knew their minds but that he desired to show us that for mankind this power lies in the realms of the impossible.
—Isocrates, *Against the Sophists*

For if everyone had recollection of the past, knowledge of the present, and foreknowledge of the future, the power of speech would not be so great. But as it is, when men can neither remember the past nor observe the present nor prophesy the future, deception is easy; so that most men offer opinion as advice to the soul.
—Gorgias, *Helen*

No one has yet seen or touched "the economy." We would never have guessed this, though, given the prolixity that attends it and the figures that purport to measure it. These words and numbers are not insignificant: presidents are voted in or out of office based on the numbers representing it; consumers spend, invest, or hide cash under their mattresses based on how they think it will "perform" in the future; and nations go to war to protect it.

Some who claim the mantle of economic experts would have us believe that the economy is a tangible, living entity, a thing that can be accurately described and observed—even predicted. The founders of the American Economics Association, owing to the Darwinian shift, referred to it as a "living organism."[1] The metaphor seems to have stuck: today, Bill Clinton, among others, talks frequently about "growing" the economy. Yet the precision implied by naming and numbering the economy should not deceive us from the truth of the matter. "Faith," after all, is the master metaphor that accompanies much of the talk about economics, and, as Robert M. Pirsig so trenchantly notes, when people are zealously dedicated to political or religious faiths, "it's always because these dogmas or goals are in doubt."[2] Murray Edelman contends further that talk of "economic faith" is to be expected, given the cognitive anxieties that usually attend the future.[3] We need to believe, and economic discourse—professional, academic, or otherwise—provides us with what Kenneth Burke terms our "secular prayer."

The significance of how the economy is symbolized has not escaped some academic economists. They comprise a contemporary movement known loosely as "the rhetoric of economics." The group's bible is Donald McCloskey's 1985 text, *The Rhetoric of Economics*. The book began a "new conversation" in economics, one concerned more with metaphors, stories, and rhetorical strategies than with testable hypotheses, observable data, and nonlinear multivariate regression analyses.

To date, the movement has produced an impressive volume of research. Yet, almost without exception, the "conversation" remains attached to a rigidly circumscribed set of rhetorical issues, principally, how academic economists talk among themselves. This has occurred despite leading exponents' admonitions to show "how the rhetoric matters to policy and in distinguishing the good stories of policy from the bad" and to attend to the terms with which ordinary citizens apprehend economic reality.[4]

But to analyze economic policy or to examine nonacademic economic rhetoric is, according to John Kenneth Galbraith, to sacrifice one's "tribal position" in the academic pecking order.[5] Institutions and disciplines are often antithetical to "conversations" insofar as they function to constrain admissible statements.[6] Given this, it remains for "outsiders" either divested of economic intratribalism or participating in a different "conversation" to plumb the importance and possibilities of economic rhetoric originating beyond the campus gates. This is my principal task—one that, as Geoff Hodgson notes, "requires interdisciplinary study which is neither fashionable nor encouraged by the structure of academia."[7]

My point of departure, ironically, is informed by an academic economist, John Maynard Keynes, who, despite his Cambridge pedigree and his Bloomsbury elitism, was never far from the wrangle of policy; in fact, his magnum opus, *The General Theory of Employment, Interest, and Money*, was written in response to the world-wide depression of the 1930s.

Keynes's diagnosis of the Great Depression was fairly complex, but his prescriptions were unambiguous and to the point: large-scale government spending financed by private dollars. But such prescriptions addressed only the material side of the Keynesian calculus for economic recovery; inseparable from economic public policy was an "immaterial" solution—namely, belief or confidence fostered by presidential rhetoric.

Keynes's acolytes and critics have searched high and low for what he "really" meant, but his remarks regarding rhetoric's role in fostering economic recovery are as lucid as the oracular Keynes gets. For example, in *A General Theory*, Keynes states, "Most, probably, of our decisions to do something positive, the full consequences of which will be drawn out over many days to come, can only be taken as a result of animal spirits—of a spontaneous urge to action rather than inaction, and not as the outcome of a weighted average of qualitative benefits multiplied by quantitative probabilities." He continues, "Thus if the animal spirits are dimmed and the spontaneous optimism falters, leaving us to depend on nothing but a mathematical expectation, enterprise will fade and die;—though fears of loss may have a basis no more reasonable than hopes of profit had before. It is safe to say that enterprise which depends on hopes stretching into the future benefits the community as a whole."[8]

In *The Means to Prosperity*, Keynes ads, "If our poverty were due to famine or earthquake or war—if we lacked material things and the resources to produce them, we could not expect to find the Means to Prosperity except in hard work, abstinence, and invention. In fact, our predicament is notoriously of another kind." "It comes," he concludes, "from some failure in the immaterial devices of the mind, in the working of the motives which should lead to the decisions and acts of will, necessary to put in movement the resources and technical means we already have."[9] And in the same text, regarding the long-term rate of interest, Keynes notes, "This requires a combination of manœuvres by the Government and the Central Bank in the shape of open-market operations by the Bank, of well-judged Conversion Schemes by the Treasury, and of a restoration of financial confidence by a Budget policy approved by public opinion and in other ways."[10] Finally, in a rejoinder in the *Quarterly Journal of Economics*, Keynes concludes, "The orthodox theory assumes that we have a knowledge of the future of a kind quite different from that which we actually possess. This false rationalization follows the lines of the Benthamite calculus." Furthermore, "The hypothesis of a calculable future leads to a wrong interpretation of the principles of behavior which the need for action compels us to adopt, and to an underestimation of the concealed factors of utter doubt, precariousness, hope and fear."[11]

The reinvigoration of "animal spirits," the movement of the "immaterial devices of the mind," fiscal policy grounded on public opinion, and the alleviation of fear, doubt, and precariousness were not the sorts of solutions that academic economists could or would carry out. It would take a rhetorical-minded political leader, someone who could reach the masses (or aggregates) so vital to national economic recovery, to fulfill Keynes's advice. This counsel is typically associated with the legislation of the New Deal and the rhetoric of hope and optimism preached by its eloquent spokesman, Franklin Delano Roosevelt. There is historical precedent for the association: Keynes implored Roosevelt by correspondence and personal visitation, and Keynes's policy of deficit spending was eventually embraced—albeit reluctantly—by Roosevelt in 1938. Less well known is the extent to which Keynes's counsel, particularly his emphasis on confidence, optimism, and hope for the economic future, was actively practiced by Roosevelt's predecessor, Herbert Hoover.

Presidential rhetoric and its relationship to the economy and to economic recovery, though, has yet to be systematically explored by rhetoricians, economists, historians, political scientists, or biographers. The Great Depression and the presidential rhetoric it engendered, moreover, have been largely ignored by rhetorical critics, a perplexing and troubling omission when we consider its profound influence on American political, social, and economic life. Both silences inform my primary objective: to write a rhetorical history of the period from 1929 to 1933 from the vantage point of economics and the presidency. Why this subject, these presidents, and this time period?

Rhetoric as Currency

If Keynes's belief concerning rhetoric's role in promoting economic recovery were idiosyncratic, we might be more inclined to dismiss it or perhaps ignore it. Yet his belief has several influential contemporary advocates. Robert Heilbroner, echoing Edelman, argues that we have "a profound human need" to hear utterances about the future. Moreover, such utterances "can affect the movement of the real economy just as decisively as they can affect the prices of securities."[12] The "real economy," the antithesis of "blackboard economics," is thus influenced by "real" rhetoric.[13]

In his seminal text on the Great Depression, Galbraith repeatedly alludes to rhetoric's pivotal role in delaying the tide of doubt that eventually overwhelmed Wall Street in October, 1929.[14] Public speaking, augmented by highly publicized acts of faith by perceived economic "experts," functioned to keep the naysayers at bay—at least for a while. Galbraith suggests that, "by affirming solemnly that prosperity will continue, it is believed, one can help insure that prosperity will in fact continue. Especially among businessmen the faith in the efficiency of such incantation is very great."[15] Galbraith's text is a testament to the destructive powers of such economic incantation.

Not to be outdone by his more traditional colleagues, McCloskey argues that "words are in fact efficacious in economics, because markets live on the lips of men and women. . . . The economy depends today on the promises made yesterday in view of the expectations about tomorrow." Invoking a quotation often mis-attributed to Herbert Hoover, she ads, "We can in fact (and in word) create prosperity by declaring it to be just around the corner. One is tempted to conclude that economies, and economics, are 'mere' matters or words . . . that words after all do have the magical power to make us safe and happy."[16]

Keynes, Heilbroner, Galbraith, and McCloskey—no economic lightweights—all point to a similar set of extraordinary possibilities: rhetoric as palpable currency; thoughts, beliefs, and emotions constitute and create our economic realities; and markets are propped up on the edifice of discourse. Or, in the Keynesian vernacular, persuasive rhetoric is the great "multiplier." Our four "modern" economists and their musings on the relationship between rhetoric and economics might have found favor with that omniscient patriarch of economic thought, Adam Smith. In his unfinished work on the history of astronomy, Smith suggests that rhetoric plays a most important role in domesticating the anxieties associated with social upheaval [17] Rhetoric, in other words, might mitigate the material damages resulting from unexpected social traumas. [18]

Each of the views articulated by these economists addresses the single most problematic issue plaguing academic inquiry this century—namely, the future and the uncertainty that always attends it. Writing in 1890, Alfred Marshall, one of the architects of modern economic thought, stated that the "element of time is the centre of the chief difficulty of almost every academic problem." [19] Despite the passing of time, the problem remains at the crucible of contemporary economic debate. That debate, moreover, has profoundly rhetorical implications that Keynes and his contemporary interpreters and followers (who label themselves Post Keynesians) anticipated and recognized.

As Philip Mirowski has chronicled, the economics discipline has self-consciously patterned its modes of inquiry on physics. [20] The analogy, of course, was flawed from the outset: predictions about human economic behavior often share little in common with predictions about natural phenomena. As such, to have any predictive power, economists, particularly neoclassical economists, have to make certain assumptions both about the models they use to describe economic behavior and the human beings represented by those models. These assumptions are objectionable to most Post Keynesians. [21]

The first and perhaps most important assumption guiding most neoclassical inquiry is a belief that we can accurately predict the economic future. Post Keynesians disagree: the economic future, to varying degrees, is always unstable, hence unknowable. [22] Or, as Stephen D. Parsons notes, Post Keynesians "reject any understanding of the future as 'predictable' by economic agents." [23] The disagreement between the two schools stems in part from how each views the human individual. Within the neoclassical framework, the economic "agent" is the transhistorical, rational utility maximizer who acts and reacts based on "perfect information." The human being within the Post Keynesian paradigm is a social, psychological, and historical being who interprets economic data selectively, if at all. Especially in times of economic flux, economic expectations about the future are uncertain. Robert Skidelsky, Keynes's most accomplished biographer, states that "the central message of the General Theory [*The General Theory of Employment, Interest, and Money*] was . . . that rational agents were bound to have uncertain expectations—expectations without probabilities." [24] Uncertainty, of course, makes for a very awkward bedfellow with theory. Alexander Dow and Sheila Dow capture the exaggerated fears of the neoclassicists: "if all decision-making is subject to the exogenous influence of expectation shifts, economists must retreat into nihilism." [25] Stated differently, neoclassical models simply cannot function with such a view of economic behavior; nihilism is thus rendered as atheoretical.

Far from nihilistic, Post Keynesians treat economic uncertainty within the broad parameters of a creative humanism. That is, "in a Keynesian world, a non-ergodic world, there are no inevitable, pre-defined paths to the economy. Agents have to create by themselves their own images of sequels and act on them. As a result, history will result from the fusion of men's actions."[26] While De Carvalho's emphasis on individual autonomy in a macroeconomic world might be objectionable, his emphasis on a creative economic reality, as opposed to a predetermined, fixed one, accurately reflects the Post Keynesian position that uncertainty is the wellspring from which economic possibility springs. As Paul Davidson notes, economic reality is thus treated as "transmutable or creative in the sense that the economic future can be created by current and future human actions."[27] So, rather than dismiss economic uncertainty as a stumbling block to economic theory, Post Keynesians see it as the starting point from which to create economic reality.

Importantly, though, Post Keynesians do not treat economic uncertainty as good in and of itself; rather, it needs to be reduced to create a positive economic climate. This point is underscored by several empirical studies that examine the role of uncertainty and its relationship to the Great Depression. Christina D. Romer, Paul R. Flacco and Randall E. Parker, and J. Peter Ferderer and David A. Zalewski have all concluded that increased levels of uncertainty functioned to exacerbate the depth and duration of the crisis.[28] In fact, Flacco and Parker conclude that income uncertainty "provides a virtually complete explanation for the initial decline in consumption that marks the onset of the Great Depression."[29] Once that decline began in earnest and uncertainty was replaced by pessimism, L. M. Lachmann notes, "it became obvious that pessimistic expectations may not only prevent recovery . . . but [they] actually set in motion multiplier processes of contraction."[30]

The economic implications of Lachmann's claim are hard to overstate: expectations about the economic future function to influence the economy today.[31] The point is fundamental to Keynes and Post Keynesians: "Keynes specifically accepted the notion that any change in expected future market demand will instantaneously alter all current (spot) market prices."[32] The rhetorical implications of the Post Keynesian logic are also hard to overstate; in fact, the rhetorical implications cannot exist independently from the economic implications. The act of *shaping* expectations about the economic future is, par excellence, the role of the rhetorician, particularly a person who can reach a "macroeconomic" audience—the president, in other words. As George Katona notes, in altering economic behavior "it is mass dynamics that matters most to the nation, not interpersonal differences that cancel out."[33] Perhaps more than any other public figure, the president attempts to engender the "mass dynamics" through a mass medium to shape economic expectations. It is no coincidence, then, that Keynes's economic epistemology "highlighted persuasion as a vehicle for transmitting grounds for belief."[34] Within Keynes's organic, non-ergodic economic system, the "selective choice of words" is the "instrument of human action whereby [the] world is changed."[35]

For Keynes and Post Keynesians words matter—perhaps so much so that not much else matters. To date, though, despite the importance of economic rhetoric for this school of thought, they have failed to consider "the processes through which expectations are formed and the social culture and structures which give them colour and substance."[36] Stated differently, "although there is a rich analysis of the effects of expectations about the future on present economic behavior, there appears to be very little on the determinants of these expectations."[37] This project is aimed, in part, at exploring some of these determinants, especially as they are manifested in the presidential rhetorical practices of Herbert Hoover and Franklin Roosevelt.

Epistemological, Social, and Economic Crisis

To examine rhetoric's relationship to economic recovery presupposes economic downturn or collapse, and collapse—economic, social, and epistemological—is an appropriate designation for what the nation experienced following the stock market crash of 1929. By the close of Hoover's presidency, the Great Depression neared its apogee. One in every three industrial workers was unemployed.[38] The nation's Gross National Product was barely half of its pre-crash level. Total personal savings dropped from $4.2 billion to a net deficit of $900 million. Prices plunged dramatically: wool dropped from nearly $1 per pound to 45 cents; wheat flour dropped from $5.79 to $3.10 per 100 pounds; the price of steak plummeted from 46 cents a pound to 29 cents. The only things that seemed to be increasing were murders, suicides, and the prison population. The total number of homicides increased from over 9,600 to more than 12,100. The nation's suicide rate jumped from 13.9 per 100,000 to 17.4 (not surprisingly, nearly all of the increase was observed among working age males). The total prison population soared from 120,000 to nearly 138,000.

Just how bad was it? As one indication, on July 28, 1932, the U.S. Army temporarily declared war on its own. Veterans from World War I had been streaming into the nation's capitol since June. They were there to lobby Congress for extra income promised them in 1925. After the Senate rejected the "Bonus Bill," coupled with veterans' unwillingness to leave their "Hoovervilles" constructed along the Anacostia Flats, soldiers led by Douglas MacArthur literally chased them out of the city. To insure their permanent evacuation, the crowd, tear-gassed and trampled by horses, watched as their makeshift dwellings were set aflame and destroyed.

Economic knowledge, as then construed, also experienced an unprecedented crisis as the predicted cyclical adjustment upward never materialized. Classical economists assumed that the economy, perhaps with the aid of the Federal Reserve or after mass liquidation, would automatically adjust itself and thereby trigger a new cycle of growth. The "reliable" orthodoxies simply did not hold: consumers did not spend despite the lowest prices in decades; businesses did not invest in capital despite extremely low rates of interest; and industries laid off workers en masse despite rapidly declining wage rates. Capitalism as a viable economic system came under serious questioning.[39]

Within this context of economic, social, and epistemological crisis and uncertainty, Hoover and Roosevelt spoke to millions of Americans. The nation's worst depression thus provides an excellent backdrop for examining their rhetorical efforts to facilitate economic recovery.

Hoover and Roosevelt—A Perennial Comparison

No two twentieth-century presidents are more frequently and inexorably linked than Herbert Hoover and Franklin Roosevelt. Popular political mythology has it that the effervescent governor from New York swept into the nation's capitol to expel the misanthropic, laissez faire mining engineer sorely out of touch with the American people. The veracity of the story has its corresponding imagery in the famous inauguration-day ride. To Roosevelt's right sits the taciturn, stolid Hoover, who is responsible for the nation's most severe economic depression. Smiles, let alone waves, to the crowd-lined streets are not forthcoming from him. Roosevelt, meanwhile, plays to the crowd, tipping his hat, waving, and smiling to the anxious onlookers. "Happy days" would indeed revisit the nation. That ride, perhaps more than any other event, encapsulates how the nation has remembered the presidencies of Hoover and Roosevelt.[40] But as with all historical mythologies, the images obfuscate more than they reveal.

As a researcher, it is easy to become ensnared in the provocative Roosevelt phalanx, what Eliot A. Rosen calls "an incredible mythology," in which the lines demarcating biography and hagiography are frequently blurred beyond recognition.[41] Roosevelt overcomes polio; Roosevelt successfully battles New York City's Tammany bosses; Roosevelt heroically flies to Chicago to receive the Democratic presidential nomination; Roosevelt saves capitalism through sweeping fiscal and institutional reforms; and Roosevelt saves the world from Nazi domination. This is the stuff of political legend. Very infrequently do we remember Roosevelt the philanderer, the aloof father, the untrusting friend, the back-biting assistant secretary of the navy, the failed vice presidential candidate, the flip-flopping presidential candidate, the manipulative administrator, or the egocentric fourth-term president.

The same sort of uncritical historical acceptance often pervades accounts of Hoover's presidency—albeit toward libelous ends. Hoover's political idealism, his philanthropic and humanitarian largess, and his unprecedented public policies have been largely shunned or forgotten. Instead, emphasis has been placed on his dislike for large crowds, his seeming unwillingness to compromise, and his disdain for the White House press corp. Always the reader is reminded of Secretary of State Henry Stimson's diary depiction:

"being in a room with Hoover is like sitting in a bath of ink." In sum, it is tempting to begin our inquiry after the motorcade arrived at the Capitol and as Roosevelt uttered the epigram forever associated with his presidency: "the only thing we have to fear is fear itself." Such a start, though, prefigures its ending. More important, it would completely ignore some of the rhetorical and legislative antecedents for Roosevelt's New Deal.

Some might find it oxymoronic to talk of the Hooverian antecedents to the New Deal; clearly, many would argue, there was a radical discontinuity between the two administrations and their approaches to the Great Depression. Such a view, though, owes much more to "partisan mythology" than historical fact.[42] The ideological continuity between the two administrations has been explored in some detail, and I will not attempt to explicate the entire literature here. I will only make mention of a few compelling accounts given by historical figures extremely close to both administrations.[43]

In 1935 the nation's most influential journalist, Walter Lippmann, claimed that Roosevelt's legislative measures represented "a continuous evolution of the Hoover measures."[44] Perhaps more persuasive are the accounts of two ground-floor architects of the New Deal, Raymond Moley and Rexford G. Tugwell. Moley, the chief rhetorical strategist and policy maker of the early New Deal, recalled that "when we all burst into Washington after the inauguration, we found every essential idea enacted in the 100-day Congress in the Hoover Administration itself."[45] Tugwell spoke of Roosevelt's "amazing resemblance to Hoover" and claimed that "practically the whole New Deal was extrapolated from programs that Hoover started."[46] More than thirty years after the early New Deal, and in the twilight of their lives, Tugwell wrote to Moley that an article Tugwell had written on Hoover "accords, I think, with your notion that we were too hard on a man who really invented most of the devices we used."[47]

Hoover and Roosevelt, as I will illustrate, both believed that public confidence was vital to economic recovery; both men, as such, could rightly be described as Keynesians, perhaps even Post Keynesians. A key point of departure, though, involves how they attempted to create public confidence and the relative weight that each ascribed to it. Roosevelt was at a distinct advantage in the game of economic symbolization: he not only employed a skilled staff of speech writers, but he also had Hoover's ineffectual example before him. Thus, Hoover's public response to the Great Depression provides an important grid for understanding the rhetorical strategies and successes his successor eventually employed and enjoyed.

But, aside from providing mere salad dressing for Roosevelt, Hoover's economic rhetoric provides a revealing window through which to view how a complex man attempted to solve a complex problem. And yet, many historians and rhetoricians have either downplayed, or completely overlooked, what Hoover introduced. Why? The possibilities are many, but Hoover had the serious misfortune of preceding Franklin Roosevelt, the consequences of which were not lost on Lippmann. He correctly predicted that "when the genuine histories come to be written scholars will not treat the Hoover Administration as a thing in itself."[48] More than sixty years later, Lippmann's prophecy continues to be played out. Such treatment does not surprise Stephen Skowronek, who insightfully notes that "it is no accident that the presidents most widely celebrated for their mastery of American politics have been immediately preceded by presidents generally judged politically incompetent."[49] Nor could Lippmann's claims have surprised Alfred Rollins, who observes that Hoover became "merely the polar opposite of those characteristics popularly arrogated to Roosevelt. He became the man that Roosevelt was not, a mere foil for his artful and persuasive adversary." Hoover thus became a "simplistic symbol for a whole era of history."[50] Ellis W. Hawley concurs: "Hoover remained an anti-Roosevelt. His activities served as backdrops or foils for the progressive innovations of the New Deal, and his accepted interpreters were historians primarily concerned with tracing, exploring, and celebrating the 'Roosevelt Revolution.'"[51]

Lippmann, Skowronek, Rollins, and Hawley each not-so-subtly suggest that the "problem" does not inhere in Herbert Hoover or Franklin Roosevelt, but in those writing about them; in other words, interpretations depend upon the personal and political convictions of the particular chronicler. Given the extent to which both men have become rhetorically charged symbols, it should not surprise us that things get a bit mixed up. Murray Rothbard, a historian by no means divested of partisanship, notes that "it is one of the great ironies of historiography that the founder of every single one of the features of Franklin Roosevelt's New Deal was to become enshrined among historians and the general public as the last stalwart defender of laissez-faire."[52] While the specifics of Rothbard's claim can be disputed, his general claim is true: Herbert Hoover, even today, remains a badly misunderstood president. This study will attempt to treat the Hoover administration both as an important precursor to the New Deal and as a "thing in itself." My aims are thus two-fold: to explore the relationship between presidential economic rhetoric and economic recovery, and, in doing the former, to gain a more thorough understanding of two complex presidents.

Matters of Method

Rhetoric's relationship to the economy and to economic recovery provides our thematic focus, the Great Depression offers the overarching historical context, and Herbert Hoover and Franklin Roosevelt function as our protagonists. The question, then, is how to proceed. Public address scholarship provides us with some alternatives. One possibility is to engage in "close readings" of significant texts. Two interrelated problems arise from this possibility.

First, just how close is close? A line-by-line and word-by-word reading sacrifices breadth for depth. Second, such a reading poses the question of selection and significance: with our very limited space, what texts should we choose, and for what reasons? The methodological quandary is extremely important, for our choice will determine what "counts" as rhetorical history. My historical prejudice, perhaps stuck forever in the modernist quagmire, is to aim for accuracy that arises from sheer coverage. I have neither the desire or the temerity to generalize about historical events, personages or meanings based on "representative" rhetorical samples. This is a roundabout way of saying that I have opted to do things the hard way. What emerges in the chapters that follow is based on a reading of Hoover's rhetorical corpus from March 4, 1929, through March 3, 1933, and a reading of Roosevelt's rhetorical corpus from January 3, 1930, through June 16, 1933. As Amos Kiewe notes, such a "longitudinal" approach to the study of rhetoric enables the critic to isolate "setbacks, changes, modifications, consistencies and inconsistencies."[53] It also gives more historical weight, according to Kathleen J. Turner, to interpretive claims insofar as it "provides an understanding of rhetoric as a process rather than as simply a product."[54]

How do I read this plethora of texts? My critical approach to the study is perhaps best represented by two seemingly divergent metaphors employed by Robert L. Scott and Martin J. Medhurst. Both conceive of critical practice as a journey. Scott's critical destination is Serendip, a place reached by "tripping," "stumbling," and going "astray."[55] Systematic readings, not readings committed to a system, provide the critical compass. Occasional detours, dead-ends and fortuitous hunches mark such journeys.

Medhurst, on the other hand, posits a more linear journey, guided by critical "landmarks" from the past. Such markers "point the way to where we still must go."[56] So conceived, the critic should travel with both eyes on the terrain ahead, but with frequent and careful looks backward.

The metaphors differ more in degree than in kind. Both openly eschew what I would term the "interstate," or theoretically driven, approach to rhetorical criticism. This approach, so pervasive in critical circles, offers a faster, less complicated, and safer route to a given destination. Moreover, the destination is known well in advance, and the travel time is predictable. Most interstate criticism is extremely boring, the view is lousy, and the food is bland. Only the occasional rumble strips jar us from our critical slumber.

Textually oriented critics, as Scott and Medhurst intimate, follow their instincts. They proceed on their hunches. Mistakes are always instructive, as they often reveal other points of access. These "back-road" critics never proceed blindly, though. Each move is carefully calculated based on the immediate landscape, and previous adventures always provide the internal compass. They are Burke's intrepid *bricoleurs* and use "all that there is to use" in confronting "nature's" labyrinths: "so we must keep trying anything and everything, improving, borrowing from others, developing from others, dialectically using one text as comment upon another, schematizing; using the incentive to new wanderings, returning from these excursions to schematize again."[57] They are also Keynes's peregrinators, those who traverse the economic landscape not from a single theoretical map, but from a variety of alternatives suggested by the immediate landscape.[58] Only upon reaching the critical destination can we fully map or retrace the route—and the point of origin always looks different with hindsight. Perhaps not surprisingly, an avid mountain climber, I. A. Richards, best summarizes my critical cynosure:

> Critical principles, in fact, need wary handling. They can never be a substitute for discernment though they may assist us to avoid unnecessary blunders. There has hardly ever been a critical rule, principle or maxim which has not been for wise men a helpful guide but for fools, a will-'o-the-wisp. . . . Even the most sagacious critical principles may, as we shall see, become merely a cover for critical ineptitude; and the most trivial or baseless generalisation may really mask good and discerning judgment. Everything turns upon how the principles are applied. It is to be feared that critical formulas, even the best, are responsible for more bad judgment than good, because it is far easier to forget their subtle sense and apply them crudely than to remember it and apply them finely.[59]

I should emphasize, though, that I am not doing "John Rambo" criticism. Such aimless wanderings, as our hero quickly learns, will get you in trouble with the authorities. My critical point of departure is economic. Hence, I will examine memoranda, telegrams, correspondence, speech drafts, press releases, messages, and addresses that broach economic matters. Several questions will guide my initial forays: how is recovery envisaged or conceived? How do Hoover and Roosevelt attempt to form economic expectations? Is recovery contingent upon non-economic factors? If so, what are they? What are the rhetorical strategies and tactics that recur over time? Which ones drop out? Why? Are there rhetorical disjuncts between Hoover and Roosevelt? Do Hoover and Roosevelt acknowledge rhetoric's role in facilitating economic recovery? If so, in what ways? How does the public, the press, and "the economy" appear to respond?

Looking Forward

In chapters 2 and 3, I examine Herbert Hoover's presidential economic rhetoric. In chapter 2, I argue that Hoover's ability to deal effectively with the crash was circumvented by a rhetorical paradox of his own making. Hoover initially contextualized the crash and its aftermath within the sphere of emotionalism, yet he disparaged presidential rhetoric precisely because it engaged the emotions.

Chapter Three covers the final two years of the Hoover presidency—a period during which his economic rhetoric shifted radically. Early in 1931, Hoover contextualized the depression as a war, and he waged it on two fronts: against the invisible forces of depression and against the advocates of large-scale federal relief. The former was fought with secular confidence and a devotion to Christ's teachings. The latter was fought by strict historical fidelity to the nation's founding documents and its founding principles. Both enemies were to be vanquished by a Christian/civic faith, not federal legislation. Hoover's rhetorical battle, though, grew silent following his realization that federal legislation was needed. He turned instead to the White House press corps to advertise the unprecedented legislative measures passed early in 1932, a major tactical error given the animosity between the president and the press.

In chapters 4, 5, and 6, I examine governor, presidential candidate, president-elect, and finally, president Franklin Roosevelt's economic rhetoric. In Chapter 4, I attempt to illustrate the extent to which Roosevelt's economic rhetoric is explicable in light of Hoover's legislative and rhetorical response to the Great Depression. Roosevelt, though, made some important amendments, most notably the relationships among sickness, health, and economic recovery. These relationships achieved their most eloquent expression in Roosevelt's July 2 speech to the Democratic National Convention.

In chapter 5, I examine candidate Roosevelt's post-Chicago campaign rhetoric—in a campaign marked by many apparent policy contradictions but recurring rhetorical strategies. Such strategies involved the role of confidence in fostering economic recovery, the translation of economic phenomenon into human/bodily terms, and the relationship of health and sickness to economic recovery. A major shift in rhetorical strategy occurred late in the campaign, as Roosevelt realized that he would win the election. The shift, a move away from health and sickness to economic warfare, presaged many of the rhetorical and legislative events following his inauguration on March 4, 1933.

These events are chronicled and explored in chapter 6, which begins with the four-month interregnum period and ends with the close of the Roosevelt administration's first one hundred days. The chapter is written, in part, from the vantage point of Raymond Moley, chief strategist during both periods. Beginning with the banking crisis and extending through to the creation of the National Industrial Recovery Act (NIRA), the administration's overriding concern was with public confidence—confidence created both by presidential rhetoric and by the sheer volume of legislative activity. In the final chapter I summarize, draw conclusions, identify implications, and discuss possibilities for further research.

Notes

1. See, for example, the "traditionalists" versus "reformists" debates in *Science* 7 (1886): 221–28, 265–71, 375–82, 485–91, 529–33, and 538–42. From volume 8 see pp. 3–6, 14–19, 25–26, 46–48, 81–87, and 103–105. See also Philip Mirowski, ed., *Natural Images in Economic Thought*.

2. Robert M. Pirsig, *Zen and the Art of Motorcycle Maintenance*, p. 134.

3. Murray Edelman, *The Symbolic Uses of Politics*.

4. Donald N. McCloskey, *If You're So Smart: The Narrative of Economic Expertise*, p. 150; Warren J. Samuels, " 'Truth' and 'Discourse' in the Social Construction of Reality: An Essay on the Relation of Knowledge to Socioeconomic Policy," *Journal of Post Keynesian Economics* 13 (1991): 511–24.

5. John Kenneth Galbraith, "The Language of Economics," in *Economics, Peace and Laughter*, ed. Andrea D. Williams, pp. 37–40.

6. Jean-Francois Lyotard, *The Postmodern Condition: A Report on Knowledge*, trans. Geoff Bennington and Brian Massumi, p. 17; John Kenneth Galbraith, "Economics as a System of Belief," in *Economics, Peace and Laughter*, p. 64.

7. Geoff Hodgson, "Persuasion, Expectations and the Limits to Keynes," in *Keynes' Economics*, ed. Tony Lawson and Hashem Pesaran, p. 39.

8. John Maynard Keynes, *A General Theory of Employment, Interest, and Money*, pp. 161–62.

9. John Maynard Keynes, *The Means to Prosperity*, p. 5.

10. Keynes, *The Means to Prosperity*, p. 21.

11. J. M. Keynes, "The General Theory of Employment," *The Quarterly Journal of Economics* 48 (1937): 222.

12. Robert Heilbroner, "Reflections: Economic Predictions," *New Yorker,* July 8, 1991, p. 70.

13. For a detailed, and humorous, discussion about blackboard economics, see Donald N. McCloskey, *Knowledge and Persuasion in Economics*.

14. John Kenneth Galbraith, *The Great Crash*, pp. 42, 78, 94, 105–106, 149, and 174.

15. Galbraith, *The Great Crash*, p. 21.

16. McCloskey, *If You're So Smart*, pp. 108–109.

17. Adam Smith, *Essays on Philosophical Subjects*, ed. W. P. D. Wightman and J. C. Bryce, pp. 34–37.

18. Charles Bazerman, paraphrasing Smith, claims that public accounts of a social trauma "calm the collective mind and allow order to ensue" ("Money Talks: The Rhetorical Project of the *Wealth of Nations*," in *Economics and Language*, ed. Willie Henderson, Tony Dudley-Evans and Roger Backhouse, p. 132).

19. Alfred Marshall, *Principles of Economics*, p. vii.

20. Philip Mirowski, *More Heat than Light*.

21. They are also objectionable to a number of other schools of economic thought, including Marxists, Austrians, Institutionalists, and Feminists, to name just a few.

22. Rossana Bonadei, "John Maynard Keynes: Contexts and Methods," in *John Maynard Keynes: Language and Method*, ed. Alessandra Marzola and Francesco Silva, trans. Richard Davies, p. 55.

23. Stephen D. Parsons, "Time, Expectations and Subjectivism: Prolegomena to a Dynamic Economics," *Cambridge Economic Journal* 15 (1991): 407.

24. Robert Skidelsky, "Keynes' Philosophy of Practice and Economic Policy," in *Keynes as Philosopher-Economist*, ed. Rod M. O'Donnell, p. 120.

25. Alexander Dow and Sheila Dow, "Animal Spirits and Rationality," in *Keynes' Economics*, p. 46. As a response to this potential "retreat into nihilism," economists have constructed an elaborate edifice to render expectations less volatile, hence predictable. That school of thought is known by the somewhat

oxymoronic label of Rational Expectations.
For the foundations of Rational Expectations,
see John F. Muth, "Rational Expectations and
the Theory of Price Movements," *Econometrica* 29 (1961): 315–35. For a devastating
critique of Rational Expectations, see Paul
Davidson, "Reality and Economic Theory,"
Journal of Post Keynesian Economics 18 (1996):
479–508.

26. Fernando J. Cardim De Carvalho, "Keynes
on Probability, Uncertainty, and Decision
Making," *Journal of Post Keynesian Economics*
11 (1988): 77.

27. Paul Davidson, "Uncertainty in Economics," in *Keynes, Knowledge and Uncertainty*, ed.
Sheila Dow and John Hillard, p. 108; see also
Rod O'Donnell, "Keynes on Probability, Expectations and Uncertainty," in *Keynes as Philosopher-Economist*, p. 16.

28. Christina D. Romer, "The Great Crash
and the Onset of the Great Depression," *Quarterly Journal of Economics* 105 (1990):
597–624; Paul R. Flacco and Randall E.
Parker, "Income Uncertainty and the Onset
of the Great Depression," *Economic Inquiry*
30 (1992): 154–71; J. Peter Ferderer and
David A. Zalewski, "Uncertainty as a Propagating Force in The Great Depression," *Journal of Economic History* 54 (1994): 825–49.

29. Flacco and Parker, "Income Uncertainty
and the Onset of the Great Depression,"
p. 169.

30. L. M. Lachmann, "G. L. S. Shackle's Place
in the History of Subjectivist Thought," in
Unknowledge and Choice in Economics, ed.
Stephen F. Frowen, p. 5.

31. Davidson, "Reality and Economic Theory," p. 485.

32. Paul Davidson, *Post Keynesian Macroeconomic Theory*, p. 302; see also, Parsons,
"Time, Expectations and Subjectivism: Prolegomena to a Dynamic Economics," p. 419.

33. George Katona, *Essays on Behavioral
Economics*, p. 35.

34. Sheila Dow, "Keynes' Epistemology
and Economic Methodology," in *Keynes as
Philosopher-Economist*, p. 146.

35. Roy J. Rotheim, "Keynes and the Language of Probability and Uncertainty,"

Journal of Post Keynesian Economics 11 (1988):
90.

36. Geoff Hodgson, "Persuasion, Expectations
and the Limits to Keynes," in *Keynes' Economics*, p. 16.

37. Philip Arestis, *The Post-Keynesian Approach to Economics*, p. 100.

38. These statistics come from *The Statistical
History of the United States: From Colonial
Times to the Present.*

39. Richard P. Adelstein, "'The Nation as an
Economic Unit': Keynes, Roosevelt, and the
Managerial Ideal," *Journal of American His-
tory* 78 (1991): 160–87.

40. The ride was pictured in newspapers
across the country on March 5, 1933. It also
figures prominently in *FDR: A Documentary.*

41. Eliot A. Rosen, *Hoover, Roosevelt and the
Brains Trust*, p. 123.

42. Walter Lippmann, "The Permanent New
Deal," *Yale Review* 24 (1935): 651.

43. The most complete historiographical
summary of the two administrations is by
Albert U. Romasco, "Hoover-Roosevelt and
the Great Depression: A Historiographical
Inquiry Into a Perennial Comparison," in
The New Deal, ed. John Braeman, Robert H.
Bremner, and David Brody, pp. 3–26. For an
excellent account of the Hoover historiography, see Ellis W. Hawley, "Herbert Hoover
and Modern American History: Sixty Years
After," in *Herbert Hoover and the Historians*,
ed. Mark M. Dodge, pp. 1–38. The most recent scholar to argue the continuity thesis is
David M. Kennedy. See his excellent study,
*Freedom From Fear: The American People in De-
pression and War, 1929–1945* (New York: Oxford University Press, 1999).

44. Lippmann, "The Permanent New Deal,"
p. 661.

45. Raymond Moley, "Reappraising Hoover,"
Newsweek, June 14, 1948, p. 100.

46. Quoted in Joan Hoff Wilson, *Herbert
Hoover: Forgotten Progressive*, p. 158; and,
R. G. Tugwell, *The Brains Trust*, p. xxii. The
third member of the Brains Trust, Adolf Berle,
said that Hoover's legislative measures constituted a "radical break" with economic

tradition; see Adolf A. Berle, "Reshaping the American Economy," *Centennial Review* 9 (1965): 211.

47. Rexford G. Tugwell to Raymond Moley, January 29, 1965, Raymond Moley Papers, "Speeches and Writings," Box 245–49, Hoover Institution on War, Revolution, and Peace, Stanford University, Stanford, Calif.

48. Walter Lippmann, "Today and Tomorrow," *New York Herald Tribune*, March 1, 1933, p. 15.

49. Stephen Skowronek, *The Politics Presidents Make: Leadership from John Adams to George Bush*, p. 8.

50. Alfred B. Rollins, "The View from the State House: FDR," in *The Hoover Presidency: A Reappraisal*, ed. Martin L. Fausold and George T. Mazuzan, pp. 123, 133.

51. Hawley, "Herbert Hoover and Modern American History: Sixty Years After," p. 5.

52. Murray N. Rothbard, N.T., in *Herbert Hoover and the Crisis of American Capitalism*, ed. J. Joseph Huthmacher and Warren I. Susman, p. 43.

53. Amos Kiewe, "Introduction," in *The Modern Presidency and Crisis Rhetoric*, ed. Amos Kiewe, p. xv.

54. Kathleen J. Turner, "Rhetorical History as Social Construction," in *Doing Rhetorical History*, ed. Kathleen J. Turner, p. 2.

55. Robert L. Scott, "Against Rhetorical Theory: Tripping to Serendip," in *Texts in Context: Critical Dialogues on Significant Episodes in American Political Rhetoric*, ed. Michael C. Leff and Fred J. Kauffeld, pp. 1–9.

56. Martin J. Medhurst, "The Academic Study of Public Address: A Tradition in Transition," in *Landmark Essays in American Public Address*, ed. Martin J. Medhurst, p. xliii.

57. Kenneth Burke, *The Philosophy of Literary Form*, 3d ed., p. 21; Kenneth Burke, *A Rhetoric of Motives*, p. 265.

58. Dow and Dow, "Animal Spirits and Rationality," pp. 61–62.

59. I. A. Richards, "An Experiment in Criticism," chap. in *Richards on Rhetoric*, ed. Ann E. Berthoff, p. 30.

Chapter Two

"Talk Is Cheap"
Herbert Hoover Responds to the Great Depression

If he had any illusions . . . one was a blind faith that some way democracy in the end would be able to see with its own eyes the truth. He believed that the people could see it clearly and logically without drama, without a hero in whose struggles they could see a story, and so feel their way to the truth. But, alas, the President was wrong in attributing a logical habit of mind to men in the mass. They must emotionalize their thinking.

They need a story. They learn their truth in parables.
—Dr. Allen White

The future can only be a matter of opinion. Until it has actually come to pass, it must lie outside the object of empirically verifiable 'scientific fact.'
—Kenneth Burke, *A Rhetoric of Motives*

As his presidency neared its torturous end, Herbert Hoover did something completely out of character. Instead of yet another grueling eighteen-hour day filled only with meeting after meeting with advisors and business leaders, Hoover isolated himself from the nation's calamitous economic situation long enough to compose two lengthy letters. The first, dated February 17, 1933, was addressed to his friend Arch Shaw. The second, dated February 21, 1933, was addressed to Ohio Senator, Simeon D. Fess (Rep.). Prior to writing these letters Hoover had been too busy for introspection, tranquility, and leisure for historical reflection. He and his administration had worked feverishly so that the country's history might continue the hallowed traditions that he had inherited under such favorable auspices in March, 1929.

On an initial reading, the letters to Shaw and Fess seem to have little in common save their reflective tone and their length. But a closer reading reveals that they are linked by the unmistakable priority that Hoover assigned to confidence—both as a cause for the Great Depression and for its solution. To Shaw, Hoover wrote, "Our whole economic system naturally divides itself into production, distribution, and finance. By finance I mean every phase of investment, banking, and credit. And at once I may say that the major fault in the system as it stands is in the financial system."[1] Part of the problem with the financial system stemmed from it being "so badly organized." More problematic, though, was that the financial system's "stability should be the particular creature of emotional fear or optimism." In a word, the nation's economic edifice was held together by a most tenuous strand— emotion. The emotion in question, the one absolutely essential to economic recovery and stability, was confidence. To Fess, Hoover explained, "What is needed, if the country is not to drift into great grief, is the immediate and emphatic restoration of confidence in the future. The resources of the country are incalculable, the available credit is ample but lenders will not lend, and men will not borrow unless they have confidence."[2] Supply and demand, the very marrow of economic inquiry and activity, were captive to an emotion that looked toward the future.

Both letters are summations, not revelations; as such, one can attempt to track Hoover's attempts to create economic confidence, beginning with the stock market crash in the fall of 1929 and stretching until the very last day of his term. Any attempt to engender mass confidence—what we might term a "macroeconomics of confidence"—involves persuasion in all of its manifold forms. This chapter examines the first two years of the Hoover administration and the creative ways by which Hoover attempted to rally the nation toward a collective perception of the economic future so as to actualize that future. The next chapter follows a similar line of inquiry, with the focus being on Hoover's final two years in office.

The Great Engineer

Generations of Americans remember Franklin D. Roosevelt's inauguration-day declaration against fear. Long forgotten in the din of national crisis and the revelry of national renewal was Herbert Hoover's far less memorable allusion to fear: "I have no fear for the future of our country."[3] Hoover was not engaging in presidential artifice; he did indeed have little cause for fear on March 4, 1929. Hoover's road to wealth, fame, and the nation's highest office began most inauspiciously. Born in 1874 to a Quaker family in West Branch, Iowa, young Herbert (or "Bert," as he was known) was exceptional only in his reticence, a trait that would accompany him throughout his long life. Hoover's Quakerism would also be a steadfast companion, especially its emphasis on voluntary community cooperation and the individual's social responsibility.[4]

By the time he was nine years old, Hoover was no stranger to adversity. His father, Jesse, died in 1880, and his mother, Hulda, died four years later. At the age of ten, Hoover moved to Oregon to live with Hulda's brother and sister-in-law. The couple owned a Quaker land-settlement business in which the young Hoover worked. At seventeen, Hoover headed south to study geology at Stanford University, where he was a member of the school's very first freshman class.

Hoover's mining career began in 1895, after his graduation. He soon moved overseas to manage the gold-mining interests of the British firm Bewick, Moreing, and Company. His work with the firm would take him across the hemisphere, which would significantly affect Hoover's views of world affairs. The job also made him wealthy. By the age of 36, Hoover had amassed a personal fortune valued between $3 and $5 million.[5] He established his own mining consulting company in 1908, and, as a result, restricted his globe-trotting travel schedule principally to the United States, Russia, and Germany. He established "home" in London. Perhaps never has geography played such a pivotal role in a person's rise to political prominence, for it was in London that Hoover displayed his organizational acumen.

At the outset of the war, thousands of stranded Americans could not secure passage back home because British banks would not accept U.S. currency. Hoover's friend, American consul General Robert P. Skinner, solicited Hoover's help—and help he got. As Liebovich details, "Hoover loaned his company's own British currency to thousands of stranded travelers, organized a volunteer staff of 500 to see to the needs of more than 100,000 Americans in Great Britain and the continent, secured temporary lodging for the refugees, and organized passage to allow them to return to the United States.[6]

Hoover volunteered for international relief work on a much grander scale before his work in London was even completed. His effort to provide food for starving Belgians made him an internationally known and respected figure. It also made him politically savvy, as he frequently had to negotiate with British and German officials to secure safe passage for food supplies. The Belgian relief effort was an unqualified victory for Hoover. As George H. Nash recounts, Hoover had saved more lives than anyone in world history. He had justly earned the title "Napoleon of Mercy."[7] Hoover was so successful at food relief that Woodrow Wilson named him to head the U.S. Food Administration upon U.S. entry into World War I.

Significantly, Wilson made the Food Administration free of any cabinet office, which allowed Hoover great autonomy in directing the nation's (and Europe's) food supplies. The non-partisan nature of the appointment also appealed greatly to Hoover's disdain for partisan politics. He was charged with seeing that American General Issues (GIs) ate well abroad and that remaining food staples were properly distributed at home. The efficiency and success of the Food Administration was a testament to Hoover's tireless efforts at organization, effective publicity and his firm belief in cooperative voluntarism.[8]

But Hoover's success and the success of the Wilson administration in helping to secure an allied victory could not mitigate the political and social fallout from America's initial foray into European politics. Despite his valiant rhetorical campaign on its behalf, Wilson's League of Nations fell victim to the country's isolationist sentiment.[9] While Wilson's political stock plummeted, Hoover's soared, thanks in no small measure to the former Princeton University President. Following the armistice on November 11, 1918, Wilson appointed Hoover to head the American delegation to the Supreme Economic Council. At Versailles, Hoover distinguished himself before an English economist whose pending fame owed much to his prophetic refutation of the council's work. Said John Maynard Keynes of Hoover:

> Mr. Hoover was the only man who emerged from the ordeal of Paris
> with an enhanced reputation. This complex personality, with his ha-
> bitual air of weary Titan (or, as others might put it, of exhausted
> prizefighter), his eyes steadily fixed on the true and essential facts of
> the European situation, imported into the Councils of Paris, when he
> took part in them, precisely that atmosphere of reality, knowledge,
> magnanimity, and disinterestedness which, if they had been found in
> other quarters also, would have given us the Good Peace.[10]

Hoover emerged from World War I a "gigantic figure," second only to
Wilson as the nation's best known political personage.[11] Wilson's Assistant
Secretary of the Navy, Franklin Roosevelt, the young aristocrat from Hyde
Park, confessed to Hugh Gibson that Hoover "is certainly a wonder, and I
wish we could make him President of the United States. There could not be
a better one."[12] Much would change in twelve years. Hoover threw his hat
into the Republican presidential ring on March 30, 1920, but congressional
Republicans were wary of his status as an outsider. As a result, he was not
seriously considered for the party's nomination, despite support from such
notable progressives as Louis Brandeis, Col. Edward M. House, William
Allen White, Herbert Croly, and Walter Lippmann.[13]

After four ballots at the Republican National Convention, party bosses
selected Ohio Senator Warren Gamaliel Harding on the fifth ballot. In the
presidential election, he trounced another Ohioan, Democratic Governor
James M. Cox, whose running mate was Assistant Secretary of the Navy
Franklin Roosevelt. While history would remember his administration to be
exceptionally corrupt, Harding was nobody's political fool: he asked Hoover
to be his administration's Commerce Secretary four months before inauguration day. Hoover accepted, despite a $500,000 per annum job offered by
Daniel Guggenheim and despite his rejection by old guard party regulars.
Hoover placed one condition on his acceptance: that he be given a voice
in all important economic policy decisions. To Harding, Hoover specified,
"I must have a voice on all important economic policies of the administration. I stated this would involve business, agriculture, labor, finance, and
foreign affairs so far as they related to these problems."[14]

Perhaps the only thing "new" about the Harding/Coolidge "New Era"
was the innovative work undertaken by "the single most important and
articulate shaper of most GOP economic policies."[15] Hoover's eight-year
tenure proved to be an invaluable training ground for the complexities of
higher office. In hindsight, his disposition and approach to problem-solving
was much better suited to cabinet head than the nation's Chief Executive.
His experiences during World War I, coupled with his engineering background, informed many of Hoover's undertakings as Commerce Secretary.

One of Hoover's first tasks was to reorganize the Commerce Department
to facilitate his vision of a decentralized, associational corporatism. More

specifically, Hoover believed that industrial waste and inefficiency could be significantly reduced if major industries shared information by organizing themselves into trade associations. With the Department of Commerce acting as the central "transforming station," many self-regulating trade associations were created. The associations were not an attempt to subvert the nation's anti-trust laws; rather, they represented a cooperative attempt toward "price stabilization and general economic stability—all without coercive federal action."[16] The idea was not a novel one: Bernard Baruch's War Industries Board (WIB) was organized during World War I along similar lines and with nearly identical goals.[17] Similarly, Roosevelt's 1933 National Industrial Recovery Act (NIRA) utilized the functional units of trade associations to set price floors and to adjudicate the supply of goods. But unlike the 1935 Supreme Court ruling, the court ruled in favor of Hoover's associational approach in 1925.

Hoover's obsession with industrial waste and duplication led to his creation of the Division of Simplified Practice within the Bureau of Standards. Hoff Wilson reports that between 1921 and 1928, eighty-six major simplifications involving standardization of specifications were effected and more than 1,200 conferences were held on eliminating waste in design, production and distribution.[18] Such standardization greatly enhanced the possibilities for mass production (and mass consumption) so vital to national economic growth.[19] Mass sameness did not much matter to Hoover: "When I go to ride in an automobile, it does not matter to me that there are a million automobiles on the road just like mine. I am going somewhere and I want to get there in what comfort I can and at the lowest cost."[20] Pragmatism could not have asked for a better spokesman.

One of Hoover's final, and perhaps most important, acts as Secretary of Commerce recalled his earlier food relief missions in Europe. Appointed by Coolidge to head the Special Mississippi Flood Committee, Hoover immediately went to work and raised $17 million from private contributions and $10 million from the federal government to provide drought relief. Hoover and his committee orchestrated the relief effort, but the work was carried out at the grass-roots level. After the initial relief effort, flood damage to crops, buildings, and livestock was estimated at $300 million—far more than private charities and federal aid could cover. In a move presaging his presidential response to the depression, Hoover organized local and regional credit facilities to provide low interest loans to financially strapped farmers. Private charity, some federal aid, abundant credit, and expert advice carried out by local officials represented an "ideal balance" for Hoover. The citizens affected agreed: "Hoover came out of the Mississippi valley a hero, with his reputation as the Great Humanitarian enhanced, and personally more popular than ever before."[21]

His life took a dramatic turn on August 2, 1927. Just as Hoover was contemplating his career options, Calvin Coolidge, in his inimical way, announced that he would not run for a second term.[22] The stock market dropped following Coolidge's announcement, but the immediate groundswell for a Hoover candidacy placated Wall Street fears. He declared his candidacy six months later. Hoover breezed through the primary season and easily defeated such hopefuls as Vice President Charles Dawes, former Secretary of State Charles Evans Hughes, and former Governor of Illinois Frank Lowden. In June, Hoover received the party's nomination on the first ballot. Although the 1928 election "generated an electric excitement not seen by Americans in years," New York Governor Al Smith proved no match for the enlightened and altruistic engineer.[23] Hoover easily outdistanced Smith, both in the popular vote (21 million to 15 million) and in electoral votes (444 to 87). The trend toward Republicanism carried over into congressional races, as the GOP claimed a 100-vote majority in the House and a 17-vote majority in the Senate.

As Michael E. Parrish notes, "seldom did a person enter the White House with stronger credentials or brighter promise" than Herbert Hoover.[24] And, as economist Herbert Stein observes, of all modern presidents, Hoover was the most familiar with scientific economics.[25] Two contemporary sources well capture the tremendous expectations for the Hoover presidency. The *San Francisco Chronicle* predicted that "Herbert Hoover will prove the greatest builder who ever occupied the White House. We predict a memorable era of constructive solutions of national problems. . . . Never before has the Presidency found a man so well equipped to grapple with large constructive problems, reduce them to order and build solidly out of their materials." They effused, "No comparison is possible. No other American has ever had the breadth of experience which Herbert Hoover brings to the tasks confronting him in the employment he takes up today."[26]

Similarly, albeit retrospectively, Anne O'Hare McCormick of the *New York Times* recounted, "We were in a mood for magic. Mr. Hoover was inaugurated, and the whole country was a vast, expectant gallery, its eyes focused on Washington. We had summoned a great engineer to solve our problems for us; now we sat back comfortably and confidently to watch the problems being solved." She added, "The modern technological mind was for the first time at the head of a government. Relieved and gratified, we turned over to that mind all the complications and difficulties no other had been able to settle. Almost with the air of giving genius its chance, we waited for the performance to begin."[27]

The grandiose expectations did not escape Herbert Hoover; in fact, they seemed to weigh heavily on him. To the editor of the *Christian Science Monitor* he confessed, "I have no dread of the ordinary work of the presidency. What I do fear is the result of the exaggerated idea the people have conceived of me. They have a conviction that I am a sort of superman that no problem is beyond my capacity." But, he warned, "If some unprecedented calamity should come upon the nation . . . I should be sacrificed to the unreasoning disappointment of a people who expected too much."[28] Prophecy, as will be illustrated, was not one of Hoover's strengths, but in this instance his fears proved prescient to a degree that even The Great Engineer could not have fathomed.

Hoover's only glaring deficiency as he entered the White House was his ineptitude for public speaking, but times of unprecedented prosperity and domestic tranquility did not require an actively rhetorical president. For the time being, the public could look past Hoover's reticence, his awkward sentences, and his uninspired delivery. As James S. Olson notes, what carried Hoover throughout the 1920s and into the Oval Office was not the quality of his speaking delivery, but the substance of his ideas.[29]

Prolegomena to Black Tuesday

While the stock market crash was nearly eight-months away, Hoover's inaugural address provides an important window on the administration's policy agenda and his rhetorical tendencies.[30] At a strictly generic level, Hoover's inaugural address is unremarkable in its thematic iterations: he unifies his audience by investing it with present and future responsibilities; the values from the past are rehearsed in the present; he sets forth his governing principles; and he shows the requisite deference and awe for executive authority.[31]

Aside from such highly generalized themes as crime, international relations, and government regulation, the text offers more subtle clues about Hoover's beliefs. The repetition of key terms is an important critical prompt, and Hoover employed several such terms throughout the address that cluster around a dominant image or series of images. Across a wide variety of topics, the text's dominant image is movement, both vertical and horizontal. Hoover characterized such movement with phrases like the "advancement" of civilization, a "course" to be pursued, a "movement" toward peace, a nation on the "march," "directing" a complex civilization, and the "road" to realization. The vertical imagery is less varied, but equally pervasive. Hoover talked of "higher" degrees of comfort and individual freedom, the nation's "high" purpose, "building" a new race, the "structure" of justice, a "crumbling" system of government, the "highest" standards, a "rise" through the ranks, a "deep" desire for peace, and the "building up" of opportunities.

The vertical and horizontal imagery intersect and are unified through the titular term "progress." Movements upward or forward were always "progressive" movements. The nation was making "progress toward" prosperity; a movement was fundamental "to the progress of peace"; the nation was building a culture which was an "impressive contribution to human progress"; and there was "great progress in the advancement of service."

We might expect that the building of progress or the road advancing toward it required an outside force or agency. Hooverian progress was governed by three external agents: law, organization/administration, and cooperation. For example, self-government "will crumble either if officials elect what laws they will enforce or citizens elect what laws they will support"; public health and judicial enforcement can be improved by "mere matters of administration"; and "our people have in recent years developed a newfound capacity for cooperation among themselves to effect high purposes in public welfare. It is an advance toward the highest conception of self government."

The formal requirement of the spatial imagery would seem to warrant an end or telos, and the text does not disappoint. For Hoover, social ills had "remedies," and, as the metaphor suggests, these ills could be completely cured. Hoover also claimed that a "permanent peace" could be attained through "greater and greater perfection in the instrumentalities for pacific settlement of controversies between nations," economic and social justice could be "perfected," international hostilities could be rendered "extinct," and poverty could be "removed." Hoover's task, then, was "to perfect the means by which Government can be adapted to human service."

Without hyperbole, Hoover's vision of the future can accurately be described as utopian: world peace could be permanent, business cycles and unemployment could be removed, and the federal government's relationship to human services could be perfected. This was not the vision of a pessimistic, hands-off, president. Hoover's vision, though, was tempered by the past, as "progress must be based upon the foundations of experience." As the *New Republic* later noted, Hoover's "look forward turns out to be really a look backward."[32] The essential form of the Hooverian entelechy was latent in existing intellectual frameworks applied to distinctly American institutions. Whether Hoover's engineering background, his Quaker heritage, his allegiance to Progressivism, or some combination of all three influenced his optimistic presidential vision is not at issue. Suffice it to say that he was committed to a dangerous course, for the pending economic collapse knew no precedents, thus rendering suspect, if not obsolete, "the foundation of experience."

Agricultural Deflation and Industrial Inflation

Hoover's inaugural address is somewhat misleading, for its vision of social and economic perfection did not reflect the state of American agriculture. Since the close of World War I, American agriculture had endured a steady free-fall. Agriculture's demise was caused by several factors. As the nation's food administrator, Hoover had pegged food prices at such profitable margins that many farmers anxiously attempted to take advantage of the situation. Not only were prices potentially lucrative, but there seemed to be an inexhaustible demand for the farmer's produce. The United States was literally feeding the world.

These conditions precipitated a huge expansion in production, but the armistice brought with it a large contraction in agricultural demand, as other countries no longer relied completely on the United States. To make matters worse, mechanization made the farmer's land and labors much more productive. Finally, like the post-war mood in the United States, many countries isolated themselves from the pre-war arteries of international trade and commerce. These factors combined to create a major problem, that of overproduction.

Hoover's involvement with agriculture dates to his work with the Food Administration under Wilson and grew while he was Secretary of Commerce. As a cabinet member, Hoover clashed frequently with Secretary of Agriculture Henry Wallace, whose socialistic ideas Hoover deplored.[33] Farm relief bills such as McNary-Haugen, Hoover argued, gave the federal government too much direct control over a private concern.[34] Hoover's influence prevailed as Coolidge vetoed two consecutive McNary-Haugen bills in 1927 and 1928.

Hoover advocated farm relief, but not in the form of federally imposed price supports at home or in dumping American surpluses abroad. The federal government should not "engage in the buying and selling and price fixing of products, for such courses can only lead to bureaucracy and domination."[35] The relief that Hoover envisioned involved communication and cooperation: if farmers organized into large cooperatives, large surpluses could be alleviated, thereby increasing prices and aggregate purchasing power. Individual farmers, not the federal government, would determine price levels and production schedules. The federal government's duty was to facilitate these goals through $500 million in loans to the Federal Farm Board, a move that would continue "the upbuilding of the farmer's own marketing organizations." A "cure" would thus be procured by the farmers and their organizations (78).

Congress eventually passed a bill resembling Hoover's vision for agricultural reform on June 12, 1929, but not without serious challenges from within Hoover's own party. Hoover lauded the bill as "the most important measure ever passed by Congress in aid of a single industry," but many western progressives wanted much more.[36] Hoover gave a four-paragraph speech at the Federal Farm Board's inaugural meeting on July 15, 1929. The board's duty, according to Hoover, was two-fold: to adjust agricultural production to existing needs, and to create marketing institutions owned and controlled by farmers. Such changes would not occur overnight; rather, change would be effected by "building steadily" on existing "foundations."[37]

Agriculture's demise coincided with the unprecedented growth of American industry and American financial markets. Following the post-war depression of 1920–21, prosperity reached new heights, spurred by greater industrial efficiency, cheap and abundant credit, and the rise of payment plans. Yet the record-shattering profits engendered by mass consumerism were not equally distributed; they were instead concentrated among a small minority of relatively wealthy capitalists. The imbalance had two inter-related consequences. First, consumer demand would remain relatively static since purchasing power was largely fixed. Second, this condition, coupled with very permissive securities regulations, insured the flow of in-vestment dollars away from industrial capital and into more speculative ventures. The problem, so it appeared to many, was structural: existing laws and income distribution patterns encouraged the speculative frenzy. Hoover, though, did not perceive the forces fueling Wall Street speculation as being exclusively structural in character. As would become clear in the fall of 1929, Hoover recognized the persuasive lure of unprecedented profits floated by loans that banks were only too willing to supply.

Rhetorical Surrogacy and the Stock Market

The "problem" of the stock market's spectacular rise and its equally spec-tacular decline was a problem for the rhetorician as much as it was for the economist, the banker, and the broker. That Hoover recognized the rhetori-cal nature of market activity is underscored by his actions less than ten days into his presidency. In private consultation with Eugene Meyer, he claimed that the stock market was too high, and that as president he should publicly state his views. Meyer convinced him otherwise: if Hoover went public with his market analysis, Meyer argued, he would be equally obliged to state pub-licly when it was too low or just right. As president, Hoover should avoid publicly indexing the stock market for fear of the future implications such indexing would entail—both on his presidency and on financial markets.[38]

Such advice, however, did not exclude the possibility that a Hoover sur-rogate might publicly evaluate the stock market and lobby for different in-vestment possibilities. Thus, on March 14, 1929, Treasury Secretary An-drew Mellon, at Hoover's request, released the following statement to the press: "The present situation in the financial markets offers an opportunity for the prudent investor to buy bonds. Bonds are low in price compared to stocks."[39] This would not be the last time that Hoover utilized a surrogate to conduct his public rhetorical business; in fact, the practice would become a hallmark of his administration. At this point in his term, though, nearly seven months away from the stock market crash, Hoover could safely speak publicly through his surrogates. The crash and its aftermath would stipu-late a more vocal, hence visible, rhetorical role for Hoover. In the meantime, such rhetorical surrogacy did not dampen early editorializing on the ad-ministration: "few could have expected his display of personal vigor, promp-titude, resolution and courageous dealing with public affairs. . . . a man of great native force and acquired skill, with no lack of initiative and boldness, is now at the head of government."[40]

The historical evidence suggests that Hoover continued his rhetorical surrogacy in voicing his concerns about the stock market, even after publication of the Mellon statement. Importantly, Hoover's private admonitions were held with one of the most important media figures of the day, Colonel Frank Knox, General Manager of the Hearst newspaper chain. And, as a revealing telegram from William Randolph Hearst to Knox reveals, Hoover's message had gotten through.

> I am very heartily in accord with the President's view on both matters he discussed with you. I agree thoroughly about danger in speculative situation and of course will cooperate to utmost. Please ask Brisbane to cooperate along these lines to discourage speculation. Also ask Ruff-skyer and all our financial people to do the same and to do it vigorously, pointing out inevitable calamities that will ensue to industry, to labor, and to business generally. And keep sounding Mellon's advice to buy bonds. I want to go even further than President and urge passage of bills to prevent speculation on margins. That is root of all the trouble. There would be no dangerous speculation if stock purchases were made outright. Please see that our papers take this attitude even if government does not, but hope you can convince the President that speculation on margin should be prevented by law. There is no excuse for allowing this marginal speculation, which is purely gambling, to endanger the prosperity of the whole country.[41]

Hoover balked at Hearst's suggestion for federal legislation to prevent stock speculation on very thin margins; any legislation applying to the New York Stock Exchange was the responsibility of New York's new governor, Franklin Roosevelt. Yet as the summer unfolded, the Hoover-Mellon-Hearst-Knox advice was not heeded by most: from June through August the value of industrial stocks soared by nearly 25 percent.[42]

The Campaign for Confidence

As in most boom periods, many recognized that stock market values would eventually decline; it was only a matter of when and how precipitate the fall would be. Despite this recognition, very few opinion leaders risked public censure by laying bare the cyclical logic of contraction. One notable exception during the summer of 1929 was the editorial board of the *Kansas City Star*. In a series of six lengthy editorials running between September 6 and September 18, the *Star* argued not only "that the end cannot be far off," but also that such an end would be beneficial for American business.[43] They also specified the noneconomic ground that kept the increasingly tottering economic edifice together, the very ground on which Hoover would wage his three-year battle for economic recovery: public confidence. "The keystone of this elaborate structure [of speculation]," the *Star* claimed, "is that unpredictable quantity known as public confidence. In the past when it has given way under such a load, there has been a crash."[44] In this case, collective belief engendered economic realities and not vice-versa.

The stock market began its historic decline on Monday, October 21. The industrials dropped thirty-one points on Wednesday. The following day brought declines of another twelve points, despite organized efforts by Wall Street elites to avert the selloff. The slide on Monday, October 28, was extreme, as the industrials lost forty-nine more points. The massive selloff culminated in Black Tuesday as the industrials dropped another forty-three points, "the most devastating day in the history of the New York Stock market."[45] The one day loss was estimated at $15 billion.

The question that immediately confronted Hoover was how to rekindle public confidence, how to catalyze collective belief in order to minimize the damage done to the nation's financial markets. His response, according to Walter Lippmann, was "utterly unprecedented in American history."[46] First, he assumed responsibility for economic recovery, a direct repudiation of conservatives' call for liquidation. Second, and equally important, was Hoover's decision to avoid institutional change and congressional action in favor of "inspiration and exhortation."[47] Economic recovery, then, would be first and foremost a rhetorical activity. As Albert U. Romasco notes, "If business men could be persuaded to retain confidence in the basic soundness of the economy, the impulse toward caution and retrenchment would be minimized. The presidential business conferences were designed to promote these ends."[48] By disposition, Hoover was ill-suited for such an overtly rhetorical role, and this trait perhaps accounts for two responses in the immediate aftermath of the crash: Hoover's initial reticence to address the situation publicly, and the anti-rhetoric that he eventually employed in framing his administration's response to it.

In a revealing volley of letters exchanged between Hoover and William Allen White, the editor of the *Emporia Gazette*, on October 26 and 28, the issue of the president's rhetorical leadership is highlighted. White judged, "The Fall verdict—and who is not sorry for the poor victim—is our evidence of a righteous wrath in the heart of the people," and that Hoover had been elected "because the American conscience was longing for a voice." The president replied, "What I really need are some suggestions as to practical devise and method by which the American conscience can be awakened and led."[49] Hoover's plea for rhetorical assistance can be productively read against the backdrop of the stock market's continued free-fall, and the nation's call for his rhetorical leadership in maintaining public confidence.

Seymour Smith, the editor of *Financial Digest*, requested, "In view of fact that your opinions have immense weight with public would greatly appreciate if you will wire us at once statement which will have constructive effect in checking a situation which may bring disaster to American finance and industry."[50] Similarly, James A. Healy suggested that

what is needed immediately is an outspoken public recognition
of the situation confronting the holders of securities . . . in the form
of a strong statement by the highest administration officials . . . the
situation is serious and is fraught with great further consequences as it
is based on and perhaps only capable of correction by the effectuation
of a complete change in the psychology of the security owning public
and I believe confidence can only be reestablished by the administration taking the perhaps unprecedented but most courageous stand.[51]

Hoover's initial response to these early calls for rhetorical leadership was to
ignore them; in fact, in his off-the-record news conference of November 5,
Hoover's first statement on the stock market crash was a non-statement:
"I see no particular reasons for making any public statements about it
[the business situation], either directly or indirectly."[52] The ostensible
justification for Hoover's silence was his mistaken belief that "there has been
a complete isolation of the stock market phenomenon from the rest of the
business phenomena in the country."[53] Any contraction in production was
"purely psychological. So far there might be said to be from such a shock
some tendency on the part of people through alarm to decrease their activities, but there has been no cancellation of any orders whatsoever."[54] While
such a claim may have comforted the White House correspondents assembled for this news conference, the nation still waited to hear reassuring
news from its president.

Predictably, requests for Hoover's rhetorical leadership intensified. E. D.
Hewins, in a telegram received on the day of Hoover's Armistice Day Address, suggested that "in your armistice day [sic] broadcast tonight you utter words of saneness to restore loss of confidence which is rapidly undermining fundamental conditions due to disgraceful speculation . . . and
purchasing power of the workers will soon be impaired unless confidence
immediately restored."[55] Hoover did not so much as mention—even
obliquely—the stock market crash in his nationally broadcast speech. The
omission brought a hostile response from the editors of the *New York Evening Post:* "It may be ungracious, but it certainly is important to say that we
wish the President of the United States could have similar sympathy [as
displayed in the Armistice Day Address] in dealing with the vast disaster
of the stock market." They continued, "Peace is centuries off. Last week's securities panic is right under the President's eyes. It affects every one in
America. Yet Washington seemed to treat it with bland, almost cheerful,
indifference."[56]

Meanwhile, telegrams imparting rhetorical advice continued to flood the
White House. On November 12, R. W. McNeel, the director of McNeel's Financial Service, called Hoover's "attention to the wave of fear now sweeping
investors of this country and threatening a national catastrophe. . . . Where
in previous panics a terrorized public caused runs on banks a similar psy-

chology now is causing run on security markets with unnecessary sacrifices and causing disaster beyond belief. Unless fears are allayed national disaster threatens." He advised, "public statement from you regarding psychology of present situation would save untold suffering and unnecessary loss."[57]

Two days later, on November 14, Hoover received two requests that may have finally convinced him to go public. The first was a strongly worded telegram from Hearst that was reprinted in newspapers around the country: "Lack of confidence is contagious; but, on the other hand, so is confidence contagious. And, in the opinion of many of your earnest friends, some reassuring utterance by the President of the United States . . . would do much to restore the confidence of the public." Hearst specified, "A statement from this authoritative source would have a great psychological effect and would do much to make the investing public realize the unusual opportunity that is now offered them. The people expect as much from you, Mr. President."[58] If the Hearst telegram and its wide dissemination were not enough, bad news from Hoover's own Cabinet seemed to dictate a rapid rhetorical response. In a personal letter addressed to the president, Secretary of Commerce Robert P. Lamont[59] countered much of what Hoover had told White House press correspondents on November 5: "I have thought it advisable to call to your attention the reactions on commerce and industry of the disastrous collapse in the stock market, as they are recorded in this Department. . . . Telephone messages this morning from the Middle West are to the effect that all sorts of stories are in circulation and there is fear of runs on the banks." As such, Lamont concluded, "Substantial and conservative business men suggest that a statement from you is needed at this time to reassure the people as to the soundness of our banking and business institutions and to prevent an already critical condition from becoming disastrous." The challenge was principally rhetorical: "there can be no doubt that the purchasing power of many of our people has been reduced. Plant operations in some lines will be affected, and unemployment will result. . . . The immediate need is to change fear and panic in the public mind to confidence."[60] In addition to the statement that Lamont requested, the other means by which the public mind might be reassured was "if some sort of cooperation among the leaders of industry could be organized for the purpose of assuring the public of their belief in the underlying soundness of our institutions . . . to the end that there shall be as full employment during the coming year as there has been on the average in recent years." The former resulted in what might best be described as Hoover's anti-rhetorical campaign for recovery, while the latter—cooperation among industrial leaders—had already been in the planning stages for more than a week.

Hoover spoke publicly about the crash, albeit through a written press release, for the first time on November 15. The message, although brief, gives us our first look at how Hoover perceived the crash, economic recovery, and the role of rhetoric in facilitating recovery. It is a most curious document, for while Hoover expressed his belief that the crash was caused by the waxing and waning of human emotion, he denigrated a most important medium for soothing such emotions—namely, presidential speech.

Hoover's opening sentence would make even the meddling stylist cringe: "I have during the past week engaged in numerous conferences with important business leaders and public officials with a view to the coordination of business and governmental agencies in concerted action for continued business progress."[61] His active role in the search for continued business progress was emphasized by his conspicuous placement of the first person. Importantly, Hoover was the figure orchestrating the conferences between business leaders and public officials; the executive branch, not greedy private interests, was calling the shots.

Hoover next announced his plans to convene a "small preliminary conference" among several industries and governmental agencies to "develop certain definite steps." The steps, indicative of a forward movement, would neither be tentative nor without purpose. Hoover could make such promises because, as was his penchant, he knew the committee's recommendations beforehand.

One such recommendation was to expand construction. This solution was the seemingly natural result of capital's diversion into speculative security markets. Construction work, in other words, had been undercapitalized because of stock speculation. Undercapitalization would not happen in the future, according to Hoover, since the nation had recently passed through the "speculative period," much like travelers pass through occasional bad weather.

Hoover was careful to appease conservatives by emphasizing the "magnificent working of the Federal Reserve System and the inherently sound condition of the banks." Plenty of relatively cheap credit was available to assure "abundant capital," but Hoover clearly knew that the nation's banks were not "inherently" stable; several thousand had closed during his tenure as Commerce Secretary. His emphasis on capital formation and lower interest rates was indicative of his top-down approach to employment: business would invest more in capital formation and thereby provide more jobs in the long run. But this view presumed stable or increased consumer demand, a view sharply at odds with existing conditions.

After describing the committee's likely course of action, Hoover disclosed his complex view of market psychology, economic recovery, and the role of presidential rhetoric. The oscillations in the market, he argued, were due to "overoptimism" and "overpessimism," and both were "equally unjustified"—to the extent that investment practices should be guided by equanimity and unemotional logical analysis, a view consistent with Hoover's approach to decision-making. But implicitly, Hoover recognized that the peaks and valleys in business cycles were directly attributable to human belief and human perception. Capital markets, as Hoover had no doubt witnessed throughout the fall of 1929, were highly influenced by words. Yet, he explicitly rejected presidential speech in particular and words in general as a mechanism for dealing with human markets and human behavior: "My own experience has been, that words are not of any great importance in times of economic disturbance. It is action that counts."

Hoover, of course, was caught in a contradiction: he downplayed the importance of words precisely as he expressed his "confidence in the economic future" of the nation. He also failed to see, at least initially, that persuasive presidential speech *was* extremely important action.[62] Instead, he concluded that business and government cooperation would provide the "forward movement" necessary for continued economic progress. Hoover's response to what history would recognize as the Great Depression's beginning is not just internally contradictory; it also reveals an antipathy for rhetorical leadership.

One senses, though, that Hoover recognized, or was at least partially attuned to, the absurdity of his anti-rhetoric. At his not-for-publication press conference on November 19, Hoover stated, "We are dealing here with a psychological situation to a very considerable degree. It is a question of fear. . . . I do not believe that words ever convince a discouraged person in these situations." Therefore, Hoover noted, "I am trying to get this problem across by action in different industries and other groups rather than by too much talking, and, therefore, I don't want to talk about it."[63]

Contrary to popular belief, following the stock market crash Hoover did not sit idly by as the nation's financial markets plunged. Instead, relying on the findings of the 1921 Presidential Conference on Unemployment and his understanding of how the public might perceive business cooperation, Hoover went to work organizing various conferences sponsored by the federal government. Cooperation between the federal government and the business community, and not legislative coercion, would minimize any widespread damage caused by the stock market crash. Moreover, such publicly proclaimed cooperation would engender the confidence so vital to continued economic activity. Confidence, in other words, would be premised less on Herbert Hoover's rhetorical leadership and more on the perception that the business community was cooperating to maintain existing wages rates, prices, and production schedules. If the "business-as-usual" perception held sway, then such business would in fact—not just in word— continue. Hoover spelled out the rhetorical logic of his plan in his not-for-publication news conference of November 19:

> We are dealing with the vital question of maintaining employment in the United States and consequentially the comfort and standard of living of the people and their ability to buy goods and proceed in the normal course of their lives. So that the purpose of this movement is to disabuse the public mind of the notion that there has been any serious

or vital interruption in our economic system, and that it is going to proceed in the ordinary, normal manner, and to get that impression over not by preachment and talks but by definite and positive acts on the part of industry and business and the Government and others.[64]

In the immediate aftermath of the crash, Hoover recruited three men to facilitate the "definitive and positive acts": Manny Strauss, the president of the Bankers Industrial Corporation and chair of the Advisory Committee on Industry Cooperation; Paul Shoup, the president of the American Electric Railway Association; and Julius H. Barnes, the chair of the U.S. Chamber of Commerce. Strauss was given the task of surveying major industrial companies, and to secure positive forecasts in order to reassure the public. The cover letter that accompanied his survey is instructive: to avert a "buyer's market," which would result "in increasing unemployment and decreasing production and consumption," Strauss requested the respondent's "opinion and forecast of conditions in your business for the next year as you see them? I am writing to the heads of all big businesses and when I receive these opinions, it is my intention to co-relate them . . . so that they may be used to the best advantage."[65] The "best advantage," of course, meant "restoring public confidence." Presumably, then, any bad news for the coming year would be scrupulously avoided.

Several respondents were quick to note that any predictions were contingent on the very confidence that Strauss asked them to voice. From S. L. Willson, the president of the American Writing Paper Company: "In forecasting the conditions in our business for the next year . . . as the recent stock market liquidations have affected general business, before it will improve to any extent a feeling of confidence must be created and maintained."[66] From Arthur J. Morris, the president of the Industrial Finance Corporation: "I hesitate to express an opinion so shortly after our recent market decline. . . . this situation [the buying power of the country] depends primarily upon the psychological influences at work in the country."[67] And, from B. F. Fairless, the president of the Central Alloy Steel Corporation: "Business conditions for the coming year will no doubt be determined by the mental attitude of the American public. . . . I would state that business for 1930 will be determined by the buyers themselves. It is within their power to make this good or bad."[68] Despite the circumspection by some respondents, Strauss largely received precisely what he was asking for: positive economic predictions for the coming year.[69]

Shoup and Barnes were recruited for different means but with similar ends: namely, restoring public confidence. Hoover figured that if he could secure the cooperation of business leaders to maintain wage rates, keep prices stable, and maintain or increase production schedules, the fallout from the stock market crash would be minimized. Along similar lines, he also wanted to secure agreements from organized labor not to demand wage increases.

Thus, any unemployment would be the result of seasonal fluctuations and not industry-wide unemployment caused by high labor costs.

Immediately after the crash, Shoup and Barnes surveyed various business leaders, principally along two lines: whether business and labor leaders would participate in White House conferences, and when such conferences might take place. In a confidential letter to Hoover, dated November 7, Shoup and Barnes detailed their secret meeting with various leaders held on the preceding day. They concluded, "It seems to us that plans for such a conference should be formulated so that they might be promptly made effective if a severe business reaction and unemployment should follow this stock market upset."[70] As for why such a conference should be temporarily postponed, Shoup and Barnes reported that "the effect upon business of the stock market difficulty" had not been adequately measured, "and the possible effect [of the conference] being misinterpreted as designed to help the stock market situation; these reactions in addition to the possible danger of over emphasis that might be given such a conference at this time." They concluded, "All were of the view that the stock market would have to be taken from 'off the front page' before constructive action in any other directions should be undertaken."[71]

Various economic reports by Hoover's Labor and Commerce Secretaries, however, soon conspired to make the conference a reality. In a letter of November 12, Labor Secretary James J. Davis reported to Hoover that "employment in our industries in [sic] decreasing, and the general conditions throughout the country are not as favorable as they might be."[72] Furthermore, the stock market crash "is very apt to bring in its wake an epidemic of fear and extreme caution, causing a retrenchment and a curtailment of buying all along the line which ultimately makes itself felt in increased unemployment. Present indications all point to an increase in unemployment." Such dire conditions required immediate action by the president, claimed Davis: "The time is opportune for you to make a move looking towards the restoration of confidence in our country and our industries. If something isn't done soon to relieve the situation . . . we shall find ourselves in the midst of an unemployment situation such as we have not experienced since 1921." Lamont argued along similar lines in a November 14 letter to Hoover, but, unlike Davis, he was much more specific in his recommendations: "there can be no doubt that the purchasing power of many of our people has been reduced. Plant operations in some lines will be affected and unemployment will result."[73] The solution mandated putting the pledges that Shoup and Barnes had received into action: "To offset this as far as possible, it will be helpful if some sort of cooperation among the leaders of industry could be organized for the purpose of assuring the public of their belief in the underlying soundness of our institutions." Hoover wasted little time: on November 21 he met in the morning with industrial leaders and in the afternoon he met with labor representatives. Both groups pledged their cooperation: from industry, construction work would be expanded in every way possible, wages would be maintained and prices would remain stable; from labor, no movement would be initiated to increase wages. Both pledges were also immediately publicized to the nation's press. In addition, Julius Barnes was selected to chair the National Business Survey Conference (NBSC), a committee designed to assist business and labor to carry out their pledges of cooperation.

Pledges of economic cooperation, though, were not Hoover's sole objective for the conferences. While the material economic effects of business-labor cooperation would no doubt be real, the principal economic stimulus was more rhetorical in nature. As Romasco notes, "While it was considered economically important that construction be expanded, it was equally important that the public should be persuaded that it was expanded."[74] Only through such persuasion would public confidence return, thus encouraging consumers to continue in their economic activities. The press duly noted the macroeconomic persuasion that Hoover had orchestrated. The *New York Times* reported that the "President's treatment of the crisis has been largely mental."[75] Similarly, the *New Republic* claimed that "This [industrial conference] was mainly a task of 'restoring confidence.'"[76]

More important were the effects of the conferences: "as a crystalizer of public opinion, in the present instance at least, he has been just about 99 percent successful."[77] Such a favorable public response seemed to hold tangible material results: from mid-November through December, industrial stocks recovered nearly three-fourths of their value.[78] Thus had Hoover "converted the simple business ritual of reassurance into a major instrument of public policy."[79] In so doing, "the President stepped forward with great promptness and vigor to assume a leadership which at once commanded the confidence and thanks of the whole country."[80] The short-term success of the conferences, according to Romasco, perhaps convinced Hoover that "the arts of persuasion would be used in place of legislative coercion to accomplish a vital national purpose."[81]

Yet, with hindsight, Hoover's short-term success contained within it two interrelated modes of action that would plague his presidency: the first involved the press and the second involved his unwillingness to speak publicly to the panic-stricken nation. The latter was symptomatic of the former; that is, because Hoover did not speak publicly to the nation, he was forced to rely on the press corp to communicate his message of confidence and cooperation to the people. The press, in other words, had a vital role to play in carrying out Hoover's rhetorical agenda. David Burner notes well the rhetorical requirements exacted by an emphasis on confidence: "But a President plodding faithfully along his own private uncommunicative course could not expect the public voluntarily to give him its trustful support. . . . The president, who knew the importance of confidence, could not bring himself to manufacture it."[82] Hoover could not expect to awaken the public's imagination or commitment in the wake of the 1929 conferences given "his own near-inability to present himself."[83] This initial unwillingness "to present himself" worried friend and confidante William Allen White. In a letter to David Hinshaw dated December 3, 1929, White noted that while Hoover had "great capacity to convince intellectuals, he has small capacity to stir people emotionally, and through the emotions one gets to the will, not through the intellect. . . . I don't think he can sublet the job of emotional appeal. People going around talking to luncheon clubs don't get very far."[84]

Confidence, that emotion so vital to economic activity, would initially have to come from some other source—in this case the press. That the press had been largely helpful in the wake of the stock market crash did not seem to temper Hoover's anger with the White House press corps. In a not-for-publication news conference on November 29, 1929, Hoover intoned,

> There is a purely personal note that I wanted to sound with you about this business situation—not for publication. All of you have been extremely helpful, and the press, in fact, has I think, performed one of the most unique services that has been undertaken in a great many years, in a general restoration of confidence. The handling of public psychology in a problem of this kind, however, is a little difficult. If we overdo our job we may create a sense that the situation is more serious than it really is. . . . I only wanted to make a minor suggestion to you, and that is that hereafter if you could confine yourselves merely to the statement of the things that actually happen. . . . I am anxious that our form of news be not so much any exaggerated statement of items as it is a definitive statement of accomplishment without overdoing the situation. . . . I am making that suggestion to you. It is not my intention to lecture the press on what they should do . . . and I merely make this suggestion on the form of news. It is not censorship.[85]

Hoover, in no uncertain terms, wanted it both ways: not only was the press to do his rhetorical work, but it was also to do it in a manner favorable to restoring the public's confidence.[86] Given such a dressing down—especially in the face of press solidarity and cooperation with the administration's aims, in addition to future condescension and disparagement—it is little wonder that "no President in modern times had worse relations with the fourth estate."[87]

Despite the acrimony between Hoover and the press and his reluctance to speak publicly to the nation, the administration had won the first major battle in the campaign for confidence. The victory, though, was brief. As the contraction deepened, confidence would be increasingly difficult to maintain and create.

Rhetorical Emotionalism vs. Rational Action

Less than a week after admonishing the press, Hoover offered his judgments on the state of the union.[88] Despite the crash, he began his report in much the same manner as he concluded his inaugural address: "The problems with which we are confronted are the problems of growth and of progress."[89] The nation's foremost problem, if we are to believe that order is indicative of priority, was foreign affairs, particularly the London conference on naval disarmament. Paring down the nation's defense expenditures was high on Hoover's list for the conference as the nation's "prospects for peace" required fiscal "moderation." Overall, though, Hoover pronounced the federal government's finances to be in "sound condition," so sound in fact that he proposed personal and corporate income tax rate cuts for the 1930 and 1931 fiscal years (408).

The nation's economic situation largely mirrored that of the federal government. Hoover claimed further that the crash was "inevitable," given the "long upward trend of fundamental progress" (411). The crash, in other words, was triggered in part by "over-optimism" arising from the perception that economic progress seemed so lucrative. For Hoover, optimism's necessary concomitant—pessimism—was caused by the threat of unemployment and by memories of the 1920–21 depression.

Hoover's earlier emphasis on a very gradual, incremental progress or advance comes into sharper relief. Progress, in his estimation, had to be slow and steady in order to avoid the emotionalism associated with unwarranted optimism or pessimism, and progress was at hand given capital's movement toward "normal channels." The return to normality, or what Hoover termed "business as usual," was further emphasized in a very rare metaphorical flourish: the stock market crash was simply a "past storm" (412). The crash was not only a natural or inevitable phenomenon, but it was also temporal: even the fiercest storms had a brief life. Hoover, though, was still largely unaware of the extent of the carnage wrought by Wall Street's unprecedented tempest.

Economic emotionalism reappeared two days later in Hoover's speech before Julius Barnes's NBSC, then meeting in Washington, D.C., under the auspices of the U.S. Chamber of Commerce. Their charge, in addition to restoring public confidence, was to alleviate industrial unemployment by encouraging both public and private sectors to expedite large-scale construction projects. The speech was Hoover's first in the aftermath of the crash; as such, he worried privately about public perceptions, and the economic consequences of such perceptions given the very tenuous "recovery" period. In a short letter of November 28 to Barnes, Hoover confided, "I have been giving some thought to your meeting. I confess that I do not think it desirable to show too much anxiety on this occasion." He continued, "It seems to me a short address from me is about all that is required, and that if we bring the whole Cabinet it will look like over-anxiety."[90] A "short address" is precisely what Hoover delivered. Ironically, an earlier draft of the speech reveals the very anxiety that Hoover had hoped to avoid. After praising the Federal Reserve System for its response to the stock market crash, Hoover remarked, "The full effect of these actions has not been shown; it is one of the problems for your consideration."[91] Instead of this sober, if more accurate, statement, in the final version of the speech Hoover claimed that the unqualified success of the Federal Reserve System's actions constituted "a magnificent tribute to the system."

The attempt to temper the perception of "over-anxiety" also informs Hoover's narrative account of his successful campaign for confidence. The "break" (no longer a "crash"), as Hoover described it, created "undue pessimism, fear, uncertainty and hesitation in business."[92] More importantly, if such emotions "had been allowed to run their course, [they] would, by feeding on themselves, create difficulties." Hoover intervened to halt the downward spiral through action, since these difficulties could not "be cured by words." "The cure for such storms," Hoover recounted, "is action." The metaphors are badly mixed, but Hoover's actions had saved the day. The text thus reveals a telling binary terminological cluster: "action" is conjoined with reason, while "words" or presidential speech are linked with a debilitating, perhaps even effeminate, emotionalism.[93] Hoover's two-and-a-half-week silence following the crash is thus explicable: his "actions" were saving the country from its self-reinforcing emotionalism.[94] Again, the contradictions are palpable: Hoover was castigating "words" precisely as he was speaking, and Hoover's attempts to "assure employment and to remove the fear of unemployment" were contingent to a great degree on the emotion of confidence.

Two days after Hoover's first public pronouncement regarding the stock market crash and its aftermath, he privately confessed that the economic news was not nearly so promising. In a letter to Barnes, he reported, "Since I saw you the news of the general situation continues to grow a little worse. For your confidential information, we are now faced with 3,000,000 unemployed."[95] Hoover advised Barnes to have his recently formed committee "send out a circular to the members of the different industries, stating the necessity for repairs, maintenance, clean-up, general betterments and improvements." Always with an eye toward the rhetorical effect of securing economic cooperation, Hoover concluded that "such an inquiry would in itself be stimulative, especially if it were phrased as a recommendation to take up the unemployment in their own business and to help out a little with others."

Barnes duly translated Hoover's private request into a persuasive public form. In the first issue of the NBSC's propaganda arm—the Bulletin of the National Business Survey Conference—Barnes reported that industries were busy "collecting the data concerning exact conditions within their industries."[96] Such "exact" knowledge held beneficial consequences (that is, confidence) for two key constituencies: industrial leaders and everyday consumers. The NBSC-sponsored surveys had created "confidence in mutual support |that| grows naturally among the directors of industry. This confidence in the ever-expanding requirements of one hundred and twenty million people leads prudent judgment to make now the extensions, re-placements and betterments of plant and equipment necessary in prepara-tion for the future." Consumer demand, in turn, would be ensured "against the timidity and hesitation which in previous recessions often has come from exaggeration." Barnes, of course, was guilty of precisely the exaggera-tion he castigated in others. To have "exact knowledge" of what 1930 would hold, businesses had to assume that which was at stake, namely, confidence. Thus, Barnes assumed the return of confidence in the economy, which, in turn, was meant to create it.

Economic Emotionalism and the Turn to Science

A fairly common present-day perception is that following October 29, or Black Tuesday, the nation began a steady, irrevocable descent into economic ruin. This simply was not the case: until May, 1930, the nation seemed to re-cover from the cataclysm.[97] Stocks recovered substantial percentages of their pre-crash values. On February 12, 1930, a *New York Times* editorial even announced, "Indication is that the patient at the end of January has be-gun to recover."[98] Hoover, despite his private concerns of December 7, agreed. In a January 21 news conference, he reported good news on the eco-nomic front, so good, in fact, that "the tide seems to have definitely turned the other way and substantially so."[99] More good news followed as the New York Board of Trade reported to Governor Roosevelt that the peak period of unemployment had passed in February.[100] Outwardly, the pledges that Hoover had secured from business and labor, coupled with his anti-rhetoric, appeared to be working. Fausold notes that the nation was confident "that the president had the economic situation in hand."[101] This belief was reflected by the nation's journalists, as the depression was not seen as a ma-jor news story during 1930.[102] Stein, moreover, claims that "until the end of 1930, President Hoover had maintained his position as the leader of the ac-tivists in dealing with the Depression."[103] The economic news appeared so positive by early spring that Hoover ventured into new rhetorical waters— those of the economic prophet. In a written statement released to the press on March 7, 1930, Hoover averred, "All the evidences indicate that the worst effects of the crash upon employment will have been passed during the next 60 days."[104]

Hoover spoke very little during the winter and spring of 1930, but when he did speak, he did so with great passion about the redemptive powers of science, always in contradistinction to emotionalism. Science applied to contemporary problems was, by Hoover's account, the hallmark of his ad-ministration. The method it had applied to such problems, Hoover claimed, was "preceded by the accretion of basic truths."[105] It was not a method that "stirred public emotions with its drama of headlines; it is rather the quiet, patient, powerful and sure method of nature herself." The imagery of scientific progress, so instrumental to Hoover's vision of the future, was not only based on truth, but it also had the virtue of being nonpartisan. Hoover could be excused for not making good copy; science needed no publicist.

Hoover continued his assault on emotionalism before the American Society of Mechanical Engineers. Hoover's unfettered praise for "engineering knowledge," "the engineer's attitude of mind," and the engineer's methods were attributable to his belief that "no emotion enters into [their] determinations."[106] He admitted that scientific progress created "emotional problems" for Americans, but such problems, in turn, were solved by "infinite patience" geared towards discovering "the economic and scientific facts." Hoover, though, went further: "Our greatest difficulty in dealing with those [emotional] problems of government is when the emotion comes first." The paradox of Hoover's relentless disparagement of emotionalism was that his conception of economic recovery and economic progress leaned heavily on a most important emotion — confidence and faith in the future.

Ambivalence?

Hoover gave his first extended discussion of the crash and its aftermath on May 1, 1930, to the Washington, D.C. Chamber of Commerce. The text is rhetorically noteworthy in several respects, but perhaps none greater than its contradictions. Perhaps the most obvious one involves Hoover's metaphorical depiction of the depression. At several points, Hoover labeled it a "great economic storm," a metaphor that denies agency to the depression's causes. Moreover, nature's whims dictated the length and severity of the storm. Humans could only heed the warning signs and take refuge. More importantly, Hoover's oft-expressed recourse to the scientific method as a problem-solving heuristic was rendered ineffectual in such a symbolic realm. Hoover, however, changed metaphors in mid-speech: "Economic health like human health requires prevention of infection as well as a cure of it."[107] The metaphor of illness and health entailed a vastly different view of human agency; doctors, via the scientific method, could both inoculate and cure. Hoover explicitly rejected "the fatalistic view," in which "disease must run its course and for which nothing could be done either in prevention, or to speed recovery, or to relieve the hardship which wreaks itself especially upon workers, farmers, and smaller business people" (173). Poverty, unemployment, and other economic ills could be completely eradicated, a view consonant with the Hoover telos. Yet, at the conclusion of the speech Hoover equivocated: "the economic millennium," he said, may not be attainable (179).

Another apparent discrepancy arose from Hoover's rhetorical foray into speculation: "I am convinced we have now passed the worst and with continued unity of effort we shall rapidly recover" (171). This statement, a reiteration of his March 7 written statement, would haunt Hoover for the remainder of his presidency—and beyond. But in this instance Hoover engaged in exactly what he deplored: "undue speculation against the future" (172). In commenting on this prophetic role, the *New York Times* sensed its political ramifications: if Hoover's prophecy went unfulfilled, "by the time the November elections roll around, it will be thrown in his face."[108]

Third, there existed a major incongruity between the cause of the economic contraction and the solutions that Hoover offered. The problem "rests mainly upon certain forces inherent in the human mind . . . the natural optimism of our people brings into being a spirit of undue speculation against the future." To date, the psychogenic origins of the depression had "proved themselves uncontrollable by any device that the economist, the business man, or the Government has been able to suggest." Hoover's solution, albeit analogized, turned its back on human emotion and psychology: leaders best served the people "by taking counsel of their charts, compass, and barometer, and by devotion to navigation and the boilers." The solution would emerge from mechanized, "reliable" instrumentalities, regardless of the human causes. Hoover was not wrong to identify human confidence, or the lack thereof, as a major factor in both starting and perpetuating the Great Depression. He erred, though, in assuming that human emotion would be automatically buoyed by his administration's science-oriented approach to the problem. A "useful discussion" of the nation's economic travails could be expressed in a language other "than the cold language of economics," but Hoover, perhaps in keeping with his personality, would not offer a "warmer" vernacular (172). Despite such waverings and incongruities, Hoover maintained the motive underlying all that had been done in the preceding five months: "Our program was one of deliberate purpose to do everything possible to uphold general confidence which lies at the root of maintained initiative and enterprise" (173).

At least one organization, however, retained the consistency between economic causes and economic solutions. In its trade publication of May 24, 1930, the American Lumberman invited anyone to join its "One Week Club." Because "the state of mind of the American people" conditioned its economic activities, business would improve if members would simply recite the following pledge: "I promise myself that, for a period of One Week, when discussing business conditions, either those relating to my own business or to those of the country generally, I will emphasize the facts that are favorable and encouraging, rather than those which incite to pessimism."[109] So much for the "boilers" and "charts"; economic reality, so several enthusiastic new members reported, could be improved by a confidence-boosting mantra.

A month and a half later, Hoover unenthusiastically signed the Smoot-Hawley Tariff Act, or what Richard Hofstadter labeled "a virtual declaration of economic war on the rest of the world."[110] Many historians and commentators have attributed the tariff act largely to Hoover; in actuality, congressional Democrats and Republicans spent nearly fifteen months hammering out its provisions.[111] Recall that part of Hoover's justification for calling the 1929 special session was to protect the farmer's markets at home: as such, in his June 16 press statement, Hoover emphasized the act's relationship to agriculture and disclaimed that no tariff bill "will be perfect."[112] Hoover's signature on the bill was obligatory, since the Republican platform urged certain tariff reforms. "Platform promises," Hoover deadpanned, "must not be empty gestures" (231).

Confidence and Culpability

The economic advance in early 1930 gave way to retreat during the summer months, despite the cooperation Hoover had so successfully achieved and promulgated, the tax rate cuts, and the expedited and increased federal expenditures for public works. As the depression deepened, and as mid-term elections neared, talk of a major political realignment surfaced. Hoover needed to make some rhetorical adjustments, which he made in abundance in his October 2 speech to the American Banker's Association in Cleveland, Ohio. This relatively long address—Hoover's Press Secretary Theodore G. Joslin characterized it as "especially significant"—represents a major rhetorical departure.[113] A word index of the text reveals a paucity of Hooverian god-terms: progress is mentioned only three times, forward motion is referenced only three times, and science receives only a passing mention. Hoover even went so far as to claim that the depression was "not a problem in academic economics."[114] A new cluster of terms appeared: "prevention," "return," "restoration," "revert," and even "retreat" dot the rhetorical landscape. Only one pivotal Hooverian term remains—"cooperation." But this term clusters around the new vernacular, indicative of a very different endstate. The Hooverian telos is entirely absent from the text.

At a thematic level, some of Hoover's conventional rhetorical strategies were dramatically altered. Perhaps the most obvious alteration involved responsibility for the depression. Hoover no longer isolated over-speculation as the sole cause for the depression. The causes were more global: "This depression is world-wide. Its causes and its effects lie only partly in the United States. . . . A perhaps even larger immediate cause of the depression [than speculation] has been the effect upon us from the collapse in prices following overproduction of important raw materials, mostly in foreign countries" (392).

After detailing the extent of the recessed markets abroad, Hoover was quick to sense the implications for foreign blame: "We can make a very large degree of recovery independent of what may happen elsewhere" (393). But, importantly, Hoover abdicated responsibility for leading the nation on the road to recovery: "I wish to revert to the influence of the bankers, through encouragement and leadership, in expedition of our recovery from the present situation" (400). And, "There is no one group of which the public expects so much in assuring stability as the bankers . . . Nor can any other group contribute so much in constructive thought and action to solve the problem either today or in the long run" (397). Why bankers? While the reason will become more obvious in 1931 and 1932, Hoover received some important economic explanations from a Cleveland lawyer, Julius B. Cohn, in anticipation of his trip to Cleveland. To Hoover, Cohn wrote, "Confidence confounded is awful, putting to rout even ordinary and necessary affairs. The bankers' organization approaches nearly to the position of psychological master of this country, and the duty largely falls on it to breathe new life into Confidence, the foundation of the business structure."[115] While the metaphors no doubt appealed to Hoover, more interesting is the extent to which Cohn's line of thinking mirrors that exhibited in Hoover's speech.

The reason for the shift in responsibility, at least according to Hoover, was rhetorical, but "for lack of better terms," he labeled it psychological. The banker "in large measure makes or tempers its [American business] psychology" since the banker can "now . . . dampen our enthusiasm and equally [he] can lift our courage and hope." The temporal marker "now" is not insignificant, for it registers a rhetorical changing of the guard, from Hoover back to New York City. Bankers could influence public opinion through a variety of channels, from assuring plentiful and low rates of credit, down to "the very atmosphere of your offices." The federal government would still cooperate with the banking community, but the rhetorical onus was clearly on its collective shoulders. Hoover, moreover, avoided an outward retreat into presidential pessimism and professed himself an "unquenchable believer in American enterprise." He added that "no one can occupy the high office of President and conceivably be other than completely confident of the future of the United States."

Hoover implicitly acknowledged his administration's inability to bring about prosperity's return. The blame was only partly his, however. In his introductory remarks, Hoover referred to the "disorganization in our economic system which has temporarily checked the march of prosperity." He added that "the problem today is to complete the restoration of order in our ranks." As the nation's master organizer and chief of cooperative associationalism, he tacitly admitted his failure to organize the necessary forces to combat the depression effectively.

Herbert Hoover did not care for partisan politics. His dislike is evident at several levels, but perhaps none is more conspicuous than the absence of overtly partisan rhetoric in 1930. Despite portents of a Democratic onslaught, Hoover made few attempts to placate voter apprehension. The closest he came to campaigning occurred early in October, when he traveled to Massachusetts. But the campaign he waged there was a referendum on the Hooverian prescription for recovery, not Republicanism writ large.

One group that Hoover had antagonized was World War I veterans. In what would be the first of several battles over bonus payments, Hoover vetoed a bonus bill in July. On October 6, Hoover defended his veto before the annual convention of the American Legion. Excessive payments to veterans jeopardized a sacred Hooverian ideal: "If we shall overload the burden of taxation, we shall stagnate our economic progress and we shall by the slackening of this progress place penalties upon every citizen."[116] Unbalancing the federal budget to pay for the bonus was not an option, because such a direct payment from the federal treasury to veterans bore a distinct resemblance to a federally sanctioned dole. Direct federal relief represented a threat to individual initiative and even to American democracy.

Hoover re-articulated these beliefs before the American Federation of Labor on the same day, but in a different nomenclature. By the fall of 1930, Progressives in the House and Senate favored some form of direct federal unemployment insurance. Hoover, to the contrary, claimed that the nationwide cooperation had "served as a practical system of unemployment insurance."[117] It should be remembered that in 1930 no accurate unemployment statistics existed; thus, Hoover could, without gross malfeasance, boast of the millions spent on public and private improvement projects and the cooperation among government, business, and labor that translated into jobs the Hoover administration had saved. Unemployment, as such, was not the principal economic problem; "stability in employment" was.

Hoover's optimism reached a crescendo the following day in a speech strongly reminiscent of his inaugural address. The nation's problems were "the problems of growth . . . not the problems of decay."[118] Unlike his uncharacteristically melancholy address before the American Bankers Association, "progress," "upbuilding," "marching," "growth," the "door of opportunity," and the "ladder to leadership" reappeared. The perfection that Hoover envisaged, however, had less to do with the cold, impersonal savior, science, than with "religious faith" (424).

This strategic shift, one that emphasized individual sin rather than adjudicating among the facts, enabled Hoover to shift the blame for the deepening depression to the American people. "We must look to our own conduct that we do not by our own failure to uphold and safeguard the true spirit of America weaken our own institutions and destroy the very forces which upbuild our national greatness. It is in our own house that our real dangers lie" (425). Crime, failure to vote, moral weakness on the part of public officials, and destructive criticism (of Hoover) threatened to undermine the true spirit of America. Perhaps even more malevolent were businesses that refused to cooperate, government involvement in business, and an increasingly centralized federal government. Goodness would win out over evil, if only "we hold the faith."

Thus, for the first time, Hoover linked economic salvation with a spiritualism manifested by the nation's founders and their founding documents that provided "a binding spiritual heritage." To veer away from them, and, by implication, from Hoover's path to recovery, would result in chaos. Economic recovery was thus contingent on a strict fidelity to the nation's

spiritual origins. A slightly different variant of confidence, "faith," would secure a prosperous future.

Victory or Defeat?

The 1930 mid-term elections must be viewed from two very different per-
spectives. Perhaps the most obvious one is from the major congressional realignment. Democrats won fifty-two seats in the House to hold a one-vote
majority. In the Senate, the GOP held on to the slimmest of majorities. From
this vantage point, the Democrats' onslaught appears uncontested and convincing. But looks can be deceiving: Republicans won more than 53 percent
of the popular vote nationwide. Perhaps more importantly for Hoover, the
burden of the depression was now a bipartisan affair.

This situation, however, did not prevent Hoover from taking a few swings
at the lame duck seventy-first Congress. As others have noted, Hoover did
not initially want a congressional solution to the depression. The executive
would lead, Congress should simply follow. Hoover was particularly wary of
profligate spenders, Republican and Democrat. Thus, in his second State of
the Union message, Hoover made a striking admonition to his foes on Capitol Hill: "Economic wounds must be healed by the action of the cells of the
economic body—the producers and consumers themselves."[119] But this
statement was largely contravened by Hoover's actions during the preceding year. For various reasons, history would largely remember the Herbert
Hoover who spoke such words, someone who resorted to organic (laissez-
faire) methods when remedies were readily available.[120] But the characterization is misleading, for Hoover's statement must be situated firmly within
his rather diffident relationship with the 71st Congress.

Summary

Lady Luck had smiled on Herbert Hoover for much of his adult life; he had
made a career of being in the right place at the right time and in making the
right decisions. In some respects, Hoover entered the Oval Office with such
public esteem and good fortune that a fall from grace was inevitable. The
editors of the *New Republic* were attuned to Hoover's impending demise:
"Mr. Hoover's apparent security at the beginning of his administration is his
greatest peril. The auspices are too favorable."[121] Despite the inevitability of
his fall, Hoover did not, as his first two years in office illustrate, take the depression lying down. "He is," Lippmann pronounced, "no true believer in
letting nature take its course."[122] Unlike his treasury secretary, Andrew
Mellon, Hoover was not content to let the business cycle wreak havoc until
a bright new day of equilibrium dawned; he was not "handicapped" by a
laissez-faire philosophy.[123]

Despite his activism, his progressive interventions, and public support for
his administration, Hoover was increasingly bitter as the mid-way point of
his presidency grew near. Much of his bitterness was aimed at the White

House press corps, a group increasingly unwilling to convey his message of optimism and confidence, in addition to excoriating him for personal aloofness and a lack of charisma. Hoover's anger boiled over in front of Washington journalists during a December 13 address to the Gridiron Club. The club's platform, Hoover mocked, included "a vigorous declaration that government must be dominated by excitement, since the honest, plodding public official, intent upon building up [the] safety and welfare of the people, is neither news nor material for Gridiron entertainment."[124] Hoover's resentment toward the press, while perhaps tempered by the spirit of Gridiron gatherings (satire and lampoon), concerned those around him. Close personal friend Edgar Rickard recorded in a diary entry for November 28, 1930, the rhetorical problem that Hoover faced: "French Strothers is on the same track as Bill Irwin in attempting to present Hoover to the public as a human being . . . rather than the Administrative machine thinking in exact engineering terms."[125] Part of the public's perception, of course, was the creation of Hoover's own hand. The question remained whether Hoover would actively attempt to recreate his public persona in a manner more amenable to "the economics of confidence," an economics based on impassioned and assertive emotion and belief rather than dispassionate and stolid logic and knowledge.

The concern of the nation's most influential journalist had more to do with Hoover's mental health than with perceptions and economic recovery. In a letter to Felix Frankfurter, Walter Lippmann confided, "I am genuinely concerned about Hoover in a human way. I felt, since before he was nominated, that he had a very bad temperament for high public office. Ambition and anxiety both gnaw at him constantly. He has no resiliency." Lippmann predicted that "if things continue to break badly for him I think the chances are against his being able to avoid a breakdown. When men of his temperament get to his age without ever having had real opposition, and then meet it in its most drastic form, it's quite dangerous."[126]

Personal and perceptual tensions mirrored the thematic tensions in Hoover's attempts to maintain public confidence despite a very precarious and uncertain economic future. The tensions were legion: amidst the pleading for public rhetorical leadership, Hoover maintained his silence, and, when he did speak, his was an anti-rhetoric; despite his overriding emphasis on the emotional states of confidence and optimism, he insisted on the cold logic of depersonalized facts and the scientific method; when the press refused to function as his faithful surrogates, he turned to America's bankers—a group whose collective credibility hurt more than it helped; and, despite his unfettered praise for, and professed adherence to, science and the scientific method, Hoover turned increasingly to prophetic incantations and religious faith. Hoover, in sum, was both confused and confusing: "In the realm of reason he is an unusually bold man; in the realm of unreason he is . . . an exceptionally thin-skinned and clearly bewildered man."[127] Confidence could not be borne of rhetorical confusion, and, as Hoover looked to 1931 and beyond, precious few signs warranted it. Increasingly, time and economic reality were conspiring against him, for "confidence, explicitly or implicitly, is confidence in something or somebody; and sooner or later it must meet the objective test."[128]

Notes

1. Herbert Hoover to Arch W. Shaw, February 17, 1933, President's Subject File, Box 155, "Financial Matters, Correspondence 1932–1933," Herbert Hoover Presidential Library, West Branch, Iowa (hereafter, HHPL).

2. Herbert Hoover to Simeon D. Fess, February 21, 1933, President's Subject File, Box 155, "Financial Matters, Correspondence 1932–1933," HHPL.

3. Herbert Hoover, "Inaugural Address, March 4, 1929," in *Public Papers of the Presidents of the United States*, p. 11.

4. Joan Hoff Wilson, *Herbert Hoover: Forgotten Progressive*.

5. Louis W. Liebovich, *Bylines in Despair: Herbert Hoover, the Great Depression, and the U.S. News Media*, p. 4.

6. Ibid., p. 6.

7. George H. Nash, "'An American Epic': Herbert Hoover and Belgian Relief in World War I," *Prologue* 21 (1989): 86.

8. A thorough account of Hoover's activities during World War I is provided by George H. Nash in *The Life of Herbert Hoover: The Humanitarian, 1914–1917*.

9. Richard Hofstadter called Wilson's speaking tour "one of the most futile stumping tours in history." See Hofstadter, *The American Political Tradition*, p. 366.

10. John Maynard Keynes, *The Economic Consequences of the Peace*.

11. Hofstadter, *The American Political Tradition*, 368; Joan Hoff Wilson, "Herbert Hoover: The Popular Image of an Unpopular President," in *Understanding Herbert Hoover*, ed. Lee Nash, p. 10.

12. Quoted in Carl N. Degler, "The Ordeal of Herbert Hoover," *Yale Review* 52 (1963): 564. In a letter to biographer Ernest K. Lindley, Roosevelt requested that two stories be taken out of the final draft. One of the stories involved Roosevelt's 1920 participation in the "Sunday Night Supper Club"—a group of young Wilsonian liberals who were attempting to recruit Hoover into the Democratic party. See Elliott Roosevelt, ed., *F.D.R.: His Personal Letters, 1928–1945, Volume Two*, pp. 193–94.

13. Hoff Wilson, *Forgotten Progressive*, p. 75.

14. Herbert Hoover, *The Memoirs of Herbert Hoover: The Cabinet and the Presidency 1920–1933*, p. 36.

15. Robert H. Zieger, *Republicans and Labor, 1919–1929*, p. 271. For a detailed account of Hoover's years as Commerce Secretary, see Ellis W. Hawley, ed., *Herbert Hoover as Secretary of Commerce 1921–1928: Studies in New Era Thought and Practice*.

16. Hoff Wilson, *Forgotten Progressive*, p. 98.

17. See Robert D. Cuff, *The War Industries Board: Business-Government Relations During World War I*.

18. Hoff Wilson, *Forgotten Progressive*, p. 110.

19. During Hoover's pioneering work at the Commerce Department, Arnold claims that he became the "father of 'big government'" (Peri Ethan Arnold, "Herbert Hoover and the Continuity of American Public Policy," *Public Policy* 20 [1972]: 526).

20. Quoted in Hoff Wilson, *Forgotten Progressive* p. 111.

21. Ibid., p. 117.

22. As was his habit, Coolidge opted for the minimalist rhetorical approach: "I do not choose to run for President in nineteen twenty-eight."

23. Liebovich, *Bylines in Despair*, p. 75.

24. Michael E. Parrish, *Anxious Decades*, p. 241.

25. Herbert Stein, "The Washington Economist," *The American Enterprise* 5 (1994): 6.

26. Newspaper clipping, the "Bible" Index, File 977, "Inaugural Address of Herbert Hoover, March 4, 1929," HHPL.

27. Anne O'Hare McCormick, "A Year of the Hoover Method," *New York Times*, March 2, 1930, sec. 5, p. 1.

28. Quoted in David Burner, *Herbert Hoover: A Public Life*, p. 211.

29. James S. Olson, "Herbert Clark Hoover," in *American Orators of the Twentieth Cen-*

tury: Critical Studies and Sources, ed. Bernard K. Duffy and Halford R. Ryan, p. 204.

30. Burgchardt claims that the address represented the high point of Hoover's rhetorical presidency. Perhaps viewed as an epideictic address, Burgchardt is right. Hoover, though, delivered many more significant speeches, with more important consequences for the nation, and with more stylistic artistry. His assertion that Hoover delivered only three "significant presidential persuasions"—the Inaugural Address, a 1931 Memorial Day Address, and the 1932 Republican National Convention Acceptance Speech—is extremely objectionable. Such characterization completely trivializes Hoover's presidency from a rhetorical point of view. Olson does even more violence to Hoover's presidential rhetoric, citing only one speech as "major"— a speech, ironically, not even included in the definitive four volume state papers of the Hoover presidency. See Carl R. Burgchardt, "Herbert C. Hoover," in *U.S. Presidents as Orators: A Bio-Critical Sourcebook,* ed. Halford Ryan, pp. 137, 144; Olson, "Herbert Clark Hoover," p. 208.

31. Karlyn Kohrs Campbell and Kathleen Hall Jamieson, "Inaugurating the Presidency," in *Form, Genre, and the Study of Political Discourse,* ed. Herbert W. Simons and Aram A. Aghazarian, p. 205. Burgchardt draws a similar conclusion regarding the critical emptiness of the inaugural topoi; see Carl R. Burgchardt, "President Herbert Hoover's Inaugural Address, 1929," in *The Inaugural Addresses of Twentieth-Century American Presidents,* p. 82.

32. "Hoover Looks Forward," *New Republic,* October 15, 1930, p. 220.

33. Hoff Wilson, *Forgotten Progressive,* p. 103.

34. McNary-Haugen was a bill designed to inflate agricultural prices at home and deflate them abroad. The federal government would prescribe acceptable prices.

35. Herbert Hoover, "Message to a Special Session of the Congress on Farm Relief, Tariff, and Certain Emergency Legislation, April 16, 1929," in *Public Papers of the Presidents,* p. 77. Subsequent references are noted in the text.

36. Quoted in Martin L. Fausold, *The Presidency of Herbert C. Hoover,* p. 52.

37. Herbert Hoover, "Remarks at the First Meeting of the Federal Farm Board, July 15, 1929," in *Public Papers of the Presidents,* p. 221. Burner refers to the Agricultural Marketing Act of 1929 as "one of the most extensive programs for the reorganization of the economy the federal government had ever undertaken." Burner, *Herbert Hoover: A Public Life,* p. 237.

38. Another possible consequence of Hoover's public expression was that it might trigger the massive selloff that many anticipated. That Hoover even considered such a public declaration was symptomatic of a radical change in presidential responsibility. According to James Truslow Adams, once Calvin Coolidge and Andrew Mellon assumed credit for economic prosperity in 1927, prosperity ceased being a non-governmental issue and, instead, "became 'presidential.'" Adams clearly sensed the importance of such a fundamental change: "If government becomes responsible for prosperity . . . will it not become increasingly necessary to forego private judgment and initiative in deference to the policy of a Coolidge, a Mellon, or a Hoover?" James Truslow Adams, "Presidential Prosperity," *Harper's Magazine,* August, 1930, p. 266.

39. Quoted in Merlo J. Pusey, *Eugene Meyer,* p. 201.

40. "The Hoover Atmosphere," *New York Times,* April 28, 1929, sec. 3, p. 4. For a comprehensive exposition of the Hoover administration's activism during the months preceding the stock market crash, see David B. Burner, "Before the Crash: Hoover's First Eight Months in the Presidency," in *The Hoover Presidency: A Reappraisal,* ed. Martin L. Fausold and George T. Mazuzan, pp. 50–65.

41. Telegram from W. R. Hearst to Colonel Frank Knox, April 9, 1929, President's Secretary File, Box 615, "William Randolph Hearst 1929–1933," HHPL.

42. William E. Leuchtenburg, *The Perils of Prosperity 1914–32,* p. 243.

43. "Hazard in the Bull Market," *Kansas City Star,* September 6, 1929, n.p.

44. N. A., "The West and the Bull Market," *Kansas City Star,* September 18, 1929, n.p.

45. John Kenneth Galbraith, *The Great Crash,* p. 116.

46. Walter Lippmann, "The Permanent New Deal," *Yale Review* 24 (1935): 652.

47. Albert U. Romasco, *The Poverty of Abundance*, p. 38. See also, Albert U. Romasco, "Hoover-Roosevelt and the Great Depression: A Historiographical Inquiry Into a Perennial Comparison," in *The New Deal*, ed. John Braeman, Robert H. Bremner, and David Brody, p. 23.

48. Romasco, *The Poverty of Abundance*, p. 35.

49. William Allen White to Herbert Hoover, October 26, 1929, President's Personal File, Box 215, "William Allen White 1929–1933," HHPL. Herbert Hoover to William Allen White, October 28, 1929, President's Personal File, "William Allen White 1929–1933," HHPL.

50. Telegram from Seymour Wemyss Smith to Herbert Hoover, October 29, 1929, President's Subject File, Box 159, "Financial Matters, New York Stock Exchange Correspondence, September–October, 1929," HHPL.

51. Telegram from James A. Healy to Herbert Hoover, October 29, 1929, President's Subject File, Box 159, Financial Matters, New York Stock Exchange Correspondence, September–October, 1929," HHPL.

52. Herbert Hoover, "The President's News Conference of November 5, 1929," in *Public Papers of the Presidents*, p. 366.

53. Ibid., p. 367.

54. Ibid., p. 368.

55. Telegram from E. D. Hewins to Herbert Hoover, November 11, 1929, President's Subject File, Box 159, "Financial Matters, New York Stock Exchange Correspondence, November–December, 1929," HHPL.

56. "Mr. Hoover on Peace and Panic," *New York Evening Post*, November 12, 1929, p. 12.

57. Telegram from R. W. McNeel to Herbert Hoover, November 12, 1929, President's Subject File, Box 159, "Financial Matters, New York Stock Exchange Correspondence, November–December, 1929," HHPL.

58. Telegram from William Randolph Hearst to Herbert Hoover, November 14, 1929, President's Subject File, Box 159, "Financial Matters, New York Stock Exchange Correspondence, November–December, 1929," HHPL.

59. Not to be confused with Thomas Lamont of the J. P. Morgan Company.

60. R. P. Lamont to Herbert Hoover, November 14, 1929, President's Subject File, Box 159, "Financial Matters, New York Stock Exchange Correspondence, November–December, 1929," HHPL.

61. Herbert Hoover, "The President's News Conference of November 15, 1929," in *Public Papers of the Presidents*, p. 382.

62. This is Roderick P. Hart's thesis in *The Sound of Leadership*.

63. Herbert Hoover, "The President's News Conference of November 19, 1929," in *Public Papers of the Presidents*, pp. 387–88.

64. Ibid.

65. Form letter from Manny Strauss, November 13, 1929, President's Subject File, Box 88, "Business Correspondence, November 1–10, 1929," HHPL.

66. S. L. Willson to Manny Strauss, November 16, 1929, President's Subject File, Box 88, "Business Correspondence, November 25, 1929," HHPL.

67. Arthur J. Morris to Manny Strauss, November 15, 1929, President's Subject File, Box 88, "Business Correspondence, November 25, 1929," HHPL.

68. B. F. Fairless to Manny Strauss, November 14, 1929, President's Subject File, Box 88, "Business Correspondence, November 25, 1929," HHPL.

69. See the President's Subject File, Box 88, "Business Correspondence, November 25, 1929," HHPL.

70. Paul Shoup and Julius H. Barnes to Herbert Hoover, November 7, 1929, President's Subject File, Box 159, "Financial Matters, New York Stock Exchange Correspondence, November–December, 1929," HHPL.

71. Paul Shoup and Julius H. Barnes to Herbert Hoover, November 7, 1929, Paul Shoup Papers, "Out Correspondence, 1928–31," Box 2, M57, File 22, Stanford University, Stanford, CA.

72. James J. Davis to Herbert Hoover, November 12, 1929, President's Subject File, Box 336, "Unemployment—PECE Correspondence, 1929," HHPL.

73. Lamont to Hoover, November 14, HHPL.

74. Romasco, *The Poverty of Abundance,* pp. 56–57.

75. "The Hoover Method," *New York Times,* December 6, 1929, p. 26.

76. "Hoover Plays His Part," *New Republic,* December 11, 1929, p. 55.

77. Alfred L. Bernheim, "Prosperity by Proclamation," Nation, December 25, 1929, p. 772.

78. William Starr Myers and Walter H. Newton, eds., *The Hoover Administration: A Documented Narrative,* p. 17.

79. Galbraith, *The Great Crash,* 149.

80. "Presidential Leadership," *New York Times,* March 9, 1930, sec. 3, p. 4.

81. Romasco, *The Poverty of Abundance,* p. 7.

82. Burner, *Herbert Hoover: A Public Life,* p. 253.

83. Ibid.

84. William Allen White, *The Selected Letters of William Allen White 1899–1943,* ed. Walter Johnson (New York: Greenwood, 1968), pp. 299–300.

85. Herbert Hoover, "The President's News Conference of November 29, 1929," in *Public Papers of the Presidents,* pp. 401–402. For a description of the press and confidence as they related to the Hoover presidency, see Craig Lloyd, *Aggressive Introvert: Herbert Hoover and Public Relations Management 1912–1932,* pp. 164–75.

86. R. C. Dillon, Governor of New Mexico, went even further than Hoover in addressing the press' proper role following the crash. Borrowing from W. Hume Logan, Dillon advised the newspaper editors of his state " 'to print failures and all depressing news under small headlines, giving such articles as little space as possible to cover news truthfully. At the same time, under larger headlines, and larger space, write up the daily items of improvements, enlargements, payrolls maintained, larger orders placed, mail-order and department store sales, and all sales of an encouraging nature' . . . No matter what the leaders in finance, commerce and industry say and do, if the consuming public gets fixed in its mind that business is bad, it will be bad" (R. C. Dillon to Newspaper Editors of New

Mexico, December 18, 1929, President's Subject File, Box 88, "Business Correspondence, December 16–31, 1929," HHPL).

87. Harris Gaylord Warren, *Herbert Hoover and the Great Depression,* p. 58.

88. The message was not delivered orally to the Congress; instead, the White House published written copies of the text.

89. Herbert Hoover, "Annual Message to the Congress on the State of the Union, December 3, 1929," in *Public Papers of the Presidents,* p. 404. Subsequent references are noted in the text. Hoover closed his Inaugural Address by stating, "The questions before our country are the problems of progress to higher standards; they are not the problems of degeneration," p. 11.

90. Herbert Hoover to Julius Barnes, November 28, 1929, President's Secretary File, Box 429, "Julius Barnes, 1929–1932," HHPL.

91. Speech draft, December 5, 1929, The "Bible" Index, Folder 1178, "Herbert Hoover Public Statements," HHPL.

92. Herbert Hoover, "Remarks to a Chamber of Commerce Conference on the Mobilization of Business and Industry for Economic Stabilization, December 5, 1929," in *Public Papers of the Presidents,* p. 453.

93. The action versus words binary recurs throughout Hoover's economic rhetoric. See, for example, in *Public Papers of the Presidents:* Herbert Hoover, "Remarks to the American Society of Newspaper Editors, April 19, 1930," p. 142; and Herbert Hoover, "Address to the Gridiron Club, April 26, 1930," pp. 162–63.

94. J. E. Edgerton, President of the National Association of Manufacturers and a member of the NBSC, responded favorably to Hoover's denigration of talk. In a December 7 letter to the president, he wrote, "I heartily believe that complete confidence will very soon be restored if, as you advised, everybody goes to work and quits talking about the securities of our economic future" (J. E. Edgerton to Herbert Hoover, President's Subject File, Box 88, "Business Correspondence, December 1–15, 1929," HHPL).

95. Herbert Hoover to Julius Barnes, December 7, 1929, President's Secretary File, Box 429, "Julius Barnes, 1929–1932," HHPL.

96. Julius H. Barnes, "Moving Ahead!" *Bulletin of the National Business Survey Conference*, January, 1930. President's Secretary File, Box 429, "Julius Barnes 1929–1932," HHPL.

97. Frederick Lewis Allen, *The Big Change*, p. 146.

98. Quoted in Myers and Newton, *The Hoover Administration*, p. 35.

99. Herbert Hoover, "The President's News Conference of January 21, 1930," in *Public Papers of the Presidents*, p. 28.

100. Myers and Newton, *The Hoover Administration*, p. 35.

101. Fausold, *The Presidency of Herbert C. Hoover*, p. 97.

102. Liebovich, *Bylines in Despair*, p. 123.

103. Herbert Stein, *The Fiscal Revolution in America*, p. 23.

104. Herbert Hoover, "Statement on Unemployment and Business Conditions, March 7, 1930," in *Public Papers of the Presidents*, 83. This statement represented a slight qualification from his oral remarks to White House correspondents: "All the facts indicate that the worst effects of the crash on employment will have been passed during the next 30 to 60 days." Herbert Hoover, "The President's News Conference of March 7, 1930," in *Public Papers of the Presidents*, p. 79.

105. Herbert Hoover, "Remarks at a Ceremony Honoring Dr. William Henry Welch, April 8, 1930," in *Public Papers of the Presidents*, p. 114.

106. Herbert Hoover, "Address to the American Society of Mechanical Engineers on Receiving the First Hoover Gold Medal, April 8, 1930," in *Public Papers of the Presidents*, p. 116.

107. Herbert Hoover, "Address to the Chamber of Commerce of the United States, May 1, 1930," in *Public Papers of the Presidents*, p. 175. Subsequent references are noted in the text.

108. "Mr. Hoover Bids Us Hope," *New York Times*, May 3, 1930, p. 18.

109. Magazine copy of the American Lumberman, May 24, 1930, President's Subject File, Box 89, "Business Correspondence,

May–June, 1930," HHPL. See also the May 31 and June 7 issue in the same file for the enthusiastic response the club engendered.

110. Hofstadter, *The American Political Tradition*, p. 398.

111. For a persuasive revisionist reading of the Smoot-Hawley tariff legislation, one that treats it as less protectionist than most, see Alfred E. Eckes, "Revisiting Smoot Hawley," *Journal of Policy History* 7 (1995): 295–310. For a similar view, see J. Richard Snyder, "Hoover and the Hawley-Smoot Tariff: A View of Executive Leadership," *Annals of Iowa* 41 (1973): 1173–89.

112. Herbert Hoover, "Statement on the Tariff Bill, June 16, 1930," in *Public Papers of the Presidents*, p. 233. Subsequent references are noted in the text.

113. Theodore G. Joslin, *Hoover Off the Record*, p. 46.

114. Herbert Hoover, "Address to the American Bankers Association in Cleveland, Ohio, October 2, 1930," in *Public Papers of the Presidents*, p. 392. Subsequent references are noted in the text.

115. Julius B. Cohn to Herbert Hoover, September 6, 1930, President's Secretary File, Box 305, "Trips, October 1–3, 1930," HHPL.

116. Herbert Hoover, "Address to the American Legion in Boston, Massachusetts, October 6, 1930," in *Public Papers of the Presidents*, pp. 408–409.

117. Herbert Hoover, "Address to the American Federation of Labor in Boston, Massachusetts, October 6, 1930," in *Public Papers of the Presidents*, p. 412

118. Herbert Hoover, "Address on the 150th Anniversary of the Battle of Kings Mountain, October 7, 1930," in *Public Papers of the Presidents*, p. 427. Subsequent references are noted in the text.

119. Herbert Hoover, "Annual Message to the Congress on the State of the Union, December 2, 1930," in *Public Papers of the Presidents*, p. 511.

120. This is precisely the quote that Frederick Lewis Allen utilizes to characterize the Hoover administration. See Allen, *Since Yesterday*, p. 29.

121. "Humpty Dumpty Hoover," *New Republic*, June 25, 1930, p. 137.

122. Walter Lippmann, "The Peculiar Weakness of Mr. Hoover," *Harper's Magazine*, June, 1930, p. 2.

123. Joseph S. Davis, "Herbert Hoover, 1874–1964: Another Appraisal," *South Atlantic Quarterly* 68 (1969): 309.

124. Herbert Hoover, "Address to the Gridiron Club, December 13, 1930," in *Public Papers of the Presidents*, pp. 565–66.

125. Diary entry of November 28, 1930, Edgar Rickard Diary, Box 1, HHPL. Strother was Hoover's Administrative Assistant, while Irwin was a friend and sympathetic biographer.

126. Walter Lippmann, *Public Philosopher: Selected Letters of Walter Lippmann*, ed. John Morton Blum, p. 268.

127. Lippmann, "The Peculiar Weakness of Mr. Hoover," p. 5.

128. Elmer Davis, "Confidence in Whom?" *Forum and Century*, January, 1933, p. 31.

Chapter Three

Recontextualizing the Depression
War, Christianity, Confidence, and Silence

It is difficult for modern politicians to be economic agnostics. The occasional skeptical conclusions of economic logic do not easily fit the necessarily confident logic of political rhetoric.
—John Zvesper, *Rhetoric and American Statesmanship*

The state of long-term expectations, upon which our decisions are based, does not solely depend, therefore, on the most probable forecast we can make. It also depends on the confidence with which we make this forecast.
—John M. Keynes, *Collected Works*

Herbert and Lou Hoover and Franklin and Eleanor Roosevelt were extremely upset in the immediate aftermath of the 1932 Annual Governor's Conference. Each couple was angry with the other, and for similar reasons. Roosevelt and his wife had taken personal offense at the president's delay in meeting the assembled governors for dinner. The delay had forced Roosevelt to stand in the oppressive heat for thirty minutes in his uncomfortable leg braces. Roosevelt might have taken a seat with his Republican and Democratic brethren, but he wanted to avoid any action that might have created more whispering about his stamina and health, especially in the context of the Democratic primary season.

Physical appearances also concerned the president and his wife. On April 30, Hoover's Press Secretary, Theodore G. Joslin, recorded in his diary, "He was wild about the movietones taken of him at the [G]overnor's Conference. 'They were horrible,' he told me after seeing them last night. 'My worst fears were realized. They make me look as though I was 82 years old.'" But Hoover, like Roosevelt, had more partisan and electoral matters on the mind: "Worst of all, posed pictures of Roosevelt and Ritchie were woven into them. They looked young and vigorous. I was made to appear aged and decrepid [*sic*]. They were entirely misrepresented to you. That is the end of indoor movietones. Mrs. Hoover was so disturbed that she broke down and cried."[1]

While Hoover's comments are revealing at face value, they also represent in microcosm much of what transpired in 1931 and 1932. First and perhaps most important was Hoover's continuing battle with the White House press corps over how his administration's policies and rhetorical practices would be represented to the nation. Hoover continued the practice of attempting to cajole the press into acting as his rhetorical surrogates, down to the very wording of their columns. Not surprisingly, the press balked. But even when

Hoover's friends in the press tried to be helpful, he ignored them, much to his own detriment.

Second, when the depression deepened, particularly in the winter of 1932, Hoover ordered an end to public contact. He remained cloistered in his office for 18–20 hour work days, far away from the daily realities of his increasingly disillusioned constituents. At the very moment when they needed to hear from their president, he fell largely silent; in fact, during an eleven-month period Hoover spoke to the nation on economic matters only once. This silence, of course, did nothing to restore the public's confidence in his administration or in their own economic circumstances.

Third, as Hoover's anger with the newsreels suggests, he was very concerned with appearances, specifically the appearance of consistency. One possible reason for Hoover's protracted silence during the winter and spring of 1932 is that his actions on the legislative front were wildly inconsistent and out of character with his earlier rhetoric. Instead of cooperative voluntarism, individual initiative, and battles on 1,000 fronts, Hoover's policy agenda suggested an institutional collectivism in which the federal government would engender confidence through balanced budgets, revenue bills, and credit facilities. Hoover's "worst fears" were likely realized: his vision for an ideal federal government was soundly repudiated. Even then, Hoover must have looked "unrecognizable" to himself, his wife and his constituents.

Hoover's Holy War and the Politics of Method

Hoover was uncharacteristically quiet during the first half of 1931. With one exception, all of his major addresses were relatively short ceremonial speeches. But he did issue frequent and sometimes lengthy statements through the press, especially following a presidential veto. The vetoes were premised on the grounds that mental confidence, in combination with private and public sector cooperation, were winning the war against the Great Depression. Material legislation, especially that which involved the federal government in relief efforts, was simply unnecessary, according to the president. Thus, Hoover vetoed the "Emergency Adjusted Compensation Bill," or the Veterans' bonus, on February 26. The measure, which would have enabled World War I veterans to receive loans on money due them in 1945, was vetoed on grounds that it was given to "a privileged class who can care for themselves." [2] Perhaps more importantly, the $1 billion outlay "breaks the barrier of self-reliance and self-support in our people" (109). Congress overrode Hoover's veto the following day. The bonus issue, though, was by no means a resolved fiscal matter.

Five days later, Hoover vetoed Nebraska senator George Norris's Muscle Shoals Bill, which would become a centerpiece of the New Deal. Hoover warranted his veto on the grounds that the federal government should regulate, not own, public utilities, and should not usurp state and local responsibility. The veto override failed by a mere seven votes.

On March 8, Hoover vetoed Senator Robert Wagner's employment bill, which was designed to create forty-eight independent state employment agencies and thereby abolish the Federal Employment Service housed in the Labor Department. Given Hoover's rhetorical emphasis on decentralization, the veto appears surprising. His major complaint was that the bill would simply take too long to implement.[3] Hoover strategically vetoed the measure while Congress was adjourned to curtail debate. Thus, within a ten-day period, Hoover seemed to serve notice to the seventy-second Congress that fiscal orthodoxy and less overtly material solutions would prevail in the Executive branch. Both, he would argue throughout 1931, had religious warrants.

Hoover raised the political stakes considerably by making the Great Depression a religious and moral matter. The method of recovery that he favored—state and local government aid, individual initiative, cooperation and confidence—offered a stark contrast to direct federal financing of relief efforts, an alternative that would lead to "the abyss of reliance."[4] Though Hoover had frequently referred to economic recovery with vertical imagery, this was one of his first overt allusions to a downward or earthly purgatory. The "abyss of reliance," moreover, "struck at the roots of self-government." Direct federal aid, in other words, would totally eradicate "American ideals and American institutions." There was simply no middle ground or room for compromise on the matter. Direct federal aid also posed a dangerous threat to the national character. Borrowing from Grover Cleveland, Hoover claimed that it would weaken "the sturdiness of our national character."[5]

The morality of recovery was featured in Hoover's February 12 address, ostensibly commemorating Abraham Lincoln. Although Hoover had invoked the moral imperative in his February 2 press conference, this was his first extended address linking morality and religion with economic depression. That Hoover recognized the potential importance of the speech is underscored by his decision to make a live radio broadcast, despite the fact that he was ill at ease with the medium. Thus, while the speech masquerades as a tribute to Lincoln, it is much more. Hoover joined God, Lincoln, and the present situation at the outset: "Lincoln was a builder in an epoch of destruction. It was his assignment by Providence to restore the national edifice," and he built "a new temple of the national soul in which our succeeding generations have since dwelt secure and free and of a richer life."[6] The metaphor of construction was a staple in Hoover's rhetoric, but he also esteemed homes and home ownership as critical to American life. Thus, to destroy or even threaten the divine dwelling sanctioned by God and forged by Lincoln's hands was both un-American and ungodly. To centralize the federal government's responsibilities was to "lay the foundation for the destruction of [peoples'] liberties" (74). While the metaphors were confused, if not contradictory, Hoover's message of unfettered individualism and local responsibility was not.

Centralization not only entailed the destruction of liberties, but it also had a distinctly ethical consequence: "The spread of government destroys initiative and thus destroys character." The nation, Hoover warned, was "passing through a critical test," a period "when character and courage are on trial, and where the very faith that is within us is under test" (74). Nothing less than the nation's future "moral strength" was at stake (75). The outcome was contingent on faithful allegiance to Lincoln's ideal of self-government, since the future, Hoover claimed, was intimately linked with the past: "This ideal [equal opportunity and individual initiative] obtained at the birth of the Republic. It was the ideal of Lincoln. . . . By [our] devotion to these ideals we shall come out of these times stronger in character, in courage, and in faith" (76). Thus, as the depression deepened, Hoover attempted to transcend "mere" materialism by cloaking his methods for recovery in the apparel of the American heritage. To depart from these ideals represented a spiritual departure from a divinely sanctioned and mandated plan.[7]

If Americans remained faithful to their past, victory in the present was assured: "Victory over this depression and over our other difficulties will be won by the resolution of our people to fight their own battles in their own communities. . . . This is not the easy way, but it is the American way. And it was Lincoln's way" (75). While the battle was something akin to a Holy War, in which American identity, American morality, and the American heritage were threatened, the warfare imagery had changed from previous speeches. According to Hoover, the war was being waged in a decentralized fashion, or "upon a thousand fronts" as he noted in June.[8]

The plan to localize warfare is significant in several respects. First, the diffusion of the front rendered the "enemy" more ubiquitous yet still largely unknowable, hardly a reassuring prospect. Second, local battles relieved Hoover of the necessity for a grand strategy unified by the commander in chief; presidential leadership, whether Hoover knew it or not, was being sacrificed. And third, recall that Hoover had frequently alluded to an economically interdependent world, one in which Europe's economic tribulations had washed onto America's shores. Given Hoover's earlier claims of causation, a macroeconomic battle plan seemed necessary, not a fragmented, microeconomic series of plans. Winning on only one front was impossible if the "enemy" was global. Prices, wages, and tax shares, after all, are determined largely in the national and international marketplace, not at the county seat. Thus, Hoover's military strategy was initially ill-defined, consigned to defeat on every front, and perhaps contributed to his ineffectual and impotent legacy.

Hoover solidified the links among the spiritual, the moral, and his economic policies in an April 13 address to the annual convention of the American Red Cross. He praised the organization both for its work during the recent drought and its unwillingness to accept "Federal appropriations as the source of its funds."[9] But the Red Cross was much more than a charitable organization for Hoover: it represented "the highest form of self government" and "the highest thing in our civilization" (179–80). This was no small claim when considered in the context of Hoover's resolute praise for self-government and his rhetorical propensity for hierarchical imagery. Institutional perfection had been achieved. Little wonder, then, that Hoover's address contained several references to spirituality. The nation's spiritual growth and actualization came in the form of charity: "A great spiritual value comes to those who give from the thankful heart, who give because of their sensibility to suffering. It is this spiritual value, which is exemplified in the Red Cross, that is of transcendent value to our Nation." The Red Cross not only appealed to Hoover's conception of direct economic relief, but the organization's mechanisms for distribution were far removed from overtly partisan matters; "need," not "claim[s] of right or influence," assured "a probity and devotion in service which no government [could] ever attain" (180).

Cooperative voluntarism stood in direct contrast to direct federal aid. This latter method, if adopted, would destroy "something even greater than voluntary service—it would [injure] the spiritual responses of the American people" (179). The administration's purported non-activism did not stem from a lack of sympathy on Hoover's part—quite the contrary. He was concerned that a nameless, faceless bureaucracy would arrogate to itself, and thus transform, the spirituality that accompanied "neighbor-to-neighbor" giving.[10] Several decades of the welfare state have largely substantiated Hoover's fears, yet as the depression deepened, charitable sources began to run dry. Spirituality, insofar as it was associated with some form of "materialism," was not immune from budget constraints.

But, as his speech two weeks later reveals, Hoover's spiritualism extended to non-pecuniary matters. Prior to this speech, Hoover had made frequent remarks on the causes of the depression that one might deem secular: World War I and its aftermath; diminished foreign trade; depressed agricultural markets; and reckless stock speculation. In his speech to the Gridiron Club, though, Hoover contextualized the depression and its causes within the Judeo-Christian tradition. More specifically, to suffer was to heed a calling: "If we shall be called upon to endure more of this period, we must gird ourselves for even greater effort."[11] The nation's suffering bore a distinct resemblance to God's suffering servant Job: "This is a period when the ideals and hopes which have made America the envy of the world are being tested." God was doing the "calling" and the "testing," and only God's gift of "spirit and strength" would carry the nation forward. It was only "natural," then, that Hoover's war on the depression was fought on spiritual fronts in which Hoover's army of volunteers could share "in the great plan of the universe and the definite order which pervades it."[12] Legislation, as such, was of little, if any use; in Hoover's later words, "We cannot legislate ourselves out of a world economic depression."[13] To a large extent, Hoover was right: federal legislation could not reverse the world-wide counter-cyclical forces. But such an avowedly anti-legislation sentiment did not necessarily make for good politics, either with Congress or the American people.

Hoover's rhetoric of recovery that conjoined warfare and spiritualism found a slightly different iteration in his May 30 Memorial Day address at Valley Forge, Pennsylvania. Hoover attempted to appropriate the legacy of Valley Forge both as a means to boost morale and as a rationale for his method of attack. The latter issue, that of method, would ultimately determine whether the nation would win or lose. At issue was not dollars and cents, but matters of the spirit. According to Hoover, the "quality of spirit" was responsible for "the success of our great democratic experiment." [14] The country's future was thus contingent on historical fidelity to the "wise national policies and fundamental ideals of the men who builded our Republic." Not surprisingly, these ideals were Hooverian staples: self-reliance, cooperation, equality of opportunity, voluntarism, and individual freedom. If, on the contrary, the nation turned its back on Washington and the lessons of Valley Forge, "we shall be writing the introduction to the decline of American character and the fall of American institutions" (276). Nothing less than the future of the country, the "American soul," was at stake.

The enemy, though, was not the depression *per se*; the depression, after all, was merely "a passing trial" (274). It was, instead, those who "sing the song of the easy way [during] the moment of difficulty" (276). The war was indeed, as Hoover claimed, a "war of independence," one in which opposing ideologies of recovery were locked in battle. The depression simply provided the battleground for the opposing forces.[15] If Americans endured the "privation and suffering," like those who had endured at Valley Forge, the victory would be a "triumph of the American soul" (277). The future was at hand, if only the country would heed the spiritual idealism of its mythic past.

Hoover's Private War

Despite the fact that Hoover's war was a decentralized one, "fought on a thousand fronts," the gravity of its outcome—the future of America—required a leader who could inspire the confidence, courage and devotion to see victory through. The nation, in sum, required a leader in whom it could trust, someone with whom it could share its suffering and from whom it could draw its inspiration. Friends and aides close to Hoover realized that one way to effect such leadership was to attempt to "humanize" the president, to depict him less as the administrative automaton and more as the kind, compassionate friend and leader they knew. This would, of course, require some cooperation with the press, a group from whom Hoover increasingly distanced himself.

He did still have some friends in the press that he trusted, perhaps most notably Mark Sullivan of the *Baltimore Sun*. As noted in the previous chapter, French Strother and Will Irwin were already, according to Edgar Rickard, seeking ways to humanize the president. On January 1, 1931, Sullivan wrote Strother with a suggestion: "The thought haunts me, however, that from the point of view of the President, the idea has value. I am impressed by certain qualities which will attend the very fact of an interview being given to a reporter of a small local newspaper." [16] Perhaps Sullivan was "haunted" by the fact that the country, after more than two years, still did not know the human side of its president.

The primary justification for the interview was made explicit by George Olds, the managing editor of the *Springfield Ledger.* In a letter to Sullivan, he noted the "amazing gap between Mr. Hoover and the great mass of socalled [*sic*] common people—the absence of a human touch that is becoming increasingly conspicuous." [17] This absence, Olds continued, had very real material consequences:

> They [the public] thought they were going to like him, they thought
> they knew him. But now, after nearly two years of his administra-
> tion, they are left perplexed and not a little hurt. They are beginning
> to associate him with all their little personal troubles. All in all, it
> is becoming a matter of considerable national importance . . . and
> one that conceivably has a direct bearing on the general economic
> situation.

Economic confidence, so Olds suggested, was suffering to the extent that it lacked personal, sympathetic embodiment.

Olds's idea, according to Sullivan, was deserving of "careful considera-tion" by the administration; as such, he encouraged Olds to forward the idea to Strother, which he did in a letter dated January 6. [18] The "human interest interview" would be conducted by Miss Doria Karell, "a genuinely 'big time' newspaper girl." It would not broach such nettlesome political issues like "the World Court situation, the Nicaraguan situation, or even the Demo-cratic situation." Rather, the interview would be conducted with a view to-ward helping the president "bridge the gap between him and the people."

On January 16, Strother acknowledged Olds's letter. He was so interested in it as to request "copies of some or all of the interviews mentioned in your letter so that I might be informed myself of the general kind of outcome that might be expected if the suggestion were adopted." [19] Olds forwarded the clippings to Strother, through Sullivan, less than a week later. [20] Based on the clippings, Sullivan reported his "favorable impression" to Strother of go-ing ahead with the interview, "with the understanding . . . that she would not print anything except with an O.K." [21] Although the documentation does not appear to exist, Hoover quashed the idea in late January or early February. On February 21, a disappointed Olds wrote to Strother, "May I be so sold [*sic*] as to recall your attention to my recent suggestion that Presi-dent Hoover be asked to receive one of our girl reporters for the purpose of obtaining an 'human interest' interview?" [22] While Olds's slip of the tongue—"sold" instead of "bold"—perhaps reveals his own economic in-

terests in printing such an interview, Hoover clearly was not sold on the idea
of allowing the reading public to see his human side. Hoover's intransigence
worried another close friend in the press, William Allen White. Evoking
Lincoln, he wrote to M. F. Amrine:

> He has to guide a people in the greatest adventure ever undertaken on
> the planet. For without leaders the people grow blind and without vi-
> sion the people perish. I am not saying this in public because I know
> Hoover is Hoover, but nevertheless I don't think his friends should fan
> him and sing to him on a flowery bed of ease made by his tempera-
> ment. The bed should be made just as thorny and the racket just as
> unbearable as possible to get the most possible leadership out of him in
> this crisis. But I haven't the heart to crash in and yell bloody murder.
> I'll let someone else do it.[23]

Others must not have had the heart either, for despite the fact that
confidence needed a visible, human face, the "real" Hoover remained
largely aloof from an eager public. As he would later confess to Joslin, "This
is not a showman's job. I will not step out of character."[24]

The International Interregnum

International events during the late spring and early summer temporarily
interrupted Hoover's spiritual assault on the advocates of federal intervention and the nation's march toward recovery. Through the winter and early
spring of 1931, the nation's economic indicators showed portents of recovery, but the indicators changed precipitously with news of the imminent
economic and political collapse of Austria and Germany. The news was no
surprise, at least to one economist—England's iconoclastic John Maynard
Keynes. Keynes had made international news in the spring of 1919, when he
unceremoniously resigned his economic duties at the Versailles Peace Conference. His resignation was a direct result of the unrealistic and unwork-
able financial impositions that the allies had foisted upon Austria and Germany. Keynes's resulting polemic, *The Economic Consequences of the Peace*,
registered a rare double result, especially for an economist: it made him famous and proved him prophetic. Twelve years after its publication, Keynes's
prophecies of German and Austrian socioeconomic rupture caused by repa-
ration treaties confronted Herbert Hoover. In the words of Hoover's secretary of state, Henry Stimson, in 1931, "the peace of 1919 was challenged and
found wanting."[25]

On May 11, the Austrian government announced that its principal private bank, the Creditanstadt fur Handel und Gewerbe, was on the verge of
collapse. The announcement, according to Elliott A. Rosen, "shattered
confidence" in other European banking institutions.[26] By the early summer,
Europe's central banks neared collapse. Germany's banking system was
particularly hard hit, as international fears of economic and political col-

lapse triggered the flight of capital away from its borders. Its cries for help only exacerbated the collapse.

The German financial crisis was caused by many factors: overseas trade was negligible due to the world-wide depression; post-war xenophobia moved former trading partners closer to autarchy; the German government's austerity budgets heightened the downward spiral of deflation; and major banks such as the Creditanstalt had invested in Austrian and Eastern European manufacturing companies that went bankrupt.[27] Such investment failures only fueled the "psychological tide" of cash withdrawals.[28] Many other major European banks suffered irreparable losses as a result of large investments in developing post-war industrial and agricultural markets. When production and profits decreased, banks could not meet demands for cash without calling in industrial loans.

U.S. interests in the German financial crisis were both financial and political. Regarding the former, the nation, particularly the banking community, could ill-afford a German collapse. Because of the attraction of high interest rates, coupled with few investment opportunities at home, American banks held between $500 million and $1.7 billion in German securities.[29] Two major New York banks, the Chase Bank and the Guaranty Trust Company, had invested nearly half of their capital in such securities.[30] Worthless securities, in other words, would have sparked a withdrawal frenzy in the nation's business capitol. New York's Governor, Franklin Roosevelt, in a letter to his former boss, Josephus Daniels, was quick to condemn the crass commercialism of the Hoover administration's response: "They [the Hoover administration] jumped into this German moratorium business on twenty-four hours notice and without previous study just because they were told by the New York Bankers that if Germany went into bankruptcy, the Stock Exchange in New York would close and most of our biggest banks would be seriously embarrassed."[31]

The political interests, linked closely with the economic circumstances, held more grave possibilities. World peace was potentially at stake. German Chancellor Heinrich Bruening warned the U.S. ambassador to Germany, Frederic M. Sackett, that unless foreign aid was forthcoming, his minority government would be ousted by either communists or Hitlerites. British Prime Minister J. Ramsay MacDonald, based on his talk with Bruening and Foreign Minister Julius Curtius, warned the United States that the collapse of Bruening's government would lead to a communist revolution on a grand scale.[32] Hoover acted quickly. In a meeting with Secretaries Stimson, Ogden Mills, and Andrew Mellon on June 5, Hoover proposed a one-year suspension of all intergovernmental debts and war reparations.

Hoover did not publicly address the matter until June 20, as he attempted to line up congressional support at home and international support abroad. While most nations pledged their support, France proved recalcitrant. Premier Pierre Laval feared that German marks originally targeted for war reparations would be used to increase armaments and dump German sur pluses on an already sated world market. The French also harbored bitter- ness over a proposed German and Austrian customs agreement made pub- lic on March 21. After much haggling, cajoling and even threatening, France finally acquiesced to the moratorium on July 6.

The Return to Confidence

In the midst of the international financial crisis, Hoover gave what he termed "a serious speech" on June 15 to the Indiana Republican Editorial Association.[33] Writing it had clearly given Hoover pause. In a diary entry of June 11, 1931, Joslin wrote, "Thank the Lord the President has completed his Indianapolis speech. Never have I seen a man work harder trying to get the words down on paper. . . . Actually there have been fourteen editions of this speech."[34] The text offers no indications that Europe's political or eco- nomic future was at stake. Hoover mentioned only obliquely that "a large part of the forces which have swept our shores from abroad are the malign inheritances in Europe of the Great War."[35] At one level, the speech is merely a repetition of now-familiar Hooverian topoi: the federal government would not legislate the nation out of the depression; industrial cooperation, tariff protection, drought relief, fiscal prudence, and increased expenditures for public works projects had tempered the depression's severity; and faith in intellectual and spiritual forces would lead the nation to future prosperity.

Yet, at another level, the speech marks an important thematic return in Hoover's rhetorical battle against the depression—a return to an emphasis on confidence. Not since Hoover's October 2, 1930, speech to the American Banking Association (ABA) had confidence been an explicit rhetorical theme; in fact, prior to his June 15 speech at Indianapolis, Hoover had made only one passing reference to confidence in 1931. Confidence was men- tioned at the outset of the speech as Hoover isolated "fear and apprehen- sion . . . [as] very real, tangible economic forces"; these forces, moreover, led people to decrease their purchases of goods and services, "thereby decreas- ing our production and employment" (298). This situation, Hoover contin- ued, "lead[s] our bankers and businessmen to extreme caution. . . . We are suffering today more from frozen confidence than we are from frozen securi- ties" (298). Notice the sequence of cause and effect: bankers and business- men merely reacted to citizens' fears and uncertainties. By the close of the speech, however, the sequence was reversed: "Our transcendent momen- tary need is a much larger degree of confidence among our business agen- cies and that they shall extend this confidence in more than words" (307).

The reversal is largely explicable within the immediate historical con- text and in relation to Hoover's October speech to the ABA. Nearly nine months earlier, Hoover had transferred the responsibility for confidence levels onto the banking community. Confidence, in other words, was a top-down phenomenon, not one from the bottom-up. This mode of thinking held important consequences for Hoover's later policy measures insofar as business, aided by bankers, might reinfuse consumer demand. Hoover's reversal is also explicable in the context of Germany's banking crisis. Shortly after the speech, Hoover asked the governor of New York's Federal Reserve Bank, George Harrison, to extend and enlarge credits to Germany's ailing Reichsbank, a request that Harrison declined. Despite having the necessary reserves, Harrison would not "extend" American banking confidence (for example, offer loans) precisely because the international scene did not warrant it, Hoover's claims notwithstanding.

Hoover's emphasis on consumer and business confidence poses a vexing question: if restored confidence was the sine qua non of economic recovery, then why did it suddenly reappear only on June 15? One plausible answer lies in Hoover's perception of the crisis. Prior to the international events of June and July, many economic experts predicted that the depression had finally run its course and that economic recovery was forthcoming. If Hoover held such convictions, he could politically afford to make the depression a tertiary issue while privileging methods of recovery and their attendant ideological suppositions. The depression, after all, was a "passing trial," one in which the Hooverian calculus for recovery appeared to be working. In contrast, by mid-June Hoover symbolized the depression as "the greatest crisis the world has ever known" (306). Given the situation's extreme gravity, it follows that Hoover might revert back, at least in part, to rhetorical basics. While his attack on the advocates of direct federal intervention persisted, the reemergence of confidence perhaps signaled that the battle had once again expanded to include the very possibility of economic recovery. This possibility, however, did not deter Hoover from continuing to argue over the means and methods of warfare.

Religion Redux

Following the moratorium, Hoover returned to grounding his recovery program along overtly religious lines. In an August 8 radio address to the World Conference of the YMCA, Hoover affirmed the organization's beliefs: "you are right in the abiding confidence that the solution of all social, economic, governmental, and international problems must be guided by an idealism which finds its firm foundations in religious faith." [36] For the first time in his presidency, and before a world-wide audience, Hoover honed in on theological specifics:

> No thoughtful person can overlook the profound truth that the ideas
> and ideals of Christ which you uphold not only have dominated the
> course of civilization since His time but are the foundations of our eco-
> nomic and social life today. Because of human weakness, the Golden
> Rule may have its daily violations, but this great principle, aimed at

the common good, penetrates and profoundly modifies all the
forces in the modern world in which we live (381).

Hoover's secularized program for national economic recovery—localized
voluntarism—had no more potent parallel than the "second greatest" commandment: love thy neighbor as thyself. Such neighbors, moreover, comprised "a great militant body enlisted in the fundamental advancement of
human progress" (382). The rightness and righteousness of Hoover's course
justified a call to arms against economic apostates.

As the summer wore on, and as the unemployment rate neared 16 percent, Hoover intimated that the war would be fought both at home and
abroad. Hoover touched briefly on each front in his unusual press conference of September 1.[37] The future fiscal position of the United States, Hoover
warned, was contingent on events abroad, as the economic climate was
"very much dominated by the European situation."[38] Meanwhile, as winter
neared, Hoover emphasized the federal government's role at home. "The
only problem in governmental fiscal questions is the maintenance of the social obligations of the Government to a population that are in difficulties,
that no government . . . will see its people starve or go hungry" (405). While
Hoover would attempt to solve both the international and domestic economic situations through voluntary channels, the divergent situations
would engender very different rhetorical approaches.

Confidence, the National Credit Corporation, and the Press

As September neared, "the European situation" no longer referred exclusively to Germany's financial crisis; gold withdrawals from England created
such a crisis that on August 25 a new national government pledged to economy measures was created. Even worse for the United States was England's
September 21 announcement that it was going off of the gold standard. The
announcement served only to accentuate the extremely tenuous banking
situation in the United States. Prior to the announcement, gold flowed freely
and abundantly into America, as many nations felt that their reserves were
most secure there. U.S. banks, in turn, used such deposits for lending purposes. England's announcement triggered a large migration of gold out of
America because many feared that the United States would also go off the
gold standard, in other words, that other nations' gold reserves would be
indefinitely frozen by American banks. As gold left the country, bank reserves dropped, which resulted in higher interest rates. At an even more localized level, depleted bank reserves triggered runs on banks as depositors
scurried to withdraw their money for fear it would disappear. The mad
scramble for liquidity forced many banks either to close their doors or to
tighten available credit.

Such caution, of course, held deleterious economic consequences for the great many in need of credit. Across the country, credit, the life-blood of commerce, was all but frozen in the fall of 1931. And where credit was frozen, there, too, was confidence frozen. Hoover explained the devolving logic of the banking situation to Harrison in an October 5 letter. Perhaps not surprisingly, much of the problem at home was attributable to a collective state of mind:

> we are in a degenerating vicious cycle. Economic events of Europe have demoralized our farm produce and security prices. This has given rise to an unsettlement of public mind. There have been in some localities foolish alarm over the stability of our credit structure and considerable withdrawals of currency. In consequence bankers in many other parts of the country in fear of the possibility of such unreasoning demands of depositors have deemed it necessary to place their assets in such liquid form as to enable them to meet drains and runs. To do this they sell securities and restrict credit. The sale of securities demoralizes their price and jeopardizes other banks.[39]

According to Martin L. Fausold, the credit crunch became an obsession with Hoover, and he swiftly went into high organizational gear.[40] Hoover initially contacted Federal Reserve Board Governor Eugene Meyer and inquired whether leading bankers might "voluntarily" form a private credit corporation to aid troubled banks. Despite their initial reluctance, major New York bankers met with him in late September at a secret meeting convened at Treasury Secretary Mellon's home. To the assembled bankers Hoover read from a prepared script: "The failure of banks in constantly increasing numbers, and the destruction of confidence and increasing fear throughout the country . . . calls for concerted action on the part of our leading bankers and strong banks to avert a possible threat to our entire credit structure."[41] That the nation's entire credit structure was in fact imperiled was underscored by Hoover's narration of recent banking history: since 1930, 2,560 banks had failed, involving $1.8 billion in deposits. The fear and uncertainty engendered by such closings had precipitated a run on banks totaling nearly $800 million—and rising.

The solution that Hoover envisioned involved "one or more central organizations which would furnish rediscount facilities to banks throughout the country on the basis of sound assets not legally eligible for rediscount at the Federal Reserve Bank." Put differently, state and local banks whose assets were sound but not liquid and who were not eligible for rediscounting of such assets from the Federal Reserve, needed stronger, more liquid, banks to help them meet the withdrawal demands of depositors. While eligibility provisions for Federal Reserve rediscounting would be expanded under the auspices of the Glass-Steagall Act, such a measure "would require time." And, Herbert Hoover was running out of time in the fall of 1931. The aims of the organization, then, were two-fold: it "would not only restore liquidity to sol-

vent institutions, but, what is even more important, we would at once tend
to restore confidence now sadly lacking among all classes of bank depositors
in all sections of the country." Liquidity was a potent sign of confidence, and
$500 million (the amount at which the organization was capitalized),
Hoover hoped, would suffice to persuade Americans to have faith in their
banks and bankers.

The bankers, despite their initial aversion to the plan, eventually acquiesced, and thus was born the National Credit Corporation (NCC). The organization, with its emphasis on coordinated cooperation and voluntarism (albeit coerced), represented the "perfect expression of Hoover's philosophy."[42]
The private organization had the additional virtue of not requiring congressional approval, though Hoover held a conference with key congressional
members on October 6. Hoover's ability to persuade such an elite body of
bankers did not surprise William Allen White. Hoover, he observed, possessed a great capacity to convince intellectuals, although he had a much
smaller capacity to stir the common emotions of the common crowd.[43]
Joslin, perhaps reflecting on the private meeting, hoped that the president
might somehow transform his private persona into his public one: "I wish
the President could show his true self in public as he does reveal himself in
private. When alone with a small group he always shines, always domi-
nates, but he does not do as well in public, because of shyness or perhaps because he is on 'exhibition.'"[44]

In keeping with Hoover's October, 1930, address to the ABA, the relationship between bankers and public confidence was an essential one. Without
confidence in the banking system, Americans would continue to take their
money out of banks, and therefore out of circulation. Moreover, such a pref-
erence for liquidity forced banks to become liquid as well, exchanging securities and loans for hard currency. As Hoover explained the situation to Harrison, "The only real way to break this cycle is to restore confidence in the
people at large. To do this requires major unified action that will give
confidence to the country. It is this that I have asked of the New York
bankers."[45] Harrison duly noted the confidence-inspiring rhetorical function of the Corporation.

> The difficulty . . . with the situation throughout the country at the
> time the credit corporation was formed, was an unholy fear on the
> part of many bankers that this unreasoning withdrawal of deposits . . .
> might continue and might put them in a position where they would be
> embarrassed. The mere creation of the corporation . . . relieved the
> minds not only of the depositors but of many of the bankers as well.[46]

Undersecretary of the Treasury Ogden Mills agreed: the NCC "had an immense psychological effect on the restoration of confidence when it was
badly needed. . . . After all, what is credit but confidence."[47]

As close allies with the administration, Harrison and Mills greatly exaggerated the effects of the NCC. Even minimal effects on confidence, though, were circumscribed by Hoover's public silence concerning the organization's goals, which were designed principally to reinstill public confidence in local banks and to reduce apprehensions feeding the withdrawal frenzy.[48] In other words, the public needed to hear from its president that its money would be safe. On October 9, in his bi-weekly press conference, Hoover broached the issue of publicity with White House reporters: "I am wondering if we could get clear possibly to the public what we are really trying to do."[49] Hoover then proceeded to detail how the NCC would work and what ailments it would cure, but it was all "background," not for attribution or quotation. Hoover concluded his credit didactic with an exhortation to the press: "some of you may want to endeavor to get this down to the understanding of the people on the street who do not ordinarily grasp the meaning of credit flow when it emanates from large institutions" (477). Hoover had unencumbered access to the nation via radio, yet he opted for diffusion and persuasion by print journalists—a group whom Hoover collectively viewed with increasing contempt and suspicion.

Hoover's decision to have the press function as his rhetorical surrogates in this instance may have been influenced by a letter he received from Robert E. Clark, head of the Clark Subscription Agency, a Chicago-based news organization. Clark wrote that the "mental effect on the public" of the NCC "is what most interests me."[50] To maximize that effect, Clark noted that "the fullest measure of your new plan cannot be realized without a concerted, intelligent, co-operation of our national press." Clark suggested the creation of a "press bureau" to publicize the NCC since many Americans could not grasp "the intricate working out of such a plan." Furthermore, "What the people want is specific examples of what this plan is actually accomplishing and as each of these examples is presented the people become more confident and confidence is now of supreme importance."[51]

While the press may have been amenable to carrying out Hoover's rhetorical duties in the fall of 1929, by the fall of 1931 the relationship had deteriorated to the point where Paul Y. Anderson of the *Nation* claimed that relations between Hoover and the press had "reached a stage of unpleasantness without parallel during the present century."[52] Anderson's remarks could not have surprised Hoover. More than a month earlier, his friend and the managing editor of the *Buffalo Evening News*, Arthur H. Kirchhofer, had written the president a ten page single-spaced letter spelling out some "newspaper fundamentals."[53] That Hoover needed such a media primer after two-and-a-half years in office speaks volumes about his relationship with the press. The situation clearly worried Kirchhofer: "I am alarmed at what amounts to a rising tide of sentiment that White House press relationships are far from satisfactory. The feeling is even apparent among men who have been most friendly to you and sympathetic with your efforts, and I suppose the whole situation is reflected in your attitude about it." Kirchhofer closed by urging Hoover to "make a radical revision in your newspaper relation-ships and get some of these publicity matters settled."

He must have been chagrined by Hoover's October 9 news conference, for the president did not even release a statement regarding how the press might relate "credit flow" to the "people on the street." Not surprisingly, the press did not follow Hoover's admonitions, and not surprisingly, the press shifted the rhetorical burden back to where it properly belonged. As the edi-tors of *Business Week* judged matters, "it [the NCC] has not been announced or explained in terms that are likely to have much effect on the man in the street. Nobody has told him his bank is now safe. Yet the whole object is to rebuild confidence. Perhaps it is not yet too late to utilize newspapers, the ra-dio, every means to convey to the small depositor the feeling that something has been done for him, personally." [54]

It was, in fact, too late: "By November, Hoover could see that the volun-tary banking-pool effort was a failure." [55] As a privately controlled body, the NCC had no legislative mandate to meet certain loan quotas. Moreover, sev-eral bankers feared that NCC loans might go to insolvent, and not just illiq-uid, banks. [56] Not surprisingly, then, the NCC loaned only $10 million of a $500 million pool. Such a paltry sum could not provide the cornerstone for national recovery, let alone inspire nationwide confidence.

Given bankers' initial reluctance to create the credit pool, Hoover per-haps knew that the organization was doomed to fail. He suggested as much in his October 7 "Statement on Financial and Economic Problems." Point number five of his "program of action" presaged Hoover's first significant move away from voluntarism—the Reconstruction Finance Corporation (RFC). In keeping with his warfare dramatization, he justified the federal gov-ernment's intervention into private finance by analogy: the RFC would be "similar in character and purpose" to the War Finance Corporation created during World War I. [57] Hoover repeated the analogy in his Decem-ber State of the Union Message. [58] What is unusual in both instances is that, beyond the analogy with World War I, Hoover did not publicly defend the seemingly radical compromise of his political and economic philosophy. The federal government would soon enter the business of direct federal aid to the tune of $2 billion, yet Hoover offered little, if any, explanation except to say that such a corporation would "strengthen confidence." What re-mained consistent was Hoover's belief that cheap and abundant credit, coupled with the concomitant return of confidence, would create the cli-mate for recovery. This presumed, of course, that there existed a demand for such credit, a view largely at odds with an underemployed and an under-consuming population.

The Winter Campaign for Recovery

The second front on which the war was fought stemmed entirely from domestic economic circumstances, and it was fought on a much more public stage. The financial events in Europe reverberated throughout the United States in the summer of 1931, which caused banks to fail, prices to fall, wages to plummet, and unemployment to swell, as the nation braced for the upcoming winter. Hoover, despite his concessions on credit backed by the Federal treasury, remained adamant that the federal government would not make direct relief payments to those in financial need. Needs would be met instead through efficient organization among local, state, and federal organizations, and through privately endowed charities.

Hoover's rhetorical campaign to effect winter relief began unofficially on September 1, as he declared "that no government . . . will see its people starve or go hungry or go cold, and every agency of a government . . . must be implemented to that end." [59] In organizing winter relief, the federal government was fulfilling its "social obligation." Ten days later, the campaign encountered its first stumbling block—media exaggeration of the relief effort's enormity. At a not-for-publication news conference on September 11, Hoover targeted unspecified members of the press for disturbing the public mind by exaggerating "the unemployment situation and what is likely to happen during the winter." [60] Hoover then proceeded to describe the extent of the relief operation in a clear and concise fashion. Yet he concluded in much the same manner as he had on October 9: it was the press' duty to reassure the public mind. "I just make that suggestion to you in the work you do that it is in national interest [sic] that we should keep the public mind properly advised and keep the people steady in the boat" (419). Once again, Hoover refused to go directly to the people over a most pressing matter.

By the beginning of October, Hoover must have felt besieged: in a twenty-two day span, from September 4 to September 26, no less than seven vast public works programs were proposed in Congress. The dollar totals ranged from $2 billion to $8.5 billion. [61] Perhaps more important was the enormous federal budget deficit projected for fiscal year 1932, a sum estimated at $2.1 billion, or nearly half the amount of the entire 1932 federal budget. Hoover's decision not to cancel his September 21 address to Detroit's American Legion in light of England's announcement to leave the gold standard makes sense: the nation simply could not afford another bonus payment to World War I veterans. Hoover pleaded, "We can carry our present expenditures without jeopardy to national stability. We cannot carry more without grave national risks." [62] He resorted to two favored images in framing the federal government's financial predicament: "The very first stone in the foundations of stability and of recovery . . . is the stability of the Government of the United States. . . . I invite you to enlist in that fight. The country's need of this service is second only to war" (432). Hoover got what he wanted. On September 24, the American Legion adopted an anti-bonus resolution.

The huge projected deficits, coupled with massive congressional spending proposals, seemed only to strengthen Hoover's resolve to make winter relief a largely local and private matter. Perhaps out of desperation, or perhaps because of his recent rhetorical success with the American Legion, Hoover took his relief campaign directly into living rooms across the nation via a radio address. Hoover employed the symbolic resources of war, Christianity, and historical continuity to contextualize the movement for relief. The tripartite appeals coalesced to form what Hoover termed the "nation's conscience." The allusion to warfare was invoked at the very outset. "This broadcast tonight marks the beginning of the mobilization of the whole Nation for a great undertaking." [63] The enemy was the "unemployment and privation" many would face "during the coming winter" (488). Additionally, the battle plan that Hoover had implemented from the depression's outset—public works, cooperation, and voluntary action—would remain in place, since it "accords with the fundamental sense of responsibility . . . upon which our nation is founded" (489). To rupture the continuity between past and present would have endangered American "ideals and the spirit of its people" (490). The nation's "final victory" over the depression had its symbolic analogue in "the victory of Yorktown," but, first, the country had to "pass through" its contemporary Valley Forge (491).

In addition to warfare and historical continuity, Hoover linked the nation's future to faithful allegiance to Christ's teachings: "This civilization and this great complex, which we call American life, is builded and can alone survive upon the translation into individual action of that fundamental philosophy announced by the Savior nineteen centuries ago. . . . Modern society cannot survive with the defense of Cain, 'Am I my brother's keeper.'" Notice that the millennial future was contingent on "individual action" and not simply "action" or "collective action." Direct federal aid, in other words, was antithetical to Biblical teaching. Hoover implied that once individuals abnegated their financial and personal responsibility to others, the vast edifice of American civilization would come crumbling down. Thus, given Hoover's explicit association between political and religious cosmologies, we can perhaps better understand his unwillingness to acquiesce both to popular and congressional mandate. In Hoover's words, "No governmental action, no economic doctrine, no economic plan or project can replace that God-imposed responsibility of the individual man and woman to their neighbors" (490).

In addition, the "national suffering" was dramatized as a "failure to observe these primary yet inexorable laws of human relationship" (490). Part of the depression (Hoover did not specify which part) was directly attributable to ignoring Christ's precepts. There was a reason, a supernatural force behind the nation's collective suffering: the nation had simply shirked its divinely imposed economic responsibilities. The economic complexities were thus collapsed into a simple economic moralism in which guilt figured prominently. The matter, Hoover concluded, was "a trial of the heart and the conscience." Not to participate in the relief campaign was, therefore, to ignore a patriotic call to arms, to sever the continuity with the nation's heroic origins, and to flaunt one's intransigence before a vengeful God. But it was also to turn the self against the self. After all, "no one with a spark of human sympathy can contemplate unmoved the possibilities of suffering that can crush many of our unfortunate fellow Americans if we shall fail them" (488).

Hoover risked a great deal of political capital with such a daring interpretation of economic events. A principal risk involved a depletion of resources: what if individuals simply had no money, food, or shelter to give? Were they, therefore, doubly unfaithful? How would an ever-critical nation view Hoover's offer of direct federal aid (RFC loans) to the nation's privileged (bankers and industrialists)? Cries of hypocrisy would indeed be heard. At a more rhetorical level, what did Hoover's departure from such staples as "confidence," "progress," and "rationality" signal? Moreover, what, if any, rhetorical resources were left should Hoover's black and white view of economic depression fail to produce recovery? Whether he knew it or not, Hoover was talking himself into a corner from which there could be no escape—save repudiating "the war" altogether.

Presidential Silence and the Reconstruction Finance Corporation

The first seven months of 1932 represent an extraordinary time in American economic history and a critical time in Herbert Hoover's presidency. The face and shape of domestic economic policy changed forever, from the minimalist state characteristic of nineteenth-century America to the bureaucratic state born of federal intervention. As many others have noted, Hoover was the last of the old-guard presidents and the first of the new, but the transition did not materialize until 1932. The transition, moreover, was reflected in a new rhetorical strategy, one in which economic recovery grew increasingly reliant on the federal government and less reliant on the American people. This shift was reflected in Hoover's increasingly limited speaking schedule; in fact, prior to his campaign for reelection, which began formally on August 11, Hoover gave six speeches, only one of which directly addressed the nation on economic recovery. Fausold, in discussing this pivotal period, claims that Hoover "was less and less able to rally the nation behind his program." [64] Perhaps a more accurate assessment is that Hoover simply did not try.

Hoover's rhetorical reticence was justified in a February 9 statement released by the White House. It announced that Hoover would no longer participate in White House receptions, since "official demands occupy his every waking hour." [65] The deepening crisis, though, required "inspirational leadership," in addition to behind-the-scenes politicking. [66] The possible explanations behind Hoover's retreat from public economic rhetoric in 1932 are many, but three seem particularly compelling. To his friend, Julius Barnes, Hoover confessed that "no President must ever admit he has been wrong." [67] In addition, by 1932 Hoover's program of cooperation, voluntarism, and public works seemed an abysmal failure in facilitating economic recovery. More importantly, his rhetorical emphasis on individualism, in its manifold iterations, was being questioned, if not repudiated, on a daily basis. Thus, given his fairly consistent rhetorical line and his intractable stubbornness (or perhaps self-righteousness), Hoover was disinclined to symbolize publicly the draconian legislative changes inaugurated in 1932. As William Appleman Williams notes, "he simply could not give over and admit through his actions that he had abandoned his commitment to an American community and to the spirit and will of the people."[68] But beyond Hoover's unwillingness to admit publicly his errors lay another problem. Stephen Skowronek, in examining why Hoover did not capitalize on his legislative departures in 1932, claims that "he could never link his initiatives with the promise of constructing a new [order]. . . . He could no more assault the received formulas directly than call his entire political career into question."[69] Direct federal intervention in economic matters was anathema to Hoover's beliefs. How could he then justify policies to which he was philosophically opposed? A second explanation, one offered by Ellis Hawley and intimately related to a role Hoover adopted in 1930, is that Hoover had become more prophet than pragmatist, especially in his public utterances. Pledged to the belief that his system was right since it was based on absolute laws of progress, Hoover was unable to admit publicly his failures and errors.[70] Walter Lippmann suggests a third possibility. In a letter of January 15, 1932, to Felix Frankfurter, he speculated, "The whole matter [of the administration's credit interventions] raises troublesome issues which it is difficult to clarify at this time, how far, for example, it is justifiable to tell the country how great the danger is, and if telling it would not multiply the danger enormously."[71] Hoover's silence, in other words, was saving the country from itself.[72] Thus, in less than three years Hoover had come full circle, as he retreated to a position of presidential silence. The silence, however, was offset by the din of a legislative barrage, the likes of which the nation had never heard during peacetime.

As his 1931 State of the Union Message presaged, Hoover proposed a comprehensive legislative agenda to the seventy-second Congress on January 4, 1932.[73] The eight-fold program was unified principally by the increase of available credit. Perhaps the two most important measures that Hoover advanced, the RFC and the easing of Federal Reserve discount rates (soon to be the Glass-Steagall Act), reflected his belief that cheap, abundant credit, loaned to reliable businesses and banks, would provide the impetus for recovery. Such a belief is not at all incommensurate with Hoover's earlier rhetoric, especially in light of his 1930 ABA speech: credit was a requisite for public confidence. The major source of divergence involved the credit source.

In 1932 the Treasury-backed RFC would take over the responsibility from recalcitrant bankers.[74] This rather dramatic change in the source of credit helps account for Hoover's otherwise anomalous pronouncement that "the Congress will go far to reestablish confidence to restore the functioning of our economic system, and to rebuilding of prices and values and to quickening employment." [75] In written, undramatic form, Hoover announced that he in fact had been at least partially wrong and that recovery had more to do with institutional mandate than with organized voluntary cooperation. Though Hoover had not given up on a bountiful future precipitated by the "unity of our people," the restoration of hope and confidence would require "prompt and courageous action" by the federal government (4). Hoover's "Special Message to the Congress" thus inaugurated a move away from public persuasion towards private negotiations with a cooperative Congress.

Congress heeded Hoover's call for prompt action. On January 11 the Senate approved the RFC by a vote of 63 to 8, and on January 15 the House passed the measure, 335 to 55. Hoover signed the bill into law one week later. Despite the lopsided majorities, the bill was unprecedented. It "launched the boldest anti-depression measure ever undertaken by the national government." [76] The Hoover administration "became the first in American history to use the power of the federal government to intervene directly in the economy in time of peace." [77] It was, as James S. Olson declares, a "revolution" in public policy.[78] Even one of the leading apostles of the anti-Hoover historians admitted that "Hoover was the first president in American history to bring any federal leadership to such an emergency." [79]

Given this shibboleth-shattering measure, some reactionary dissidents predictably saw it as a move toward bolshevism.[80] Even the progressive Nebraska Senator, George Norris (Rep.), said in response to the RFC, "I have been called a socialist, a bolshevik, a communist, and a lot of other terms of a similar nature, but in the wildest flights of my imagination I never thought of such a thing as putting the Government into business as far as this bill [the RFC] would put it." [81] The RFC's ostensible purpose was to lend taxpayer dollars to rescue banks, savings banks, trust companies, credit unions, insurance companies, and, after Interstate Commerce Commission approval, to make loans to financially strapped railroads.

Privately, though, in two letters to Colonel Frank Knox of the Hearst newspaper chain, Hoover acknowledged that the RFC, along with banking legislation pending congressional approval (the Glass-Steagall Act) was aimed principally at restoring public confidence. In a February 11 letter Hoover noted, "It is our belief that with the completing of the Reconstruction organization through the country and the passage of the banking bills we should have a further strengthening of public and banking confidence by the week of the 22nd [of February]." [82] Two days later, Hoover was more emphatic: "The general idea is that by the end of this week we will have our two major financial measures completed [the RFC and Glass-Steagall] . . . The two combined should enable us to restore confidence so far as confidence can be restored by reopening the flow of credit."[83] While restoring confidence may have still been Hoover's overriding goal, the agency responsible for it, in particular, had a decidedly anti-Hooverian ring—namely the federal government. What the voluntary NCC could not do, was not willing to do, the RFC, capitalized by the U.S. Treasury at $2 billion and enacted by congressional approval, was forced to do.[84] Importantly, though, Hoover had not surrendered the idea that cooperative, voluntary organizations could also help restore confidence as evidenced by the voluntary sister of the RFC, what Hoover named the Citizens Reconstruction Organization (CRO).[85] Given the importance of the RFC measure, combined with its wide bipartisan support, one might logically expect a major address; instead, Hoover issued a brief, three-paragraph written statement. The reason was simple: passage of the RFC signaled that "voluntarism had failed," and Hoover was none too eager to symbolize this ideological about-face to his detractors.[86]

Hoarding, Confidence, and the Citizens Reconstruction Organization

As his creation of the NCC and the RFC suggest, Hoover understood the relationship between the country's credit structure and national confidence; that is, should people fear for the safety of their bank deposits (the Federal Deposit Insurance Corporation—or FDIC—was still more than a year away) and withdraw currency, credit would contract, thereby bringing commerce to a near standstill. Bankers were perhaps even more aware than Hoover of confidence's role in keeping banks viable. In a January, 1932, trade publication of bank auditors and comptrollers, confidence was presented as sacrosanct. "What is the foundation of the structure of every bank?—Confidence. Without the faith of the community which a bank serves it cannot exist."[87] Confidence, though, transcended banking: "what is this world dependent upon?—Confidence, and heaps of it. Confidence in our fellow man; confidence in his undertakings; confidence in our Government, and last but not least, confidence in ourselves." Not surprisingly, then, any citizen not displaying confidence (for example, by trading in one's bonds for gold) was a traitor to his country: "Such a man, if he is an American citizen, has no doubt lost faith in his God and all mankind. If he isn't an outlaw to society he may become one."

Hoover was attuned to the gravity of the banking situation, but he was not content to allow the government-sponsored RFC to do all the confidence-restoring work; such work needed also to come from a national voluntary movement. To facilitate the publicity incumbent on such a movement, Hoover selected Knox of the *Chicago Daily News* and a key Hearst insider. Knox and forty-eight other community and business leaders were invited to the White House on February 6 to receive their charge from the president, as well as to hear from such administrative insiders as Mills, General Charles G. Dawes, the president of the RFC, and Julius Barnes, the chairman of the U.S. Chamber of Commerce.[88] Confidence—specifically how the fledgling organization might go about restoring it—was the theme of the conference.

Hoover narrated the causes for the banking crisis that had caused mass hoarding, while at the same time vindicating his administration's actions over the previous nine months.

> It [hoarding] began in April last year in consequential amounts. The disturbances in Austria, which finally culminated in the German panic, showed paralleled increase of hoarding in the United States, which rose at one time to about seventy or one hundred million a week. Bank failures necessarily both arise from and are the cause of hoarding, but the movement of bank failures has the same parallel. We then brought the German moratorium to restore confidence in the world. It served that purpose, and our hoarding and our bank failures ceased, but then for the first time we noticed a phenomenon which we have to deal with today, and that is that the money taken out did not return. We went along after that until the disturbance began in Great Britain which finally resulted in the British abandonment of the gold standard. Instantly, within 24 hours after the Bank of England ceased paying gold, hoarding jumped in the United States to $250,000,000 a week. Bank failures followed. We then brought on the National Credit Corporation as a measure to restore domestic confidence. The hoarding stopped instantly, bank failures ceased, but the money did not come back. Following that, a month later I addressed Congress upon the necessity of creating an institution [the RFC] which would stand behind the whole credit structure of the country and thus assure confidence. . . . Hoarding has largely ceased with the passage of this legislation. But nothing has come back.[89]

In this remarkably aggrandizing passage, uttered safely out of range from the press and public, Hoover literally professed to having saved the world. And while he eventually needed legislation to do it, the end—confidence—was the guiding principle in his administration's heroic actions.

Treasury Secretary Mills[90] was next on the dais, and he explained that the hoarding problem was caused not by a "lack of patriotism or selfishness," as the Association of Bank Auditors and Comptrollers had claimed, but by the "average man's ignorance of the complex mechanisms of credit." Based on our late-twentieth-century sensibilities, such a problem would seem rife for public presidential leadership. Mills (and Hoover) thought otherwise: your "job is to explain the situation. You cannot do it entirely through the press, because after all a story is only news once. In order to get a story into all the papers it probably has to come from the President, and he cannot keep telling the story of hoarding every day in the week." Rather than concerted presidential rhetorical leadership of public opinion, "what we must do to cut this great evil is to organize on a national basis in order to combat it." Ignorance, a relatively benign condition caused by complexity, had become a great moral issue inside of four sentences.[91]

Voluntary organization, a key component of Hooverian problem solving and rationality, was not the solution that the President of the RFC envisaged. According to Dawes, the hoarding problem required a less reasoned approach: "Millions of people are slowly committing economic suicide. The American people of all others! Slowly strangling themselves to death. It is not a situation where you can reach the people by reason. It is a mob situation—mass psychology, mass conditions." Hoover, seated next to Dawes, must have cringed at the General's unscripted foray into the American psyche. Dawes, though, was just getting started: "you cannot reach it [a solution] through argument. You must reach [it] through men's feelings and instincts. That is the thing that brings men together to create atmosphere. Approach this doctrine as you would approach war." Dawes continued, "If we are going to go into this thing to reach it through reason instead of instinct, you are making a mistake." The General was not yet done; one final blow to the administration remained: "It [the solution] can only be reached by leadership, and this the people of our country have not had. When they get it, they will rise to the situation. . . . Here are the people of the United States, through lack of leadership at this time destroying themselves." Hoover and Joslin were panic-stricken by the General's ravings. In his diary shortly after the conference ended, Joslin recorded,

> The real news of the hoarding conference did not get out. Dawes went haywire, saying we were dangling on the brink of complete disaster. If his remarks are made known by any of the conferees they may start a panic. To the credit of the 70 [*sic*] men present they did not mention the matter to the press. Very possibly half of them didn't understand him, for he talked so fast, shouted so loud and pounded the table so hard that he was almost unintelligible.[92]

Also militating against Dawe's comments leaking to the press was the matter of placement: several more reasonable positions were articulated following the General's anti-administration tirade.

Hoover had the last word, and that word is revealing for what it says about his expanding understanding of the grounds for confidence, a grounding apparently much more material and tangible in nature: "We are making war on depression. War against a lack of confidence. Our people must have something tangible to do in the fight. There is no use to go out and say 'Have confidence, courage and faith.' They must have something positive to bite on and they can bite on the question of hoarding." At closer inspection, however, Hoover's war for confidence was nothing if not a war of the spirit. While hoarded currency was no doubt real, to return it to banks required a faith that transcended the "biting" that Hoover awkwardly described. Perhaps not surprisingly, then, Hoover's materialism was premised on incorporeal matters of the spirit: "I have felt all along that this is a question of the spirit of a people. What we need is more courage and more recognition of moral responsibilities. What we require are the forces in this country which penetrate into [a] spiritual movement of the people."

At the heart of the confidence problem lay a profoundly rhetorical one: the incipient movement would be appealing to its audience to return its hard-earned and imperiled currency to a group whose collective credibility was negligible. After all, popular wisdom had it that bankers were largely responsible for Wall Street's speculative orgy by offering loans on thin margins at exorbitant interest rates. Additionally, as a group they were too selfish to offer anything but a fraction of the $500 million NCC pool. Hoover was thus attuned to the rhetorical problems faced by Knox's organization; as such, he offered the following advice: "I stated yesterday to the press that we were not undertaking this as a bank relief program; we were undertaking it as a patriotic program to return . . . the dollar to work in the United States." In other words, "it is not a question of the community appealing for a return of this money to the banks themselves. It is an appeal to the community to put its money to work." Putting money to work, though, meant precisely returning it to banks and bankers—the very institution and group increasingly blamed for the deepening depression.

One week later, as bankers threatened to interfere with Knox's organization, he implored Hoover by telegram, "I plead with you not to let cowardice of bankers interrupt the splendid and gratifying progress which we are making back toward prosperity under your leadership."[93] Such interference on the part of bankers threatened the very mission with which Knox had been charged: "you wanted me to help because of my understanding of public psychology. If I know anything about public psychology the thing to do now is to keep driving and harness the public enthusiasm of which I have multitudinous evidences now in the movement already started." Knox closed his missive by imploring Hoover not to give in to the banking community: "Throughout this entire crisis [the] banking business has shown not the slightest capacity for leadership and an utter lack of understanding of public psychology. If confidence is to be restored in the banks I am convinced it will have to be done without help from that quarter." Knox repeated his warnings to Hoover in a second telegram:

> the people have not and apparently cannot be induced to have any
> confidence in a banker spnosored [*sic*] movement[.] Some of the criti-
> cisms of bankers and banking methods and security selling may be un-
> just but they represent a definite and dangerous public point of view[.]
> This state of mind is confirmed by the action of a number of bankers

who have been asked to serve in this organization[.] They [are] declining on the ground that it would not be wise to have any banker concerned in it.[94]

Hoover, though, had more in mind than merely ignoring bankers, as
per Knox's suggestion; instead, in a February 13 letter to Knox, Hoover
expanded the confidence-creating mission of the CRO to include a propaganda campaign against potentially uncooperative banks and bankers.
Hoover recognized that restoring confidence in this instance meant restoring confidence in banks; in other words, "the banks [must] start functioning
as public institutions," which meant they had "no justification for further
strangulation of the country by withdrawal of loans and failure to support
little business."[95] To urge banks to function for the public good, Hoover
noted "that we will need to use some propaganda on the banks." By the close
of his letter, Hoover was more specific: "We must undertake propaganda
that the bank serving its community must be a borrower or it is not serving
the community. In other words we will undertake an anti hoarding campaign against the banks themselves." Two days later, Knox privately registered his reactions to Hoover: "I cannot tell you how great the relief was
when I read your letter of Saturday."[96]

While Hoover and Knox concurred privately on the CRO's relationship to
banks and bankers, the methods for how to bring nearly $1.5 billion out of
hiding and back into circulation were split along a material and rhetorical
axis. While Hoover had stated his intention of giving the American people
"something positive to bite on" at the February 6 Hoarding Conference, rhetorical solutions to the problem proliferated, three of which Knox related to
Hoover in a mid-February letter. First, "a score of the biggest advertisers on
the air" would work "into their broadcasts references to hoarding, its unde-
sirability and its dangers."[97] Second, an editorial campaign by major newspapers would be undertaken. And third, Knox had coordinated "a very effective series of page advertisements dealing with the subject of hoarding" to
be published in "four hundred of the biggest newspapers in the country." In
addition, each of the three solutions would be augmented by educational
community programs conducted by local chapters of the CRO during the
week of February 22.

Knox and Hoover, however, both agreed that something more was
needed, something more tangible—something to "bite on." Perhaps because the anti-hoarding campaign specifically and the depression generally
were metaphorized as "war," Hoover in concert with his Treasury Secretary
conceived the idea of offering a government-sponsored security aimed at
hoarders and their sense of patriotism. While Hoover did not want the sale
of such securities to approach the magnitude of the World War I Liberty
Loan Campaign, it could play a vital role in returning currency back into
banking channels. Mills and Hoover suggested a one-year Treasury

certificate, bearing interest at an annual rate of 2.5 percent and issued in denominations of $50, $100, and $500.[98] While Knox responded that the "rate of interest seems pretty low" and that "denominations lower than fifty dollars" were needed, he was in substantial agreement with Hoover and Mills: the security issue should go forward in late February or early March.[99]

One problem, however, remained unresolved, that of cumulative effect. Hoover and Mills both worried that the Treasury certificates might actually deplete existing bank deposits further, since some might choose to purchase certificates with money already safely deposited in local banks. As Mills put the matter, "the great danger in the whole proposition is that an obligation sufficiently attractive to the hoarder will be equally attractive to the depositor and might result in wholesale withdrawal of deposits from banks."[100] And, although Hoover sought to counter this scenario by targeting only hoarders and by offering a low rate of interest on the certificates— "thereby not competing with the banks or other securities"—caution prevailed. No government-backed securities were offered in the wake of the hoarding. The nation was thus left to masticate on the increasingly bland and insubstantial diet of Hooverian confidence. That the diet was indeed empty is reflected by Hoover's February 16 written statement: only an estimated $34 million of the more than one billion of hoarded currency had returned to circulation.[101]

These meager scraps did not deter Knox. If he could not have the material help of the U.S. Treasury, he would simply extend the rhetorical axis further. Thus, on February 25 he wired Hoover Secretary Lawrence Richey the following inquiry: "Please learn from the President whether he has any objection to a coast to coast broadcast in support of our drive against hoarding on Sunday night March sixth. Have wired him on subject but have received no reply."[102] The slight perturbation caused by Hoover's refusal to acknowledge Knox's request for rhetorical assistance likely increased with receipt of Hoover's reply. To Knox he wired back, "I will go on the radio for you but as you sense the situation in the country I wish you would dictate and telegraph me early tomorrow about a thousand words of a statement I can properly make. I am so close to the situation that I feel it would help if I could have a new vision from the outside on it."[103] Knox ignored both of Hoover's requests: he sent a draft containing only four hundred words, and he sent it five days later, on March 1. While Hoover borrowed generously from Knox's draft, he made significant additions—most notably repeated allusions to warfare and the role of the federal government in facilitating recovery.

Hoover repeatedly emphasized that the people had a crucial role to play, but it was largely derogated to the federal government, since only the latter could "liberate the inherent resources and strength of the American people."[104] The efforts to restore "economic stability and prosperity" were now a "joint effort," but one in which the people responded to the federal government's actions (95). Throughout the speech, Hoover attempted to straddle the people versus the government fence. At times, he sounded like the pre-1932 Hoover, as he championed "the private citizen of the United States," who, "coerced by no authority save his conscience," could be counted on to "meet every emergency in the Nation's economy" (96). But Hoover's ambivalence resurfaced in the conclusion: "The true basis of wealth and the creator of prosperity are the industry and resourcefulness of the people when inspired by vision and sustained by faith" (96). The subtle qualifier is extremely important, as it indicates a subservience to an external agent—in this case the faith and vision procured by balanced federal budgets.

Perhaps motivating the shift in responsibility away from the individual to Washington was the type of war Americans were then waging. Specifically, the localized war that Hoover had earlier sanctioned—battles on 1,000 fronts—had resulted in the selfish fragmentation that might logically result from such a war. One of its material manifestations, not surprisingly, was hoarding, or protecting one's assets, in this case from villainous bankers. Hoover's ill-defined war had effectively imploded. The enemy was now within: "the individual American has not realized the harm he has done when he hoards even a single dollar away from circulation" (94). "The enemy," no longer the "individual American," "strangles our daily life, increases unemployment, and sorely afflicts our farmers" (95). Hoover's war against hoarding was not unlike the traitorous actions described by the Bank Auditors and Comptrollers: "To join in this effort and to respond to this appeal becomes a measure of your faith in our country; it will be the touchstone of your loyalty and of your sense of individual responsibility for the welfare of the whole community; it is your opportunity to prove again that the private citizen of the United States . . . can be counted upon to meet every emergency in the Nation's economy and to rout every foe of the nation's security" (95–96). The last passage is particularly alarming: Hoover's war was increasingly a civil war, one in which "enemy" activity was carefully delineated and presidential sanction was given to "rout" them. Moreover, Hoover's war was being waged in a more centralized fashion. Instead of 1,000 battles on 1,000 fronts, there now existed "100 battles on 100 fronts" (94). What started as a campaign for confidence had become, in exactly one month, a "great war" (94). But unlike World War I, Hoover's war was being fought on American soil, by Americans, against Americans.

Compromises, Congress, and Centralization

Change was also brewing on a different front in the early winter months of 1932. Despite the continued free fall in employment, prices, and tax revenues, Hoover repeatedly urged the adoption of a balanced budget for fiscal year 1933 on the grounds that it would restore confidence. Such a measure required cuts in government spending, but also massive increases in taxes, an action that appears farcical within the context of the Great Depression. A balanced budget, Hoover contended, would increase confidence in America's financial stability, both at home and abroad. The move would also remove the federal government from the securities markets and thereby free up dollars for private investment opportunities. The idea for a balanced budget was not Hoover's alone. The Senate and the House both concurred that a balanced budget was of the utmost importance. Speaker of the House John Nance Garner, in a moment of high drama, asked all of his colleagues who believed that a balanced budget was necessary to rise from their seats. Not a single representative remained seated.

Hoover, in press conferences and written statements, campaigned at great lengths for a balanced federal budget. Yet the campaign appears to make little sense given the deficit incurred during the two preceding fiscal years. Hoover made little ado about deficits of $900 million and $2.1 billion, respectively. He even claimed during a May, 1931, cabinet meeting that no one balanced budgets in wartime, not even a metaphorical one.[105] While Hoff Wilson suggests that Hoover's decision to press for a balanced budget resulted from his willingness to compromise his position on federally sponsored relief, a more plausible fiscal explanation is offered by William J. Barber. He argues that Hoover refused to compromise on a balanced budget because government deficits would have simultaneously deflated bond prices and increased interest rates. In other words, a balanced budget meant higher bond prices for beleaguered bank portfolios and it meant lower interest rates, which, in turn, would invite more capital investments.[106] Thus did Hoover battle nearly seven months with congressional leaders in order to arrive at a legislative package suitable to his demands. He signed the largest peacetime tax increase in the nation's history on June 6, a series of increases aimed primarily at the wealthy and projected to raise more than one billion dollars annually.

One aftermath of the RFC was that it "opened the floodgates to a torrent of demands for federal relief legislation." [107] One such demand, in the form of a bill sponsored by Wisconsin's Robert La Follette, Jr., and Colorado's Edward Costigan, was designed to create the Federal Emergency Relief Board. Based on hearings conducted during the winter, many states reported that relief funds had run dry. As a result, La Follette and Costigan proposed that a federal board provide $375 million worth of direct grants (not loans) to needy states. While the bill fell fourteen votes shy in the Senate, a similar proposal comprised part of the Emergency Relief and Construction Act, a bill that Hoover eventually signed on July 23. Though the measure provided direct federal assistance, Hoover made sure that the need-based state loans were distributed under the auspices of the RFC. Degler and Hoff Wilson claim that Hoover's economic principles were stretched to their limits during the summer of 1932, but this provision, more than perhaps any other, seemed a direct repudiation of Hooverian economic doctrine.[108] In a moment of rare public compromise, Hoover admitted as much in a speech to the Senate. "The time has come," Hoover announced, "when we must all make sacrifice of some parts of our particular views and bring these dangers and degenerations to halt by expeditious action." [109]

Other demands for federal relief legislation were more amenable to Hoover's views, particularly those related to easing credit restrictions. On January 23, Hoover signed the Federal Farm Loan Act, a bill that provided $125 million in federal loans to the federal land banks. A little more than one month later, Hoover signed the Federal Reserve Act (known more commonly as the Glass-Steagall Act), which lowered Federal Reserve Banks' rediscount rates and freed up $750 million for lending purposes. Later in the summer, Hoover signed the Federal Home Loan Bank Act, a bill designed to create discount banks for home mortgages. And, although it had nothing to do with easing credit, Hoover signed the progressive Norris-LaGuardia Act on March 23. The bill essentially allowed labor organizers much easier access to a given group of laborers.

The seven-month period from January to July, 1932, dramatically transformed the character of the federal government. Whereas Franklin Roosevelt's first one hundred days as president became a national baseline from which to judge future presidents, Hoover's first two hundred days of 1932 represents an equally significant benchmark for comparison.[110] Roosevelt, after all, had precedent, a honeymoon period, urgency, oratorical talents, and a huge democratic majority in both houses of Congress. In contrast, Hoover was increasingly unpopular with Congress and the larger public. He was painfully shy in a crowd; and he had no precedent, save World War I, to guide his policies. The label of bold, courageous experimenter, a label commonly attributed to Roosevelt, could be judiciously applied to Herbert Hoover. He was, as Degler describes, "one of the truly activist presidents of our history"; indeed, "no other president had done so much so soon." [111]

Yet, the same seven-month period, despite the unparalleled flurry of legislation, was accompanied by a marked contraction of presidential rhetoric. Hoover simply chose not to symbolize verbally the progressive legislative measures that he had signed into law, and this, no doubt, further undermined his prestige and popularity with the American people. There is evidence, though, that Hoover had come very close to going public with his legislative achievements, among other things, in the spring of 1932. Specifically, on the afternoon of May 6, Knox wired Richey the following: "The President advises me he is going on the air in [a] day or two in appeal to [the] country. This must be well advertised in advance. The broadcast should not take place until [the] country is thoroughly expectant and waiting for it." [112] Attached with this cover note was an eight-page speech, written by Knox, in which he urged the electorate to support Hoover's call for a balanced budget, financed by higher taxes and spending cuts. Not only was the speech never delivered, but Hoover did not address the American people on economic matters until the fall campaign.

The potential explanations for Hoover's decision not to address the nation are legion. One explanation, though, suggests itself, especially if the president was relying exclusively on Knox for his rhetorical materials: namely, the speech simply does not "sound" like Hoover. While Knox correctly emphasized that the administration's legislative agenda "had for its sole purpose the restoration of public confidence and the calming of public fear," little else could have been familiar to Hoover.[113] The speech is rife with hyberbole—"no more ignominious chapter has been written in a grave hour of crisis in the nation's history"— and colorful language—"this mad orgy of demagoguery and blind partisanship." More importantly, Knox called attention both to the passage of the RFC and the Glass-Steagall Act— each of which represented major compromises of Hoover's governing philosophy. And, most significantly, Knox broke the vow Hoover had made earlier to Barnes: "I have failed to accomplish this [getting legislation approved by Congress] through my own personal efforts and now I appeal to the American people to come to my assistance." If Hoover had to admit any compromises or defeats he would do it through less visible channels, such as news conferences and written press releases.

Summary

Well before John Maynard Keynes wrote to Franklin Roosevelt pleading his case for presidential rhetoric attuned to the "animal spirits," Hoover was actively practicing it.[114] But the larger, more important, issue is that of effect: if presidential rhetoric is linked to economic recovery, as has been posited, then why did Herbert Hoover apparently fail so miserably? His presidency seems to offer a compelling rejoinder to the Keynes-Galbraith-Heilbroner-McCloskey hypothesis.

Can we, however, in good historical conscience, unequivocally declare that Hoover's rhetorical campaign was a failure? While it failed to bring about the desired ends, it was not, therefore, a failure. Failure always requires a benchmark, a baseline of comparison, and Hoover's benchmark has usually been the Roosevelt administration. Such a comparison, though, invokes the absurdity of a historical contrary-to-fact conditional: it assumes a contextual uniformity that never existed nor could exist. Implicit in nearly every historical account of Hoover's "abject failure" is the assumption that Roosevelt would have done better. The inevitable comparisons, and their absurdity, are insightfully noted by Alfred B. Rollins: Hoover became "merely the polar opposite of those characteristics popularly arrogated to Roosevelt. He became the man that Roosevelt was not, a mere foil for his artful and persuasive adversary."[115]

But if we can agree that Hoover's confidence economics specifically and his presidency generally failed to achieve the desired results, we should inquire why. There are several possible reasons. First, Hoover may have been too faithful to the Keynesian prescription: economic confidence needed to be at least partially rooted in economic circumstance. After more than two years of "confidence economics," the editors of the *Nation* had grown impatient: Hoover "must some day be brought to recognize that confidence itself must in its turn be based on something." [116] The "something" was optimistic predictions about the depression's impending end. Such an appeal, though, cast Hoover in the unenviable role of economic prophet—a position, as Hofstadter notes, that went a long way toward ruining his reputation.[117] Each unfulfilled prediction only made the next one even less likely to come to fruition.

After a while some pundits sensed the ostensible economic trickery behind Hoover's recovery rhetoric. On July 26, 1931, Brand Whitlock wrote to Colonel Edward M. House, "And Hoover seems to think that the world may be saved by something he calls confidence—a word, incidentally, much used by card-sharpers. The new theory of economics teaches a kind of Cueism [*sic*, for "coueism"], so that if you can convince yourself that business is good, it will be good." [118] By this time, most were not convinced and much of the blame could be attributed to Hoover's overwhelming emphasis on confidence. One of the great ironies of Hoover's presidency is that despite his emphasis on persuasion, belief, and faith, he often shied from employing the rhetoric that might shape them. By emphasizing action and devaluing words, Hoover effectively undermined his own position.

A second explanation favored by many Hoover scholars is a rhetorical one, specifically his inability and unwillingness to persuade a mass audience. The following represents only a partial list of scholars who have adopted such a view. According to Barber, Hoover viewed the White House less as a bully pulpit than as a "site for quiet and undemonstrative persuasion." "At the heart of the problem," claims Richard Norton Smith, "lay Hoover's own inability to fill the role of presidential persuader." William Leuchtenburg states that Hoover "did not have the personality to inspire the people." According to Henry Stimson and McGeorge Bundy, Hoover "seemed unable to present himself to the people as a confident, fighting, democratic leader." For Walter Johnson, Hoover "was unable to put into memorable words what the people were striving to achieve." He was "not a dynamic figure who believed in rallying the public to help him push a program through Congress." "He lacked that one spark necessary to stir men's hearts," claims Harris Gaylord Warren, "The people en masse do not follow reason, but only emotion." According to Arthur Krock, "In public appearances this most delightful and witty of companions was dour. His speech delivery was monotonous." Wilton Eckley notes that Hoover had a "distaste for public speaking." White complained that Hoover "cannot dramatize his leadership. A democracy cannot follow a leader unless he is dramatized. . . . He must talk and explain as he acts." Gerald Nash claims that Hoover needed to dramatize his actions. He had little inclination to stir people emo-tionally. Liebovich argues that the depression brought a new focus to the presidency and "only those who could influence reporters, look presidential, speak with authority, and appear sincere would be able to claim success in the White House. Herbert Hoover . . . was a victim of circumstance and changing times to which he could not adjust." And, according to James David Barber, Hoover "avoided and detested the rhetorical demands of the office." [119]

There is a kernel of truth in what each of these writers claims. Herbert Hoover was not a very good rhetorician, and this clearly affected his at-tempts to lead the nation out of the Great Depression. Yet, the explana-tions are too easy. Not only do they largely attribute a single cause to Hoover's "failed" presidency, but that cause should give us pause. That is, if Hoover's rhetorical deficiencies are largely to blame for his inability to lead the nation, what are we to make of his election just four years earlier? Robert F. Himmelberg asks a similar question: "How can we . . . square the difference between Hoover's apparent success as a politician, public figure, and administrator in the 1920's with the failure" that many have "charge[d] him with as president?" [120] He notes further that "it is difficult to understand why one should not turn to changed times and conditions as the answer to why Hoover's stock fell after the crash rather than to supposed severe limi-tations in his personality and leadership capability." As Himmelberg cor-rectly notes, Hoover was the same rhetor in 1928 as he was in 1932—and the nation responded by making him president by an unprecedented elec-toral majority. We would be better advised, then, to discuss Hoover's failures at the level of what he did or did not say rather than how he said it or in what directions his personality led him rhetorically.

Despite the fact that Hoover eventually opted for legislative solutions to the Great Depression, the end toward which they were aimed remained constant—confidence. The RFC, the Glass-Steagall Act, various bills ex-panding credit, revenue bills, the Emergency Relief and Construction Act— all were geared toward revitalizing the nation's collective confidence. So, too, were the two major voluntary organizations created by Hoover, the NCC and the CRO. And while these organizations and measures continue to be dis-cussed in the context of anticipating Roosevelt's New Deal, they should also be situated firmly in their rhetorical context. All too frequently Hoover's pol-icy innovations were followed by presidential silence. Collective confidence simply could not be borne in the face of such silence. Equally important, col-lective confidence could not be expected to come from Hoover's rhetorical surrogates, the White House press corps. The feelings of animosity and even hatred between Hoover and the press escalated through most of 1931 and reached a climax during the summer of 1932. Joslin's succinct description of the situation in his diary summarizes the relationship well: "There is almost as much love lost between the President and the press as between god

Almighty and the devil himself."[121] Yet, remarkably, Hoover entrusted the press with his rhetorical duties. In news conference after news conference the message of surrogacy remained constant. Not only did Hoover need to make economic information available to the public, but as George Katona notes, such information needed to be readily understandable and filtered through the right frame of reference.[122]

On those rare occasions when Hoover did speak publicly on economic matters, the message had to be dispiriting to a dispirited people. The leaderless, fragmented war fought on 1,000 fronts in 1931 was transformed into an increasingly centralized civil war by the spring of 1932. Perhaps it was not altogether surprising when the U.S. Army literally waged war on its own veterans in the nation's capitol during the summer of 1932, in what became known as the Bonus Army riots.[123] Hoover was not unaware of what the people wanted and needed: they needed the type of confidence that was tangible and active, something that they could "bite on." He mistakenly believed that the campaign against hoarding would meet this need. He was wrong insofar as the confidence he kept describing was a psychological condition premised on individual belief. When the nation did not bounce back from repeated psychological shocks in 1929, 1930, and 1931, metaphors of health and sickness came to dominate popular understanding of the Great Depression.[124] The nation was rendered mentally ill; it was in the throes of a deep depression. The entailments of Hooverian confidence had effectively been internalized on a mass scale. Metaphors of health and sickness, combined with metaphors of warfare, formed a potentially volatile cluster: Hoover's incorporeal war was being fought, not by experienced and kindly doctors, but by the self against the self. The enemy to be vanquished appeared every day in the mirror. Hoover's war was largely a passive psychological war in which active bodies mattered little. Not surprisingly, Hoover's physical presence had also disappeared, barricaded from view at the White House. As we will see in the next chapter, Franklin Roosevelt capitalized on the passive, bodiless war stipulated by Hooverian confidence. It was a war that he was uniquely experienced to wage given his lengthy convalescence from infantile paralysis.

Notes

1. Diary entry of April 30, 1932, Theodore G. Joslin Papers, Box 10, Herbert Hoover Presidential Library, West Branch, Iowa (hereafter, HHPL).

2. Herbert Hoover, "Veto of the Emergency Adjusted Compensation Bill, February 26, 1931," in *Public Papers of the Presidents, 1931*, p. 108. Subsequent references are noted in the text.

3. Herbert Hoover, "Statement on the Disapproval of a Bill To Provide for the Establishment of a National Employment System, March 8, 1931," in *Public Papers of the Presidents, 1931*, pp. 132–33.

4. Herbert Hoover, "The President's News Conference of February 3, 1931," in *Public Papers of the Presidents, 1931*, p. 50.

5. Herbert Hoover, "Statement on Public vs. Private Financing of Relief Efforts," in *Public Papers of the Presidents, 1931*, p. 54.

6. Herbert Hoover, "Radio Address on Lincoln's Birthday, February 12, 1931," in *Public Papers of the Presidents, 1931*, p. 71. Subsequent references are noted in the text.

7. For the classic formulation of the relationship between religion and American politics see Robert N. Bellah, "Civil Religion in America," *Daedalus* 96 (1967): 1–21. See also Roderick P. Hart, *The Political Pulpit* (West Lafayette, Ind.: Purdue University Press, 1977); and John Frederick Wilson, *Public Religion in American Culture.*

8. Herbert Hoover, "Address to the Indiana Republican Editorial Association at Indianapolis, June 15, 1931," in *Public Papers of the Presidents, 1931*, p. 299.

9. Herbert Hoover, "Address to the Annual Convention of the American National Red Cross, April 13, 1931," in *Public Papers of the Presidents, 1931*, p. 179. Subsequent references are noted in the text.

10. At his February 3 press conference, Hoover complained that he "should [not] be charged with lack of sympathy for those who suffer" (Herbert Hoover, "The President's News Conference of February 3, 1931," in *Public Papers of the Presidents, 1931*, p. 52).

11. Herbert Hoover, "Address to the Gridiron Club, April 27, 1931," in *Public Papers of the Presidents, 1931*, p. 223.

12. Herbert Hoover, "Address to the Annual Convention of the American Red Cross, April 13, 1931," in *Public Papers of the Presidents, 1931*, p. 180.

13. Herbert Hoover, "The President's News Conference of May 22, 1931," in *Public Papers of the Presidents, 1931*, p. 263.

14. Herbert Hoover, "Memorial Day Address at Valley Forge, Pennsylvania, May 30, 1931," in *Public Papers of the Presidents, 1931*, p. 274. Subsequent references are noted in the text.

15. Ellis W. Hawley also notes the two-fold front on which Hoover fought: to cure the nation's economic ills and to prevent the cure from being worse than the disease. See Hawley, in *Herbert Hoover and the Crisis of American Capitalism*, ed. J. Joseph Huthmacher and Warren I. Susman, p. 23.

16. Mark Sullivan to French Strother, January 1, 1931, President's Secretary File, Box 883, "Mark Sullivan, 1929–1933," HHPL.

17. George Olds to Mark Sullivan, December 27, 1930, President's Secretary File, Box 883, "Mark Sullivan, 1929–1933," HHPL.

18. George Olds to French Strother, January 6, 1931, President's Secretary File, Box 883, "Mark Sullivan, 1929–1933," HHPL.

19. French Strother to George Olds, January 16, 1931, President's Secretary File, Box 883, "Mark Sullivan, 1929–1933," HHPL.

20. George Olds to Mark Sullivan, January 20, 1931, President's Secretary File, Box 883, "Mark Sullivan, 1929–1933," HHPL.

21. Mark Sullivan to French Strother, January 22, 1931, President's Secretary File, Box 883, "Mark Sullivan, 1929–1933," HHPL.

22. George Olds to French Strother, February 21, 1931, President's Secretary File, Box 883, "Mark Sullivan, 1929–1933," HHPL.

23. William Allen White, *The Selected Letters of William Allen White 1899–1943*, ed. Walter Johnson, p. 311.

24. Quoted in Theodore G. Joslin, *Hoover Off the Record*, p. 3.

25. Henry L. Stimson and McGeorge Bundy, *On Active Service in Peace and War*, p. 191.

26. Elliott A. Rosen, *Hoover, Roosevelt, and the Brains Trust*, p. 68.

27. Ibid.

28. Ibid., p. 77.

29. Ibid., pp. 68–69.

30. Ibid., p. 69.

31. Elliott Roosevelt, ed., *F.D.R.: His Personal Letters, 1928–1945, Volume Two*, p. 209.

32. Rosen, *Hoover, Roosevelt, and the Brains Trust*, p. 70.

33. Hoover made the reference in his brief remarks at Charleston, West Virginia, on June 15; see *Public Papers of the Presidents, 1931*, p. 293.

34. Diary entry, June 11, 1931, Theodore G. Joslin Papers, Box 10, HHPL. Unfortunately, none of the drafts have survived.

35. Herbert Hoover, "Address to the Indiana Republican Editorial Association at Indianapolis, June 15, 1931," in *Public Papers of the Presidents, 1931*, p. 297. Subsequent references are noted in the text.

36. Herbert Hoover, "Radio Address to the World's Conference of the Young Men's Christian Association, August 8, 1931" in *Public Papers of the Presidents, 1931*, p. 380. Subsequent references are noted in the text.

37. The press conference was unusual to the extent that Hoover talked at length about the nation's economic future.

38. Herbert Hoover, "The President's News Conference of September 1, 1931," in *Public Papers of the Presidents, 1931*, p. 404. Subsequent references are noted in the text.

39. Herbert Hoover to George Harrison, October 5, 1931, President's Subject File, Box 158, "Financial Matters, NCC Correspondence, September–October 7, 1931," HHPL.

40. Martin L. Fausold, *The Presidency of Herbert C. Hoover*, p. 152.

41. Draft of speech to bankers, President's Subject File, Box 158, "Financial Matters, NCC Correspondence, September–October 7, 1931," HHPL.

42. Michael E. Parrish, *Anxious Decades*, p. 250. For a similar view, see James S. Olson, "The End of Voluntarism: Herbert Hoover and the National Credit Corporation," *Annals of Iowa* 41 (1972): 1104–13.

43. Carl N. Degler, "The Ordeal of Herbert Hoover," *Yale Review* 52 (1963): 576.

44. Diary entry of October 15, 1931, Theodore G. Joslin Papers, Box 10, HHPL.

45. Herbert Hoover to George Harrison, October 5, HHPL.

46. Quoted in Albert U. Romasco, *The Poverty of Abundance*, p. 93.

47. Quoted in Romasco, *The Poverty of Abundance*, p. 93.

48. Hoover mentioned the NCC in only one paragraph of a written statement released on October 7, 1931: "Statement on Financial and Economic Problems, October 7, 1931," in *Public Papers of the Presidents, 1931*, pp. 465–68. See also Romasco, *The Poverty of Abundance*, pp. 77, 93.

49. Herbert Hoover, "The President's News Conference of October 9, 1931," in *Public Papers of the Presidents, 1931*, p. 476. Subsequent references are noted in the text.

50. Robert E. Clark to Herbert Hoover, October 9, 1931, President's Subject File, Box 158, "Financial Matters, NCC Correspondence," October 9–10, 1931.

51. Similarly, Arthur S. Draper of the conservative *New York Herald Tribune* noted in an October 7 letter to Hoover that "in the building up of confidence you have not enlisted some outstanding journalist. I venture to suggest that in the final analysis the American press will be the greatest factor in the restoration of confidence." Hoover wryly cribbed at the top of the letter, "Thanks—who is the outstanding journalist?" (Arthur S. Draper to Herbert Hoover, October 7, 1931, President's Personal File, Box 181, "Newspapers, New York Herald Tribune, 1930–1932," HHPL).

52. Paul Y. Anderson, "Herbert Hoover and the Press," *Nation*, October 14, 1931, p. 382.

53. Arthur H. Kirchhofer to Herbert Hoover, September 1, 1931, President's Personal File, Box 180, "Newspapers, Buffalo Evening News, 1930–1931," HHPL.

54. "Still To Be Done," *Business Week*, October 14, 1931, n.p.

55. Fausold, *The Presidency of Herbert C. Hoover*, p. 153.

56. George Harrison expressed such a concern in a lengthy letter to Hoover dated October 7, 1931; see *Public Papers of the Presidents, 1931*, pp. 455–59.

57. Herbert Hoover, "Statement on Financial and Economic Problems, October 7, 1931," in *Public Papers of the Presidents, 1931*, p. 467.

58. Herbert Hoover, "Annual Message to the Congress on the State of the Union, December 8, 1931," in *Public Papers of the Presidents, 1931*, p. 590.

59. Herbert Hoover, "The President's News Conference of September 1, 1931," in *Public Papers of the Presidents, 1931*, p. 405.

60. Herbert Hoover, "The President's News Conference of September 11, 1931," in *Public Papers of the Presidents, 1931*, p. 417. Subsequent references are noted in the text.

61. Herbert Stein, *The Fiscal Revolution in America*, p. 23.

62. Herbert Hoover, "Address to the American Legion at Detroit, Michigan, September 21, 1931," in *Public Papers of the Presidents, 1931*, p. 431. Subsequent references are noted in the text.

63. Herbert Hoover, "Radio Address to the Nation on Unemployment Relief, October 18, 1931," in *Public Papers of the Presidents, 1931*, p. 487. Subsequent references are noted in the text.

64. Fausold, *The Presidency of Herbert C. Hoover*, pp. 156–57.

65. Herbert Hoover, "White House Statement About Presidential Receptions, February 9, 1932," in *Public Papers of the Presidents, 1932*, p. 48.

66. Fausold, *The Presidency of Herbert C. Hoover*, p. 156.

67. Quoted in Hoff Wilson, *Herbert Hoover*, p. 154.

68. William Appleman Williams, *Some Presidents: From Wilson to Nixon*, p. 38.

69. Stephen Skowronek, *The Politics Presidents Make: Leadership from John Adams to George Bush*, p. 283.

70. Ellis Hawley, in *Herbert Hoover and the Crisis of American Capitalism*, ed. J. Joseph Huthmacher and Warren I. Susman, pp. 12–13.

71. Walter Lippmann, *Public Philosopher: Selected Letters of Walter Lippmann*, ed. John Morton Blum, p. 285.

72. Hoover, in fact, attempted to legitimate his presidential silence in his first major campaign speech in Des Moines on October 4: "Many of these battles have had to be fought in silence, without the cheers of the limelight or the encouragement of public approval (?), because the very disclosure of the forces opposed to us would have undermined the courage of the weak and induced panic in the timid and would have destroyed the very basis for success. Hideous misrepresentation and unjustifiable complaint have had to be accepted in silence for the national good. It has been as if a great battle in war should be fought without public knowledge of any incident except the streams of the dead and the wounded from the front. There has indeed been much of tragedy, but there has been but little public evidence of the dangers and enormous risks from which a great national victory has been achieved" (Herbert Hoover, "Address at the Coliseum in Des Moines, Iowa, October 4, 1932," in *Public Papers of the Presidents, 1932*, p. 463).

73. Skowronek is perceptive in noting that a "new Hoover" emerged in his 1931 annual message to Congress; see Skowronek, *The Politics Presidents Make*, p. 280.

74. For the standard historical works on the RFC, see James S. Olson, *Herbert Hoover and the Reconstruction Finance Corporation;* and James S. Olson, *Saving Capitalism: The Reconstruction Finance Corporation and the New Deal, 1933–1940.*

75. Herbert Hoover, "Special Message to the Congress on the Economic Recovery Program, January 4, 1932," in *Public Papers of the Presidents, 1932*, p. 3. Subsequent references are noted in the text.

76. Parrish, *Anxious Decades*, pp. 253–54.

77. Hoff Wilson, *Forgotten Progressive,* p. 156.

78. James S. Olson, "Herbert Hoover and the 'War' on the Depression," *Palimpsest* 54 (1973): 29.

79. Richard Hofstadter, *The American Political Tradition,* p. 395.

80. Jordan Schwarz, *The Interregnum of Despair,* p. 92.

81. Quoted in Richard Lowitt, *George W. Norris: The Persistence of a Progressive,* p. 498.

82. Herbert Hoover to Frank Knox, February 11, 1932, President's Subject File, Box 172, "Hoarding Correspondence, February 11–15, 1932," HHPL.

83. Herbert Hoover to Frank Knox, February 13, 1932, President's Subject File, Box 172, "Hoarding Correspondence, February 11–15, 1932," HHPL.

84. Importantly, the $2 billion capitalization was off budget, thereby not adding to the burgeoning budget deficit for fiscal year 1932. See William J. Barber, *From New Era to New Deal,* p. 177.

85. In his February 11 letter to Knox, Hoover stated that "The best suggestion we can make as to name is the 'Citizens Reconstruction Organization'" (Herbert Hoover to Frank Knox, February 11, 1932, President's Subject File, Box 172, "Hoarding Correspondence, February 11–15, 1932," HHPL).

86. Hoff Wilson, *Forgotten Progressive,* p. 156.

87. "Confidence," *National Auditgram,* January, 1932, n.p. This document was found in the President's Subject File, Box 172, "Hoarding Correspondence, February 1–5, 1932," HHPL.

88. The group also heard briefly from William Green, the president of the American Federation of Labor (AFL), Harry J. Haas, the president of the American Banking Association, Samuel McCrea Cavert, the general secretary of the Federal Council of the Churches of Christ in American, Michael J. Ready, the assistant general secretary of the Catholic Welfare Association, Mrs. John F. Sippel, the president of the General Federation of Women's Clubs, A. C. Pearson, the president of the National Publisher's Association, and Magnus Alexander, the president of the National Industrial Conference Board. For a complete list of the conferees, see *Public Papers of the Presidents, 1932,* pp. 46–47.

89. Transcript of the President's Conference on Hoarding, February 6, 1932, President's Subject File, Box 173, "Hoarding—White House Conference, 1932," HHPL.

90. Mills was promoted to Treasury Secretary in early February, after the increasingly unpopular Andrew Mellon was "reassigned" to be the U.S. Ambassador to Great Britain.

91. Hoover realized that any effective campaign to bring money back into circulation required the press; as he noted later in the conference, "We are going to be dependent on the press for success," "Hoarding—White House Conference, 1932," HHPL, p. 24.

92. Diary entry, February 6, 1932, Theodore G. Joslin Papers, Box 10, HHPL.

93. Telegram from Frank Knox to Herbert Hoover, February 13, 1932, President's Subject File, Box 112, "Hoarding Correspondence, February 11–15, 1932," HHPL.

94. Telegram from Frank Knox to Herbert Hoover, February 13, 1932, President's Subject File, Box 172, "Hoarding Correspondence, February 11–15, 1932," HHPL.

95. Herbert Hoover to Frank Knox, February 13, 1932, President's Subject File, Box 172, "Hoarding Correspondence, February 11–15, 1932," HHPL.

96. Frank Knox to Herbert Hoover, February 15, 1932, President's Subject File, Box 172, "Hoarding Correspondence, February 11–15, 1932," HHPL.

97. Frank Knox to Herbert Hoover, February 15, 1932, President's Subject File, Box 172, "Hoarding Correspondence, February 11–15, 1932," HHPL.

98. Herbert Hoover to Frank Knox, February 16, 1932, President's Subject File, Box 172, "Hoarding Correspondence, February 16–29, 1932," HHPL.

99. Telegram from Frank Knox to Herbert Hoover, February 16, 1932, President's

Subject File, Box 172, "Hoarding Correspondence, February 16–29, 1932," HHPL.

100. Quoted in Herbert Hoover to Frank Knox, February 16, 1932, President's Subject File, Box 172, "Hoarding Correspondence, February 16–29, 1932," HHPL.

101. Herbert Hoover, "Statement on Hoarding of Currency, February 16, 1932," *Public Papers of the Presidents, 1932*, p. 56.

102. Telegram from Frank Knox to Lawrence Richey, February 25, 1932, President's Subject File, Box 172, "Hoarding Correspondence, February 16–29, 1932," HHPL.

103. Telegram from Herbert Hoover to Frank Knox, February 25, 1932, President's Subject File, Box 172, "Hoarding Correspondence, February 16–29, 1932," HHPL.

104. Herbert Hoover, "Radio Address on the Hoarding of Currency, March 6, 1932," in *Public Papers of the Presidents, 1932*, p. 94. Subsequent references are noted in the text.

105. Fausold, *The Presidency of Herbert C. Hoover*, p. 140.

106. Hoff Wilson, *Forgotten Progressive*, p. 157; Barber, *From New Era to New Deal*, p. 135.

107. Schwarz, *Interregnum of Despair*, p. 233.

108. Degler, "The Ordeal of Herbert Hoover," p. 571; Hoff Wilson, *Forgotten Progressive*, p. 159.

109. Herbert Hoover, "Address to the Senate on the National Economy, May 31, 1932," in *Public Papers of the Presidents, 1932*, p. 244.

110. Fausold and Mazuzan compare Hoover's first one hundred days in 1932 to Franklin Roosevelt's first one hundred days in 1933. See their introduction to *The Hoover Presidency: A Reappraisal*, ed. Martin J. Fausold and George T. Mazuzan, p. 16.

111. Degler, "The Ordeal of Herbert Hoover," p. 571; Alan Dawley, *Struggles for Justice*, p. 351.

112. Telegram from Frank Knox to Lawrence Richey, May 6, 1932, President's Subject File, Box 173, "Hoarding Correspondence, May–December 1932," HHPL.

113. Frank Knox, Speech Draft, May 6, 1932, President's Subject File, Box 173, "Hoarding Correspondence, May–December 1932," HHPL.

114. Davis W. Houck, "Rhetoric, Science and Economic Prophecy: John Maynard Keynes's Correspondence with Franklin D. Roosevelt," in *The New Economics Criticism*, ed. Martha Woodmanssee and Mark Osteen, pp. 352–64.

115. Alfred B. Rollins, "The View from the State House: FDR," in *The Hoover Presidency: A Reappraisal*, p. 123.

116. "Christian Science Economics," *Nation*, February 17, 1932, p. 185.

117. Hofstadter, *The American Political Tradition*, p. 391.

118. Brand Whitlock to Edward M. House, July 26, 1931, President's Personal File, 1820, Container 11, Franklin D. Roosevelt Presidential Library, Hyde Park, New York.

119. Barber, *From New Era to New Deal*, p. 191; Richard Norton Smith, *An Uncommon Man*, p. 129; William E. Leuchtenburg, *The Perils of Prosperity 1914–1932*, p. 264; Stimson and Bundy, *On Active Service in Peace and War*, p. 283; Walter Johnson, *1600 Pennsylvania Avenue: Presidents and The People, 1929–1959*, pp. 25, 26; Harris Gaylord Warren, *Herbert Hoover and the Great Depression*, p. 167; Arthur Krock, *Memoirs*, p. 125; Wilton Eckley, *Herbert Hoover*, p. 61; White, *Selected Letters of William Allen White 1899–1943*, p. 329; Gerald Nash, in *Herbert Hoover and the Crisis of American Capitalism*, p. 95; Liebovich, *Bylines in Despair*, p. 211; James David Barber, "Classifying and Predicting Presidential Styles: Two 'Weak' Presidents," *Journal of Social Issues* 24 (1968): 57, 77.

120. Robert F. Himmelberg, in *Herbert Hoover and the Crisis of American Capitalism*, p. 130.

121. Diary entry of July 23, 1932, Theodore G. Joslin Papers, Box 10, HHPL.

122. George Katona, *Psychological Analysis of Economic Behavior*, p. 288; see also George Katona, *The Powerful Consumer*, p. 239.

123. For historical studies of the Bonus Army, see W. W. Waters and William C. White, *B.E.F.: The Whole Story of the Bonus Army;*

and Donald J. Lisio, *The President and Protest. Hoover, MacArthur, and the Bonus March.*

124. The number of popular and scholarly articles that framed the Great Depression in the vernacular of health and sickness is too large to cite here, but several representative articles include: "A Plea for Convalescence," *Commonweal*, April 27, 1932, pp. 705–706; George E. Putnam, "The Hardened Arteries of Business," *Atlantic Monthly*, October, 1931, pp. 504–13; "The Wrong Medicine," *Business Week*, January 21, 1931, p. 44; Elmer Davis, "Hoover the Medicine Man," *Forum*, October, 1930, pp. 195–99; W. Beran Wolfe, "Psychoanalyzing the Depression," *Forum*, April, 1932, pp. 209–14; Nelson H. Cruikshank, "Prosperity by Suggestion," *World Tomorrow*, March, 1931, pp. 85–87; James Bayard Clark, "A Doctor Looks at Economics," *Review of Reviews*, June, 1932, pp. 29–31; "One Hundred Doses, One Dollar," *Saturday Evening Post*, September 26, 1931, p. 22; Louis T. McFadden, "Convalescent Finance," *Saturday Evening Post*, February 15, 1930, pp. 5, 145, 146, 149; "The Castor-Oil School of Economics," *Business Week*, July 9, 1930, p. 40; F. W. Taussig, "Doctors, Economists and the Depression," *Harper's Magazine*, August, 1932, pp. 355–65; Roger W. Babson, "How to Cure the Blues," *Collier's*, March 28, 1931, pp. 12, 13, 60; William Trufant Foster, "When a Horse Balks," *North American Review*, July, 1932, pp. 4–10; Georges F. Doriot, "Our Sick Industries," *Yale Review*, March, 1931, pp. 442–55; "Major Surgery for the Depression," *New Republic*, November 2, 1932, pp. 314–15; "Nature's Course," *Saturday Evening Post*, October 1, 1932, p. 20; Roger W. Babson, "Everybody Has a Job," *World's Work*, February, 1931, pp. 67–69.

Chapter Four

"A Satisfactory Embodiment"
FDR's "Run" for the Nomination

Socrates: And you would agree that there is bodily health and spiritual health?
Gorgias: Yes.
Socrates: And also such a thing as an unreal appearance of health? For example, many people appear to enjoy health in whom nobody but a doctor or trainer could detect the reverse."
Gorgias: "True."

At 10:45 in the evening of November 7, 1932, Franklin Roosevelt made what would be his final pre-presidential speech. To his assembled neighbors along the Hudson River in Poughkeepsie, New York, Roosevelt waxed nostalgic and humble:

> Out of this unity, this unity that I have seen, we may build the strongest strand to lift ourselves out of this depression. If all of this multitude of my friends (and)—of my neighbors—give expression tomorrow to your united confidence in this invigorating tonic of a change, I may in some modest way bring this unity of purpose to practical fulfillment. A man comes to wisdom in many years of public life. He knows well that when the light of favor shines upon him, it comes not, of necessity, that he himself is important. Favor comes because for a brief moment in the great space of human change and progress some general human purpose finds in him a satisfactory embodiment. To be the means through which the ideals and hopes of the American people may find a greater realization calls for the best in any man. I seek to be only the humble emblem of this restoration of America.[1]

Roosevelt knew that he would soon be the nation's thirty-second president, but this peroration hints at the ideological ambivalence so characteristic of his 1932 presidential campaign. In one breath, Roosevelt could talk of "progress" and "change" and in the next, the "restoration" of the nation. The ambivalence is reflective of the different constituencies that Roosevelt had to juggle in order to win his party's nomination and then to defeat Herbert Hoover. But juggling loyalties was nothing new to the squire from Hyde Park; it was one constant in an otherwise discontinuous life.

Roosevelt's word choice in this final, pre-presidential peroration is also of interest. The rhetoric is muscular, active, vigorous. To "have seen," to "lift ourselves," to be part of an "invigorating tonic of change," and to be an "emblem of this restoration of America"—these references suggest a corporeal presence, or, in Roosevelt's words, "a satisfactory embodiment." The irony is palpable: "some general purpose" had situated itself squarely on Roosevelt's body—a body badly ravaged by the effects of infantile paralysis, a body carefully concealed even when revealed to the American people. That Roosevelt would refer frequently to his body in the 1932 presidential campaign, though, is not surprising: it had repeatedly been under attack politically for nearly eight years. He needed to defend his body, yet to have mentioned explicitly the effects of polio would have been electoral suicide: crippled presidential candidates evoke sympathy, not votes.[2] But, ever the opportunist, Roosevelt exploited the rhetorical possibilities of popular understanding of the Great Depression—understanding metaphorically contained in terms of health and sickness. While metaphors of health and sickness recur frequently in Roosevelt's pre-nomination rhetoric, they achieve their most eloquent and forceful expression in his dramatic address to the assembled delegates in Chicago, as he displayed his healthy body to the nation both visually and discursively.

The Squire from Hyde Park

If Herbert Hoover was weaned on the sobering sustenance of death and poverty, Franklin Roosevelt cut his teeth on the gilded pabulum of wealth and privilege. Born on January 30, 1882, the only child of Sara and James Roosevelt, young Franklin grew up in the aristocratic enclave of Dutchess County—seventy-five miles north of New York City. By all accounts, his childhood was marked by tutors, extensive travels, and frequent frolics in and around the bordering Hudson; he was reared in a manner befitting a country gentleman.

The wrangle of politics, despite familial antecedents, was far removed from the family estate. Perhaps his first prolonged contact with public service occurred at age fourteen, when Roosevelt headed east to attend school in Groton, Massachusetts. Over the course of the next four years, Roosevelt was under the watchful eye of Groton's rector, Endicott Peabody. The traditional curriculum was augmented by a monastic reverence for scripture— the Bible was read cover to cover three times during a student's six-year matriculation—and by an emphasis on public service.[3] Peabody once stated that "If some Groton boys do not enter political life and do something for our land, it won't be because they have not been urged."[4] Roosevelt did not distinguish himself academically, athletically or socially at Groton; presidential portents were not in evidence.

In 1900 Roosevelt left one cloistered environment for another as he migrated forty miles south to Harvard. During his freshman year, his mother, Sara, moved to Boston to be near her only son. James, twenty-six years her senior, had died from heart disease. Another death figured prominently during Roosevelt's early tenure at Harvard—that of President William McKinley in 1901. His assassination, by Leon Czolgosz, a twenty-eight-year-old Polish anarchist, elevated Roosevelt's idol, cousin Theodore, to the nation's highest political office. The family name was forever after a household one. Never one to shy from making the social rounds, Roosevelt was a frequent guest at 1600 Pennsylvania Avenue.

If imitation is the highest form of flattery, cousin Teddy could not have lacked for a more obsequious acolyte. On the way to becoming president, Theodore Roosevelt held the following political posts: New York state senator, assistant secretary of the Navy, governor of New York, and vice president. Though the chronology differed slightly, Franklin followed the identical political trajectory—and, as he unabashedly confessed in 1907 to his fellow law clerks, it was all quite purposive.[5] Presidential aspirations were forthcoming from as early as 1905. While he was on his European honeymoon with distant cousin Eleanor, Roosevelt reported in a letter to his mother that a clairvoyant by the name of Madame de Noel foretold his presidency.[6]

Roosevelt stayed an extra year at Harvard to edit the *Crimson*, the student newspaper.[7] He eventually graduated with his "gentlemanly C" average intact and proceeded to enroll in law school at Columbia in the fall of 1904. Despite Columbia's lofty reputation, "the professors elicited little response from Roosevelt."[8] He left after three years, having passed the bar but without having completed his LL.B. degree. After clerking in one of Wall Street's leading firms, Roosevelt, largely at his cousin's behest, "decided to turn toward the excitement of politics rather than the dullness and security of a career in corporate law."[9]

One of Roosevelt's first political juggling acts involved family and politics. By inheritance, Roosevelt was a Cleveland Democrat, but in 1900 he joined the Harvard Republican club and later cast his first vote for his Republican cousin. "When it came down to specific cases," Burns notes, "he supported Republicans."[10] According to both Freidel and Burns, Roosevelt's willingness to run as a Democrat for New York's State Senate in 1910 had more to do with the party seeking him out than any ideological commitments on Roosevelt's part.

Roosevelt's first campaign was not easy: his district had gone Democrat only once in nearly fifty years, and his incumbent opponent, John Schlosser, "was a man of substance and reputation."[11] But with the help of an open-canopied Maxwell—the only car in the area—and with Schlosser's associations with old-guard Republicans then under assault by president Roosevelt, the squire squeaked out a narrow victory.[12]

He wasted little time in getting enmeshed in the state's affairs at Albany. In what would be a three-decade juggling act with the party's New York City Tammany Hall bosses, Roosevelt thrust himself into the vortex of an intraparty conflict shortly after he was sworn in. He led a group of young Democrats in the fight to block Tammany's candidate for the U.S. Senate, Billy Sheehan. Although his side eventually gave in to a compromise candidate, Roosevelt served notice to Tammany bosses that he would not be a passive tool in their hands. In so doing, he garnered national headlines as his progressive campaign for direct senatorial elections struck a responsive chord with the public.

Within two years, Roosevelt established himself as a progressive reformer by supporting labor measures, workman's compensation, and child labor laws. He also lobbied for his agrarian constituency back home by supporting agricultural reforms such as cooperative marketing and low interest loans. Perhaps more importantly, Roosevelt had won the good graces of New Jersey's governor, Woodrow Wilson, by aligning himself with Wilson's 1912 presidential aspirations.

One of the recurring themes in Roosevelt's life was his ability to transform personal misfortune into political capital. The first incident occurred in 1912, when Roosevelt was stricken with typhoid fever: being bed-ridden greatly imperiled his reelection possibilities. To his rescue came an unsavory looking newspaperman by the name of Louis McHenry Howe—a behind-the-scenes player zealously dedicated to protecting and promoting Roosevelt's political aspirations.[13] In 1912 Howe did the seemingly impossible: he got Roosevelt reelected in absentia. Roosevelt reciprocated his loyalties, as Howe never left his side. In 1913 Roosevelt took Howe with him to the nation's capitol when Wilson's secretary of the Navy, Josephus Daniels, invited the upstart senator to be his assistant. Roosevelt eagerly accepted: "It would please me better than anything in the world."[14]

Roosevelt's seven-and-a-half years in Washington, D.C., were invaluable to his political education; it was during this period that he learned the fine art of national and international politics as well as administration. Socially, Roosevelt ran in fairly elite circles: associating with Oliver Wendell Holmes, Louis Brandeis, Felix Frankfurter, and Henry Cabot Lodge, to mention only a few. Politically, he drew Democratic praise for his stances on labor, industrial trusts, efficient administrative organization, and his support for Wilson's progressive legislative agenda. Roosevelt also displayed an aggressive internationalism. Like his cousin, Roosevelt was a big Navy man who consistently favored militancy in resolving foreign entanglements. Following the start of World War I, he was a leading advocate of preparedness within the Wilson administration. Once the United States entered the war, he went into high gear "to make the naval participation in the war as large and vital as possible."[15] He was frustrated, though, that Wilson and Daniels would not permit him to join American doughboys fighting in Europe. The possibility of thus emulating cousin Teddy's heroics on the battlefield was the only significant thing missing from his political facsimile.

Roosevelt's tendency toward political epigonism got him in trouble on the voyage home from the Versailles conference. At a luncheon aboard the

George Washington, Wilson lectured Roosevelt on the need for U.S. participation in the League of Nations. "Roosevelt was profoundly impressed and thereafter an ardent advocate."[16] His unreserved support for the League would not only plague him in 1920, but it would come back to haunt him twelve years later.

Before the armistice had been reached, however, crisis befell the Roosevelts. In the fall, while her husband convalesced from influenza, Eleanor helped him keep up with his correspondence. Their relationship changed forever with her discovery of a packet of love letters from her social secretary, Lucy Mercer. "She was long despondent and never entirely recovered from the shock."[17] Franklin rejected Eleanor's overture for a divorce, as marital contretemps would have ended his presidential aspirations. Their common meeting ground from then on was politics—specifically, furtherance of Franklin's political career. Along with Howe, Eleanor kept her husband's name in the Democratic hopper, even after his second consecutive electoral defeat.[18]

The 1920 presidential campaign was a referendum on U.S. involvement in the League of Nations, and Roosevelt allowed his political allies to place him at the center of the maelstrom. Perhaps out of fidelity to his ailing cousin, or perhaps out of potential political advancement, he agreed to Ohio Governor James Cox's overtures to be his running mate. The post-war environment simply was not conducive to Democratic insistence on League entry. The nation was much more amenable to Ohio Senator Warren Gamaliel Harding's appeal for "normalcy, not nostrums." Although the League issue proved decisive, Roosevelt did not help his cause when, on a campaign swing through Butte, Montana, he boasted of the dozen votes the United States would command in the League Assembly. Moreover, Roosevelt and Daniels controlled two of the votes, "for they 'had something to do with the running of a couple of little republics.'"[19] Roosevelt wryly joked that he had written Haiti's constitution while in the Navy. As Burns reports, "it was a dreadful boner."[20]

In spite of Roosevelt's "high hopes," the Harding-Coolidge ticket scored a resounding victory, winning the popular vote by a total of 16 million to 9 million. The "earthquake," as Wilson's private secretary, Joseph P. Tumulty, described it, continued at more local levels: Republicans controlled the House of Representatives by the greatest majority ever—309 to 132—and they held firm control in the Senate—59 to 37. The "New Era," was about to begin—and for the first time in nearly ten years, Roosevelt was without a job.

"Franklin Has Been Quite Ill"

Roosevelt's life from 1921 to 1928 represented the best of times and the worst of times. His remarkable recrudescence at the end of the decade is all the more so in light of his battle with infantile paralysis and the psychological depression that accompanied it.

On August 10, 1921, after taking a dip in the Bay of Fundy off of Campobello Island, Roosevelt took his last unaided steps. He initially thought he had simply caught a chill from the Bay's frigid waters. Four days later, Eleanor reported to her husband's half brother that paralysis had set in. She was quick to sense the potential political ramifications of the illness: "I do not want particulars to get in the papers so I am writing the family that he is ill from the effects of a chill and I hope will soon be better." [21] After the diagnosis of infantile paralysis was made, Louis Howe, Roosevelt's long-time personal secretary and confidante, was more emphatic: "I'm not going to mention the word 'paralysis' unless I have to. If it's printed, we're sunk. Franklin's career is *kaput,* finished." [22] Thus did the twenty-four-year veil of secrecy and deception begin. Importantly, Tony Gould refers to this concealment as "the necessary deception," given the social stigma then attending physical disability generally and polio specifically. [23]

In her revealing look at the social construction of polio, Naomi Rogers details how the lay public came to understand polio—and the social opprobrium attending those unlucky enough to have been infected by the virus. In general, the early twentieth century witnessed the continuation of the longstanding belief that linked moral rectitude to physical health. Illness then had its antecedents in ill-conduct. Even with the rise of germ theory, moralism did not relent: "Germs, in lay thought, did not spread randomly; infection depended on the class, ethnicity, and personal habits of individuals." [24] Even though Roosevelt's background contravened popular associations about the disease—it was a disease of the unhygienic, the lower class, and immigrants—he could not, at least initially, "escape" it. More importantly, Roosevelt's political aspirations made the affliction even more insidious and cruel: disabled politicians had little if any electoral hopes—especially when those hopes involved the nation's highest, and most visible, elected office. As Theo Lippman, Jr., recounts, "Roosevelt and especially Howe always feared that part of the public did want a leader who was as physically able-bodied and impressive as he was mentally astute . . . A conscious or unconscious yearning for a symbol of masculinity in the state house or White House." [25] Thus, "if he had been candid about his disability at the beginning of his career," concludes John Duffy, "he would probably have had no career." [26]

That these early efforts at deception—so crucial if the deception was to be persuasive in the long term—were successful is illustrated by press accounts. On August 25, Dr. Robert W. Lovett diagnosed the affliction as Poliomyelitis. Two days later, the *New York Times* reported that while Roosevelt "has been seriously ill . . . he is now improving." [27] On August 29, the *New York Times* stated that Roosevelt had "caught a heavy cold and was threatened with pneumonia" and that he was "recovering slowly." [28] Nearly three weeks after the initial diagnosis, the official line was that Roosevelt showed "gradual improvement" from the threat of pneumonia.[29]Finally, on September 16, with Roosevelt's harrowing train ride from Campobello

Island to New York City, the fact of the illness could no longer be hidden; the extent of it, however, could. While the front page of the *New York Times* blared "F. D. Roosevelt Ill of Poliomyelitis," his doctor in New York City, George Draper, attempted to temper the possible political effects: "you can say definitely that he will not be crippled. No one need have any fear of permanent injury from this attack." [30] Draper was lying. The extent of the paralysis was such that he worried that his famous patient "might never be able to sit up again, much less stand or walk." [31] To Lovett, Draper confided, "He has such courage, such ambition, and yet at the same time such an extraordinarily sensitive emotional mechanism that it will take all the skill which we can muster to lead him successfully to a recognition of what he really faces without crushing him." [32]

Publicly, Roosevelt expressed his optimism of a complete recovery; to coaching legend Walter Camp he reported that his "rebellious legs" would allow him to "join in another course of training sometime in the future." [33] To those around him, he maintained that he would walk again—a conviction that appears to stem equally from personal and political considerations. "Despite uniformly discouraging counsel from his doctors," Geoffrey C. Ward notes, "he remained determined that he would somehow find a way to restore his wasted muscles to something like their old strength. . . . The laws governing ordinary polios, he remained convinced, did not apply to him. He could not be President unless he could walk; therefore, he would walk.[34] As for his personal motivations for walking again, Roosevelt confided to therapist Helena Mahoney, "I'll walk into a room without scaring everybody half to death. I'll stand easily enough in front of people so that they'll forget I'm a cripple." [35] Walking and standing were thus part and parcel to his personal and political identity. Not walking was not an option, hence "the fierce physical agony he suffered, the dark nights of utter despair through which he had passed, the incredibly harsh regime he now imposed upon himself as he struggled to walk again—all were designed to prepare him for the great historical tasks that must ultimately be his." [36]

Sara Roosevelt urged her only child to return to the protective clutches of Hyde Park, where he could pursue his philatelic interests full time and she could watch over him. Roosevelt rejected her offer. In the autumn of 1922 he resumed his business affairs, and in 1925 he formed a law partnership with Basil "Doc" O'Connor. Meanwhile, Eleanor, with Howe's supervision, stumped to keep her erstwhile husband's name and career before party regulars. Yet Roosevelt's hoped-for recovery was not forthcoming. Partly as an excuse to exercise in a warmer climate and partly to escape his "unbearable" life in New York City, Roosevelt went in on a houseboat purchase with John Lawrence. The vessel, docked near Miami, was christened the "Larooco" in early 1924.[37] Over the next three years, Roosevelt fished, swam, and entertained political friends and acquaintances—frequently for months at a time. The boat served an important psychological purpose according to biographer Doris Kearns Goodwin: The Larooco "allowed him a haven to be able to be sad, to mourn the loss of the body that had once been his." [38] But Roosevelt's escape took its toll on the family: son James would remember this time as "the lonely years."

The first major break in Roosevelt's seven-year political sabbatical came in the spring and summer of 1924: at New York Governor Al Smith's request, he agreed to manage Smith's pre-convention campaign for the Democratic presidential nomination. More importantly, Smith asked Roosevelt to give the address placing his name in nomination. The result was the soon-to-be-famous "Happy Warrior" speech, the only bright spot in what would be one of the Democratic party's darkest hours. After 14 days and 102 ballots, the party compromised on the conservative John W. Davis, a former Ambassador to England during the Wilson administration. The wounds the party received at Madison Square Garden would not begin to mend until July 2, 1932. While Coolidge and Charles Dawes eventually returned to the nation's capitol, Smith went on to claim victory in New York's gubernatorial race. Roosevelt's speech was remarkable not only in content, but also in the physical demands it exacted. Importantly, Roosevelt did not use his wheelchair to get to the speaker's podium; instead, he propelled his body forward on crutches—his first major public exhibition of his ability to walk. The reasoning behind the perilous act was simple: "no political leader of modern times had managed to reach the top rung without standing alone and giving the appearance of being in good health and in physical command." [39]

Roosevelt's performance was greeted with mixed reviews, but even the most favorable were tempered by mention of his disability. Ralph E. Renaud reported that "Franklin Roosevelt, who hobbled painfully on his crutches toward the microphone, looked every inch the splendid gentleman." [40] The *New York Herald Tribune* offered, "Roosevelt's appearance on the speaker's platform, robust and ruddy and with ringing voice, gave such evident proof of his general health that those responsible for the boom effort felt that his physical shortcomings would offer no insurmountable difficulty." [41]

Others reported a much different version of Roosevelt's health. "Delegates . . . had in their minds a picture of a young man in the flower of his manly vigor stepping briskly to the podium," noted Kyle D. Palmer. "Today they saw him virtually carried there, crippled by the creeping inroads of infantile paralysis, and obliged to prop himself against the speaker's desk once he had been lifted to this feet." [42] Robert M. Lee was even less kind in his appraisal: "He is hopelessly an invalid, his legs paralyzed. Wheel chair [*sic*], crutches and attendants are with him wherever he goes." [43]

But if he could only surmount his physical handicap, if could make his recalcitrant legs obey, there was hope. "Were he physically strong," editorialized Oswald Garrison Villard, "it seems to me that he would be the ideal compromise candidate for the Presidency from the Democratic point of view." [44] Similarly, the *New York Herald Tribune* concluded, "Four years from now and another Democratic convention may see him present without crutches and in full health. Then, and only then, another story may be written." [45] Roosevelt set out to write that story himself following the convention, an effort aided by the warm spring waters in the hills of north Georgia. In the meantime, notes Frank Freidel, "Despite his splendid appearance at Madison Square Garden, the consensus was that he was through." [46] Thus did Roosevelt's body enter the crucible of electoral politics and public speculation.

In the meantime, Roosevelt bided his time between frequent bacchanals on the Larooco and a remote tourist area in Georgia known as Warm Springs. He had heard about Warm Springs through a friend who claimed that the area's 90-degree springwaters had enabled one victim of polio to walk with the aid of canes. Roosevelt arrived in October, 1924, and he transformed the once-vibrant town into an infantile paralysis treatment center. [47] Much of what would eventually become the Warm Springs Foundation was initially bankrolled out of Roosevelt's own pocket. [48] Roosevelt's initial visit to Warm Springs left him ecstatic. To Eleanor he wrote, "This is really a discovery of a place and there is no doubt that I've got to do it [water exercises] some more." [49] More strategically, to his mother he related, "I feel that a great 'cure' for infantile paralysis and kindred diseases could well be established here." [50]

Though his health continued to improve, Roosevelt was not yet ready to run for political office. In 1926 he turned down Democratic overtures to nominate him for a run at the U.S. Senate, and as 1928 neared he sensed that the Republican prosperity would keep the GOP firmly in control of national politics. The planned political comeback, according to Howe, would occur in 1932, a year in which Roosevelt presciently forecasted a depression. [51] This did not stop him from actively working for Smith's second bid for his party's presidential nomination. Roosevelt again delivered Smith's nomination speech, and again it met with journalist praise.

Smith anticipated a close race, so close that he needed New York's forty-five electoral votes to win. They could only be secured, he figured, if the party ran a strong Democratic candidate for Governor—Roosevelt, in other words. Smith lobbied Roosevelt extensively, but he would not budge. In September, Roosevelt left for Warm Springs, content to convalesce for four more years. Smith would not take "no" for an answer, however; more importantly, neither would the state delegates meeting in Rochester. Even the new Democratic National Committee Chairman, the wealthy General Motors executive John J. Raskob, entered the fray: he promised to help finance Roosevelt's fledgling Warm Springs Foundation. [52] On October 2, 1928, the convention nominated Roosevelt for governor; this time he finally capitulated. Yet by initially declining the nomination out of concern for his health, Roosevelt unintentionally created more concern about it. "Having agreed to run for governor," notes Finis Farr, "Roosevelt saw that his most serious campaign problem would be to convince the voters of New York State that he was not a physically handicapped man." [53] The media sensed a political

sacrifice for Al Smith—with Roosevelt's body as the offering. Republican papers in particular "portrayed him as a dangerously ill man, warned by his
physicians not to run, forced by Smith's ambition to risk perhaps even his
life." [54] Freidel's point is born out in particular by the *New York Herald Tribune.* The day after the nomination, they opined, "Let the desperation of
the Democratic cause in the nation and in this state be conceded. Who
can defend the risking of another's health and whole future career in the
cause of one's own vanity and ambition. The nomination is unfair to
Mr. Roosevelt." [55]

Even state Democratic leaders were concerned: they made plans "to
make the burden as light as possible for Franklin D. Roosevelt." [56] But in the
relatively short period of time before election day, Roosevelt went to work
combating the popular perception that he was an invalid—on his own
terms. [57] In less than three weeks, Roosevelt delivered more than fifty
speeches and covered more than 1,300 miles by car. Such a display
prompted surprise: "the nominee is surprising his associates by his vigor after four hard days of campaigning. He has been described as an invalid who
was sacrificing his health for the Democratic Party, but in actuality he is in
better condition today than any one else in the [campaign] party." [58]

But even Roosevelt's whirl of physical activity could not dissuade many
from what appeared to be an unreasonable sacrifice. Less than two weeks after his nomination *Time* reported, "In another two years, his doctors said, he
might go without braces and canes—if he stayed at Warm Springs. If he did
not stay, he would risk being crippled for life." [59] The sacrifice was so severe
and imperiled his health to such a degree that the *New York Times* could not
recommend voting for him:

> A noble character, a devoted public servant, a man of the finest in-
> stincts, highly cultivated—what a shame that in his poor condition of
> health he has been called upon to make such a sacrifice! If the Demo-
> cratic Party had only waited two years and nominated him for Gover-
> nor in 1930, then all of us independents and Republicans would have
> been delighted to vote for him, but this year, as you see, the thing is
> sorrowfully impossible for us. [60]

Despite the concerns and reservations of many of New York's political and
media elite, Roosevelt narrowly defeated Albert Ottinger. Ironically, Freidel
attributed the victory to Roosevelt's ubiquitous physical presence: "the spectacular display of physical endurance helped endow him with glamor." [61]

Smith's augury proved wrong on both accounts: he lost badly to Herbert
Hoover, and, despite Roosevelt's narrow victory over Albert Ottinger, Smith
did not even carry his home state. [62] Smith experienced further rejection
prior to Roosevelt's inauguration—a rejection that eventually led to a bitter
rift in 1932. Instead of kowtowing to the Smith forces entrenched at Albany,
Roosevelt immediately fired two of Smith's most important lieutenants—

Belle Moskowitz and Robert Moses—and thereby served notice to the Tammany Progressive that he would be calling the shots.

Governor Roosevelt

As in his term as state senator, Roosevelt immediately went to work on the state's upstate agricultural problems, which had grown even more acute during the postwar period. Most of the agricultural legislation that Roosevelt eventually signed involved tax relief measures, not the controversial measures that required government intervention to limit agricultural supply. Roosevelt also wanted to offer relief to his constituents in the form of cheaper electricity. The physical source of power was the St. Lawrence River; the state government could insure lower rates to consumers. The plan, though, met with stiff resistance in the Republican-controlled legislature, a common occurrence during Roosevelt's first term.

Having helped to orchestrate several campaigns, Roosevelt was keenly aware of the need for political organization, and for this role he hired the secretary of the State Democratic Committee, Jim Farley. Farley was instrumental in organizing moribund upstate Democratic committees, so much so that in 1930 Roosevelt appointed him chairman of the State Democratic Committee. Farley's upstate efforts were made more difficult not only because the area was traditionally a Republican stronghold, but also because it received most of its political information from predominantly Republican news organs. It was to overcome this predicament that the "fireside chat" was created.[63] Farley's efforts at party organization, Roosevelt's frequent radio appeals and his progressive record, all in the context of a deepening depression, had Republicans worried—and not just New York Republicans. President Hoover clearly sensed Roosevelt's burgeoning political status: he sent Henry Stimson, Ogden Mills, and Patrick Hurley to New York to stump for the party's gubernatorial nominee, Charles Tuttle. Their efforts proved futile. Roosevelt was reelected by a huge margin; he even captured a majority of the votes north of New York City, a feat of which not even Smith could boast. More importantly, the landslide victory catapulted Roosevelt into the national spotlight as a leading Democratic presidential candidate.

Roosevelt, though publicly dismissive of the speculation, privately agreed with Howe and Ed Flynn: he would run for president in 1932, thus expediting his initial plan by four years.[64] Howe and Flynn agreed to do the necessary groundwork in New York; Farley would sound out other states' Democratic organizations and leaders as to a possible Roosevelt candidacy. Farley had the perfect cover for the clandestine mission: he was Exalted Ruler of the Benevolent and Protective Order of the Elks, a position that obliged him to visit Elk lodges throughout the nation. Farley's cross-country journey in the summer of 1931 proved invaluable in getting the electoral ball rolling.[65]

Insofar as labels often think for us, it would be easy to adopt the standard interpretation that Roosevelt was a progressive governor, which would au tomatically differentiate him from Herbert Hoover. In this case, the designation is misleading, for while Roosevelt did propose progressive measures in such areas as prison reform, mental hygiene, education, agriculture, old-age pensions, and public power, he clung tenaciously to fiscal orthodoxy and to relatively traditional views of federal, state, and local government responsibilities. This was particularly so during the two year period following the stock market crash, to which I now turn.

Roosevelt's Hooverian Rhetoric

Roosevelt spoke frequently to his New York constituents, typically about state issues and how his administration proposed to deal with them. Perhaps because of the circumstances in which he often spoke, and perhaps because he employed only one principal speechwriter, Samuel I. Rosenman, his gubernatorial rhetoric is pedestrian, especially when compared to his presidential rhetoric. More important for our purposes is how Roosevelt publicly responded to the depression and to what extent, if any, economic recovery could be facilitated by rhetorical means. As I will illustrate, Hoover could hardly have asked for a better spokesman.

Shortly after the crash, on January 16, 1930, Roosevelt heartily endorsed Hoover's proposal to increase government-financed construction projects: "I was in hearty accord at all times with the suggestion of the President that this was a good time to do all the construction work that we possibly could."[66] He also agreed with Hoover that cooperation with business leaders was instrumental in mitigating unemployment. But he went further: "we have got to have a State financial policy that is sound, and we cannot get it unless we get the intelligent interest of the business men of the Nation" (686). Later in the year, Roosevelt proudly announced that business leaders had cooperated with his administration to maintain employment levels.[67]

Aside from expediting government construction projects and securing cooperation with business leaders, recovery was largely a private matter. To the Knights of Columbus, Roosevelt stated that "government, whether it be state or local, could not undertake more than a limited amount of welfare activities. . . . To private organizations, however, must be left the training and care of the hundreds of thousands who, in order to insure better citizenship, require some kind of outside assistance."[68] Here, at the local level, was "the chance to help the individual neighbor" and the opportunity to "live up to the second great commandment" (741). As the election of 1930 neared, Roosevelt reduced economic recovery to its most indivisible unit: the individual:

> The responsibility for the upward climb rests not on conferences, not
> on commissions, not on government . . . The primary responsibility
> rests upon the individual. We cannot legislate a return to prosperity,

we cannot force factories to open by commission fiat, we cannot per-
manently feed and clothe the unemployed through the operation of
mere charity.[69]

Prosperity would return, Roosevelt promised, if "every man and woman"
would simply "do one good turn daily for the purpose of bringing industry
and business back where it belongs."[70] This "one good turn," Roosevelt explained in several speeches, amounted to "persuad[ing] the purchasing public of this country to go about their business of purchasing in a normal way"
(812). If only people with purchasing power would spend, "the economic
level of the whole population" would increase (813).

Roosevelt, it should be emphasized, never declared that the government
should not intervene, but the sort of intervention to which he subscribed
was radically de-centralized—what he termed "Home Rule." He wanted to
avoid "the regulations and legislation by 'master minds'" that had been so
"glaringly apparent at Washington during these last ten years."[71] He ab-
horred the idea that "all authority and control be centralized in our National
Government." De-centralized government was a "necessity if we are to remain a truly united country" (710).

Roosevelt reiterated the theme of Home Rule at no small length in what
would appear to be an inopportune time and place—his second Inaugural
Address. After his resounding victory over Tuttle, he quickly became the
Democratic presidential frontrunner. Because of this, one of Roosevelt's
closest advisors, Colonel Edward M. House, advised him to strike a "high and
progressive note" in his Inaugural Address, since the whole country would
be listening.[72] Instead, Roosevelt struck what appears to be a low and conservative note, that of local government and its manifold responsibilities.

The speech resembles a rudimentary lecture on the divisions of government, but it also had a moral: "Let us not at this time pursue the easy road
of centralization of authority lest some day we discover too late that our liberties have disappeared."[73] The country was in the midst of a "dangerous
tendency" of increased government centralization, a structure "alien to our
system and more closely akin to a dictatorship or the central committee of a
communistic regime."[74] Relief, in other words, was to be effected at the most
localized levels of government, where officials were highly attuned to the
needs of their own communities. To do otherwise was to usurp the civic responsibilities and duties bequeathed by the Constitution.

The federal government did have a role to play in the depression, but that
role was circumscribed by Roosevelt's abiding fear of centralization. In his
speech to the annual Conference of Governors on June 2, 1931, he advised
his fellow state heads that "we should not put all of our eggs into one bas-
ket," since conditions "vary greatly in different sections of the country."[75]
The best alternative was a state-by-state provisional approach in which
each state functioned as its own "experimental laboratory." But each state,

Roosevelt realized, needed data to carry out the experiments, and here the federal government was needed:

> The state requires, of course, the sympathetic cooperation of the National Government as an information gathering body. The National Government can well act as a clearing house for all of us Governors to work through and I think that is the correct and most useful function of Washington. Instead of trying to run the whole works and to dictate methods and details to all of the states along some hard and fast program which may or may not apply in the different sections of the country.[76]

Roosevelt's altered his position, though, following the Hoover administration's moratorium on intergovernmental debts and reparations as the 1932 presidential campaign neared. At Charlottesville, Virginia, on July 6, 1931, he made his first equivocal statement on increased centralization: "the larger units of government have been properly and logically forced to assume functions that once belonged to the lesser units. The demands of a different sort of civilization and a different sort of national economy have forced us to redistribute the burdens which the public service imposes."[77] Roosevelt's verb construction is telling: the situation had effectively coerced government officials into seeing the need for increased centralization. There was even precedent for the largely unprecedented move: the country's founders "were wise enough to look into the future and to recognize that the conditions of life and the demands upon government were bound to change . . . so the plan of government that they prepared was made, not rigid, but flexible—adapted to change and to progress" (751). Political observers must have been perplexed at some point during the summer of 1931: the Founding Fathers were being pulled in opposite directions to sanction very different ends. They might well have been equally nonplused by a careful reading of Roosevelt's speeches. In a radio address later in the summer, he stated that "many of our new problems can best be solved by federal jurisdiction and yet I am very certain that in the days to come nothing can be bettered by a fundamental change of the theory government [sic] which was set up in the year 1789."[78] Perhaps never were the Constitution or the motives that helped to frame it so malleable. Only one thing was increasingly clear: the federal government, either because of situational exigencies, constitutional mandate, or both, had to become involved.

The involvement Roosevelt favored appeared to stem from an admixture of Frederick Jackson Turner's frontier hypothesis and urban economic theory. While Roosevelt took Turner's "famous course" at Harvard, Freidel downplays any influence.[79] Roosevelt's economic rhetoric suggests otherwise. To a group of agricultural economists, for example, he noted that "many economists are seriously questioning whether we have not for the time being reached the saturation point of industrial production calling for a period of digestion for a number of years to come." [80] Similarly, to the nation's governors, he recounted,

> Our country was of necessity developed in a highly individualistic way. Hardy and determined men went into a new wilderness to carve out homes, to gain a living for their families and to build a future for their race. But the settling of all the land on the continent, the development of a highly organized system of industry and the growth of a huge population have created new and highly complicated problems. [81]

The country, in other words, had reached its economic limits; the inexorable march of prosperity had stopped at the nation's industrial and geographical limits. Within this context of satiation, government planning, not unfettered capitalism, provided the only solution to the depression.

Within a closed or bounded system, expansion was impossible. The solution, as such, required redistribution: "the machine is today out of balance and the principal effort of the next few years will be to restore that balance." [82] Economic equanimity was to be achieved by planning "a better distribution of our population as between the larger city and the smaller country communities." [83] This meant a mass migration, "a considerable movement of workers from city to country" (757). Many of the nation's agricultural problems would be solved, since distribution costs would shrink prices and thereby encourage greater consumption of the farmers' produce. The exodus from the city would be facilitated by industrial relocation into rural areas; the population's balance would thus be restored. [84] Roosevelt, like many of his contemporaries, focused attention primarily on the supply side of the scale; demand, or getting people to actually spend more, still needed fixing.

Like Hoover, Roosevelt initially attempted to boost demand by increased spending on public works projects and by securing cooperation from business and labor leaders. But Roosevelt tried to differentiate his economic leadership from Hoover's by calling attention to the president's "futile attempt to restore prosperity by means of proclamations from Washington." [85] Hoover had misled the American people by offering "messages of good cheer" when workers were being "discharged by the thousands." "Nothing happened," Roosevelt admonished, "but words." But, like Hoover, Roosevelt fell prey to his anti-rhetoric. To the New York Advertising Club, he encapsulated his remarks "into this thought: that we as a nation have got to persuade the purchasing public of this country to go about their business of purchasing in a normal way and in a different spirit from that in which they are now acting." [86] The "big objective" that government at all levels shared with the advertising industry was to restore "normal business through a re-establishment of confidence in American business" (813). Consumer confidence, Hoover and Roosevelt both agreed, would trigger economic recovery—and persuasive rhetoric would provide the means. The emphasis on confidence was not a recurrent feature in Roosevelt's gubernatorial rhetoric, which is perfectly explicable in light of its preponderance in the Hoover corpus: mimicking the enemy makes for bad electoral politics. Nonetheless, at this point Roosevelt viewed consumer confidence as a vital first step toward economic recovery.

The purpose of this brief overview of Roosevelt's gubernatorial rhetoric is not meant as a comprehensive survey; rather its purpose is three-fold: to draw parallels and distinctions with Herbert Hoover; to provide a rhetorical and ideological backdrop to the 1932 presidential campaign; and to understand how Roosevelt conceptualized government's role, at all levels, in combating the depression. This thumbnail sketch reveals a Governor aligned with Home Rule and national centralization, individual responsibility and federal planning, and anti-optimism and pro-confidence—all within a two-year span. In sum, we have been duly warned that consistency might not be a hallmark of Roosevelt's campaign rhetoric. He indeed possessed a "swift shiftiness of footwork" that, on the surface, enabled him to appeal to diverse factions within the Democratic party.[87]

Stumbling Out of the Blocks

Though outwardly the Democratic party appeared to have mended its fences by 1928, it was still deeply divided on such vital issues as tariffs, prohibition, and agriculture. To complicate matters, the pro–big business Smith appointed fellow Roman Catholic John J. Raskob as chair of the Democratic National Committee. Raskob's views on economic policy were predictably conservative given his affiliations with General Motors and the DuPonts. Raskob, in turn, summoned another wealthy businessman to committee headquarters in 1929, Kansas City's Jouett Shouse, who "shared Raskob's wholehearted devotion to a business-governed America."[88] Thus, the party's leadership structure was top-heavy with a pro-business, top-down approach to economic issues. Their views, in sum, scarcely differed from the pre-1932 Hoover administration.[89] Within this context, Roosevelt's progressive measures on labor legislation, unemployment insurance and old-age pensions were seen as "dangerously radical" proposals.[90]

Not only was Roosevelt anathema to Smith's circle on business matters, but his pro-internationalism did even less to ingratiate him with party leaders. In 1920 Cox and Roosevelt ran on a pro-League platform, a position that cost the party dearly at the polls, and by 1932 Roosevelt had done little, if anything, to indicate that he had sworn off his Wilsonianism. To make matters worse, he had greatly incensed the titular head of the party, Smith, by not consulting with him on the impending presidential candidacy. To Roosevelt ally Clark Howell, Smith exploded, "Do you know, by God, that he has never consulted me about a damn thing since he has been Governor? He has taken bad advice and from sources not friendly to me. He has ignored me! By God, he invited me to his house . . . and did not even mention to me the subject of his candidacy."[91] Roosevelt would learn the hard way that an unhappy "Happy Warrior" could make for a trying primary season.

Less than one month after Smith's private outburst, publishing titan William Randolph Hearst went public with his preferred presidential candidate: the isolationist Speaker of the House, John Nance Garner. Garner's candidacy would tie up ninety delegates from California and Texas who initially appeared to be leaning toward Roosevelt. One week later, before Roosevelt had even declared his candidacy, his presidential qualifications were seriously impugned by the nation's most influential journalist.

In his syndicated column, Walter Lippmann admonished the New York Governor for his ideological inconsistency:

> The reason [for the inconsistency], is that Franklin Roosevelt is a highly impressionable person, without a firm grasp of public affairs and without very strong convictions. . . . [he] is no crusader. He is no tribune of the people. He is no enemy of entrenched privilege. He is a pleasant man who without any important qualifications for the office would very much like to be President.[92]

Lippmann and others saw Roosevelt as a "Democratic Harding," someone charming, good-looking and friendly but lacking in intellect and convictions.[93] Ten days later, on January 17, 1932, Hearst struck again: his front page newspapers indicted Roosevelt for being a League supporter.

The Candidate Strikes Back

Against this backdrop of candidacy jockeying and editorial censure, Roosevelt declared his presidential candidacy in a most understated way— through a January 22 letter to North Dakota's Democratic Committee. But before his official announcement, he delivered an important speech on January 14 in New York City. It is an odd amalgamation of Democratic party history, campaign ethics, and tax policy—"odd" primarily because the occasion, a Democratic Victory Dinner, was right for epideictic generalities, not pedagogy and policy. Roosevelt also used the occasion to declare war, albeit subtly, on the party's national leaders.

In the first third of the speech, Roosevelt told his version of the party's origins, but with a particular emphasis on class and class distinctions. The party's initial identity was a response to the Hamiltonian principle "that a small element in the population, composed of the rich, of the well-educated and of the aristocratic families, should constitute a ruling class."[94] Thomas Jefferson and the friends of Jefferson looked for support from "the average citizen in the small town and in the vast areas of the country." The Democratic party had its origins in class and the aristocratic Governor maintained that this point of origin must not be forgotten or overlooked in the present.

If the party lost sight of its class origins, its future "success" would be impeded. And class applied also to the party's leadership (Raskob, Shouse and Smith). Although Roosevelt purported to address his "Republican brethren," the Democratic triumvirate could not have been pleased with his class exhortations:

> The appeal is not . . . to the rich alone, to those few who though perhaps they may have the means have no right to be the sole custodians of the party itself. It is an appeal rather to the rank and file of a party which has continued to exist through more than six generations because its foundations are laid in the first instance in the membership of the party rather than in a few chosen or self-appointed leaders (542).

Though Roosevelt thanked "Mr. Raskob" for disseminating the party's agenda to the public, he was not "solely responsible" for its continuation. Such a duty resided with the "party as a whole," particularly the Democratic rank and file.

Privately, Roosevelt was no fan of John J. Raskob. Though his wealth and connections went a long way toward resuscitating an enervated party, Roosevelt was highly suspicious of the party's chairman—perhaps with good reason. The Raskob-Smith forces quickly translated Roosevelt's 725,000 vote majority in the 1930 gubernatorial election as a portent of presidential aspirations. The day after the elections, Raskob and Shouse penned a letter to Herbert Hoover pledging Democratic support for his administration's recovery measures—traditionally conservative measures at that.[95] The letter was signed by Smith, Davis, Cox, Garner, and Senator Joseph Robinson— an elite congregation of party conservatives. Roosevelt interpreted the epistolic gesture as hostile to his future plans, since it pledged the party to an alliance with big business.[96]

Roosevelt's suspicions of Raskob multiplied during the winter of 1931. On February 10, Raskob announced a special meeting of the Democratic National Committee to be held, remarkably, on March 5. The interval was purposefully brief: Raskob wanted a meeting to commit the party to a platform of continued high tariffs and an outright repeal of prohibition—planks he personally favored. Perhaps more importantly, Raskob was flouting party policy: the national convention was in charge of platform formulation. Roosevelt eventually diffused the potentially volatile situation, but it was no secret that the party's leadership hierarchy harbored no desires for a Roosevelt candidacy. Thus, the motives behind Roosevelt's initial appeals to class and the party's rank and file come into sharper relief. They also point to a skill at rhetorical nuance: praising the party while simultaneously damning its leader was no mean task.

In the second third of the address, Roosevelt continued his veiled assault on Raskob—albeit under the guise of campaign decorum. Recalling the 1928 campaign, in which Smith's Catholicism was a frequent topic,

Roosevelt urged his listeners to conduct themselves so "that we shall never be made the object of the accusation that we have dealt our opponents a blow below the belt" (543). Hoover, he declared, had been the victim of malicious gossip, especially in magazines and the daily press.

That Roosevelt singled out these two sources is not insignificant: Shouse, with Raskob's approbation, had hired Charles Michelson to direct the Democratic National Committee's publicity division in 1929. Michelson immediately began churning out near-libelous anti-Hoover propaganda for the remainder of his presidency. Thus, given the machinations of Raskob-Shouse-Michelson, he could empathize with Hoover's plight: "He is perhaps the victim of a theory which holds that the control of the Republican party reins entitles the holders to use that historic party for the purposes of personal gain" (543).

Roosevelt concluded the speech with a strange transition into tax policy. More specifically, he proposed a plan to enhance tax revenues through more equitable and efficient means—a plan that privileged state sovereignty over federal centralization. Roosevelt made no mention of budget cuts; rather, he proposed to increase the "flow" of tax revenues by expanding the tax base. This would address "the problem of balancing budgets" and, thereby, aid "the maintenance of the credit structure of each of the governmental units" (543–44). Though he might, with some exaggeration, describe the means as "progressive," the ends were the stuff of fiscal orthodoxy.

But he was not finished; he intimated vaguely that economic recovery could be facilitated by other avenues:

> If we believe in the Democratic doctrine that the functions of our government should be exercised to stimulate not "big business" nor "little business" but all enterprise so as to prevent unfair aggression by the strong against the weak; if we believe that we must return to the principle of giving an equal chance to everyone . . . we must insist that this foundation principle be observed by those in control of government.
> So only can we translate a depression into a mere transition period before we construct a sounder economic edifice (544).

The metaphors were not the only thing reminiscent of Herbert Hoover; equality of opportunity was also a Hooverian mainstay, but Roosevelt steered safely from recovery specifics. Was he hinting at tougher enforcement of anti-trust laws? Was he referring to a reduction in the pro–big business Smoot-Hawley tariffs? Was he instead alluding to industry's advantages over agriculture? More importantly, how would the government, aside from maintaining equal opportunity, stimulate "all enterprise"? Was this perhaps a veiled reference to Roosevelt's earlier emphasis on economic balance, wherein recovery was contingent on a redistribution of purchasing power? To direct such queries to Roosevelt presupposed that he possessed the answers—a highly dubious assumption given both his then limited knowledge of economics and his Albany advisors' lack of economic expertise.[97] But at this point, he was under no obligation to discuss policy specifics. The expectations mounted, however, following his official entrance into the presidential race eight days later.

Forsaking the League

If we were to take the editor of *The Public Papers and Addresses of Franklin D. Roosevelt,* Samuel I. Rosenman, at face value, we should begin our investigation of his 1932 presidential campaign on April 7, the date of Roosevelt's "Forgotten Man" speech—on Rosenman's account, his first "official" campaign speech. Yet biographers Kenneth S. Davis and Frank Freidel and historian Eliot A. Rosen give another speech primary importance in Roosevelt's bid to secure his party's nomination. The speech in question was Roosevelt's first as a declared presidential candidate: an address given on February 2 to members of the New York Grange. It aptly illustrated Lippmann's complaint that Roosevelt carried buckets of water on both shoulders.

In late January, Jim Farley privately admitted to Hearst's New York editors that Roosevelt had changed his mind on U.S. entry into the League of Nations. Farley's confession was meant to temper Hearst's vitriol aimed at Roosevelt's perceived internationalism. Hearst did not want a Wilsonian in the Oval Office, as he had made clear throughout January. Farley's private efforts to assuage Hearst's fears backfired, however, and on January 31 the front page of every Hearst paper blared: "If Mr. Roosevelt has any statement to make about his not being an internationalist he should make it to the public publicly, and not to me privately."[98] Public words were much harder to recant than private ones. Roosevelt responded publicly two days later.

Howe and House, then Roosevelt's principal advisors, threw together a hasty draft. It would prove to be one of their last joint rhetorical creations—with good reason. The speech, as it has come down to us, is awful, both thematically and stylistically. It was, as Richard Oulahan states, "an astonishing, inconsistent, weaseling speech."[99] It was so offensive to Eleanor that she did not speak to her husband for several days. It also provoked the wrath of Wilsonian liberals who had thought that Roosevelt would not capitulate to the party's conservative faction. One can, therefore, perhaps understand the motives behind Rosenman's strategic omission.[100]

Roosevelt called initially for international solidarity, yet he later espoused rabidly nationalist sentiments. In a word, the speech is schizophrenic. The bulk of the text is addressed to the farmer's problems—"problems that are world-wide in their scope."[101] The problem redounded, according to Roosevelt, to the matter of markets: the nation needed either to increase its consumption of goods or find foreign markets. He strategically ignored the former; the latter was being thwarted by the Smoot-Hawley tariff bill. The solution required merely "a little horse sense," a reciprocal method of exchange in which the United States bartered its goods for another nation's goods.[102] Trade agreements would be simple: other countries "will meet us half way and put all [their] cards on the table for the purpose of breaking an actual deadlock" (551). The United States and other nations would no longer engage in poker diplomacy, or so Roosevelt had "good reason to believe" (551). At this point in the speech, though, the international accord ended and intranationalism took its place.

First, trade agreements, Roosevelt assured his audience, were not indicative of a desire to join the League of Nations. Europe had so bastardized Wilson's founding vision that it would not serve U.S. interests to join. Roosevelt's main rationale for avoiding membership—the lack of resemblance to Wilson's plan—is absurd: in European hands, the League might plausibly concern itself with European problems. Roosevelt rejected League entry for one and only one reason: it was politically expedient, and those closest to him knew it.

Roosevelt then moved, albeit obliquely, to the recently enacted moratorium on intergovernmental war debts, as if to underscore his point that most, if not all, European countries were dishonorable. At this point the speech turned isolationist:

> What the world needs most today is a *national* policy which will make us an example of *national* honor to other nations. The first lesson for all the world is recognition that a treaty is a *nation's* word of honor to another *nation* and that all just *national* debts are debts of honor (552; emphasis added).

This was the same speaker who, three paragraphs earlier, had spoken of international trust and cooperation. He added belligerently, "Europe owes us. We do not owe her." Economic diplomacy never lacked for a more one-sided card game, but Roosevelt was far from through.

He continued his anti-European harangue: the United States should "demand an understanding" from Europe; it should insist on an accord; Europe had been "crippled" by "an orgy of spending" and had engaged in "reckless vituperation" against the United States. In spite of this xenophobic tirade, Roosevelt had the audacity to conclude with a plea for "economic co-operation" and an "adherence to the principles of Washington. But U.S. imperialism would hold sway: the nation would singlehandedly steer "the world ship of state" back to a "safe course to port" (552).

Lippmann's hypothesis rang true: the wild ambivalence in the text "conformed precisely to the behavior pattern [Lippmann] had described and deplored."[103] The speech was not only "an abject capitulation to a hateful and much hated man," but Roosevelt was ready to yield even further. "He was prepared, should Hearst demand it, to add a statement saying he no longer favored U.S. participation in the World Court!"[104] The formerly strident Wilsonian was more willing to embrace isolationism than even the autarkic duo of Harding and Coolidge.

Aside from the national/international thematic tension, the speech offers more subtle clues as to Roosevelt's views on economic recovery. Despite its relative brevity, the address contains numerous references to sight, such as "make it clear," "let us see," and "she should look." The repetition of the ocular sense makes it conspicuous. The frequent object of Roosevelt's gaze involved matters of health and sickness. He mentioned, for example, nations that "are suffering," "paralyzed" world trade, Europe's "crippled" financial position and its fiscal "ills," and America's attempts to "revive the trade of the world."

It is tempting to speculate at this point whether Roosevelt's references to paralysis and crippling were, consciously or otherwise, motivated by his own physical condition. Whatever the case, the maladies that afflicted the world's economy were not permanent: a "helping hand" would help "revive" economic conditions at home and abroad.[105] The patient, in other words, could be healed if only it would follow Roosevelt's vision. Economic recovery was akin to science: the ailments simply needed to be seen in the proper light. So, like Hoover, Roosevelt initially conceptualized recovery within a largely scientific matrix. But unlike the president, Roosevelt did not denigrate the power of words, nor did he emphasize confidence.

Roosevelt's troubles increased exponentially following the speech. He not only infuriated many of his political allies and his wife, but the speech may have signaled to Smith that Roosevelt was too weak and too malleable to survive the rigors of a presidential race.[106] Six days after the speech, Smith announced that he would be available should the party seek to nominate him. His announcement complicated matters for the Governor, for it immediately put him in a difficult political bind.

Raymond Moley to the Rescue

In August, 1931, Roosevelt helped to appoint appellate court judge Samuel Seabury to investigate allegations of Tammany Hall corruption. By January, Seabury had concluded part of his investigation, and he requested that Roosevelt remove from office the Honorable Thomas M. Farley, the sheriff of New York County, on corruption charges. To do so, though, would anger Tammany, not to mention other big city bosses. But, on the other hand, if Roosevelt succumbed to Tammany's pressure, the nation would see him as ineffectual, as a mere tool of the bosses. To make matters worse, Smith was a born-and-bred Tammany politico. Convention delegates, from New York and elsewhere, hung in the balance. As he would do frequently in the next year, a Columbia University political science professor, Raymond Moley, came to Roosevelt's rescue.

Howe recruited Moley in 1928 to aid Roosevelt in crafting a message on judicial reform, which was his area of expertise. Moley agreed, but on one condition: that Roosevelt appoint him to a state commission on the administration of justice. Moley upheld his end of the bargain: Roosevelt delivered a well-received speech on prison and court reform on October 28, 1928.

Although it took him close to three years, Roosevelt eventually appointed Moley as the commission's research director in the summer of 1931.[107]

Roosevelt was impressed with Moley's work on the committee—so much so that he invited Moley to lunch in early January. There Moley volunteered his services for the upcoming campaign; approximately one month later, Roosevelt accepted the offer. Because of Moley's prior work with the Seabury investigations, Roosevelt asked him to write Farley's removal statement, a statement legally justifying Roosevelt's bold indictment of Tammany corruption. The statement played well with two very different audiences: to Tammany, Roosevelt claimed that he was forced to act; to the public, he claimed that he had acted with "unprecedented boldness." [108] The successful rhetorical tightrope act thus commenced a most important political alliance.

That Moley was taken with his new boss is attested to in a very revealing and insightful letter to his sister, Nell, composed in April, 1932. Regarding his manner:

> The idea people get from his charming manner—that he is soft or flabby in disposition and character is far from true. When he wants something a lot he can be formidable—when crossed he is hard, stubborn, unremorseful—relentless. I used to think in the hours of casual observation that his amiability was "lord-of-the-manor"—"good with the peasants" stuff. It isn't that at all.[109]

He also commented on Roosevelt's effect on people: "He is wholly conscious of his ability to send callers away happy and glowing and in agreement with him and his ideas. And he particularly enjoys sending people away who have completely forgotten (under his spell) the thing they came to say or ask."

In addition, he characterized Roosevelt's intellectual and political habits:

> I've been amazed with his interest in things. It skips and bounces through seemingly intricate subjects and maybe it is my academic training that makes me feel that no one could possibly learn so much in such a hit or miss fashion. . . . What he gets is from talking to people and when he stores away the net of a conversation he never knows which part of what he has kept is what he said himself or what his visitor said.

As for the all-important health issue, Moley was a believer: "The stories about his illness and its effect upon him are the bunk. Nobody in public life since T.R. has been so robust, so buoyantly and blatantly healthful as this fellow. . . . The man's energy and vitality are astounding." Roosevelt had thus convinced the man who would play a most crucial role in getting him elected that he was presidential material.

The origins of what Roosevelt initially termed his "privy council" are uncertain. Rosenman claims that in mid-March he suggested that Roosevelt solicit some college professors to help develop his political positions. Moley argues that his January luncheon presaged the group's formation.[110] Origins in this case are immaterial. What is very clear, however, is that the Howe/House team had been stretched to its limits. Thus, Moley recruited some of his Columbia colleagues to come to Roosevelt's aid in March. Two of his recruits stuck: agriculture expert Rexford G. Tugwell and credit whiz Adolf A. Berle. The academics teamed with Farley, Howe, and O'Connor to form what *New York Times* reporter James Kieran later designated the "Brains Trust."

Some questioned Roosevelt's willingness to entrust his political fortunes to a small group of largely untested university faculty, a group that was, Rosenman claimed, "notoriously impractical."[111] Roosevelt's faith in academic expertise, however, had been rewarded frequently during the preceding three years, and he obviously felt no compunction to change. As his comments of January 20 indicate, his adoration for academic experts bordered on the religious. To the New York State Agriculture Society he declared,

> if we wish to save ourselves from a stupendous waste of public and
> private funds, we need to know what is going to be the future of farm
> development and the general use of the lands of the state. We should
> hire a few prophets to tell us. And that . . . . is just what we are doing.
> Prophecy along certain lines is not an impossible thing.[112]

The prophets Roosevelt had hired were soil experts and agricultural economists from Cornell University. He hoped that his other Ivy League clan would be equally prescient.

Before he could offer their work for public consumption, however, Roosevelt needed first to deal with the machinations of the burgeoning "Stop Roosevelt" coalition. Raskob had called a meeting of the Democratic National Committee's Subcommittee on Arrangements for April 4, during which it would select the convention's temporary chairman. Shouse openly coveted the powerful post, but the Roosevelt forces wanted Kentucky Senator Alben Barkley, who was much more amenable to a Roosevelt candidacy. The meeting was immediately deadlocked, as both coalitions announced their preferences. Virginia Senator Harry Byrd proposed a compromise: the committee would recommend Barkley as temporary chairman, and it would recommend Shouse for permanent chairman.[113] Roosevelt gave his assent to Farley, but with an important semantic qualifier: he would "commend," not "recommend," Shouse for the position. Such a distinction, Roosevelt maintained, would give him the necessary room to maneuver at the convention. No one, save Farley, apparently noticed the rhetorical hair splitting. Three days later, Roosevelt gave his first nationally broadcast campaign speech.

The Forgotten Man

The ten-minute radio address, the Brain Trust's first rhetorical creation, did not lack for controversy. It was immediately hailed as the "Forgotten Man" speech, because of its emphasis on those at "the bottom of the economic pyramid."[114] Many, including Smith, labeled it a demagogic appeal designed to foment class antagonism. Tugwell may well have wished it were so, given his affinity for Marxist economic doctrine, but Moley's hand tempered the text's nascent radicalism.

At one level, the speech was a rejoinder to the Hoover administration's proposals for recovery, specifically the Reconstruction Finance Corporation. By making $2 billion worth of federal funds available to those at the top of the economic pyramid, Hoover had effectively forgotten "the infantry of our economic army." Permanent relief would come from the bottom up rather than the top down. Roosevelt's overt emphasis on class, coupled with his frequent allusions to planning, would have frightened most fiscal conservatives.

But the "concrete" solutions that he offered were not only far from radical, but they also had next to nothing to do with those lowest in the economic hierarchy. His three objectives—increased purchasing power for farmers, easier credit for homeowners and small banks, and reciprocal tariff agreements—did not directly address "the seven or ten million people who are out of work." The measures were so benign as to be favorable to those at the economic summit: increased purchasing power, easier credit, and broader markets might make big business salivate, not quiver. But Roosevelt went further to placate the economic elite: he would not turn to "the illusions of economic magic." He denounced the "huge expenditure of public funds by the Federal Government and by State and local governments" in order to employ the unemployed. It was time for the country "to get back to fundamentals," to "kill the bacteria in the system" rather than conceive a new economic body. Any conversion to Keynesianism and the start of the great class struggle would have to wait.

Roosevelt was not only fairly close to Hoover on economic means and ends, but his contextualization was nearly identical: the Great Depression was "more grave" than World War I. But unlike Hoover's initially fragmented battle plan, Roosevelt envisaged an organic plan in which the "whole Nation" was "gathered into a vast unit." The implications were clear: the federal government would assume the responsibility for battle plans and troop movements. Hoover deplored the leadership required by such an emergency; Roosevelt appeared to revel in it.

The speech, as Oulahan reports, may have "had an electrifying effect," but it was not a promise of "drastic social and economic reforms."[115] The conservative reform measures must also have been lost on Al Smith. At a Jefferson Day Dinner in Washington, D.C., the Happy Warrior declared, "I will take off my coat and fight to the end against any candidate who persists in any demagogic appeal to the working people of this country to destroy themselves by setting class against class, and rich against poor."[116] Roosevelt's ostensible response to Smith's challenge would again prove Lippmann correct.

On April 18, at a Jefferson Day Dinner in St. Paul, Minnesota, Roosevelt squelched rumors and accusations that he was fomenting class warfare. But before he headed west, he delivered a speech to the Catholic Charities of New York City that gently amended Hoover's Judeo-Christian position on charitable relief efforts. Like Hoover, Roosevelt viewed charity as a necessary and desired concomitant of democracy; moreover, it was rooted in the Christian tradition. But, whereas Hoover praised organizations such as the Red Cross for refusing state aid, Roosevelt took a different approach: public service, he claimed, was "really neighborliness on a large scale."[117] State and federal governments were not usurping duties that, by theological mandate, belonged only to private citizens; instead, they were acting as any concerned neighbor might. Intimacy, not remoteness, was the hallmark of publicly sponsored relief. The imagery conveyed by government neighborliness dovetailed nicely with his earlier emphasis on Home Rule: local autonomy would hardly be threatened or undermined by an unintrusive "neighbor."

"A Concert of Interests"

While he was clothing government relief in the garb of populism, Tugwell crafted Roosevelt's response to his intraparty critics. The address would become known as "The Concert of Interests" speech, but Roosevelt did not deliver it as initially drafted by Tugwell and refined by him and Moley. The version that he eventually delivered was, in Tugwell's words, "terrible."[118] Tugwell's judgment stemmed from Roosevelt's lengthy digression on public utilities regulation—a digression that comprised nearly 40 percent of the entire speech. Others were more kind, most notably Lippmann, who said that the speech reflected a "breadth of vision and an understanding of principle which are entitled to ungrudging praise."[119]

Like the "Forgotten Man" speech, economic recovery was the principal issue under consideration. It was also similar in that it offered very little in the way of specifics: better economic planning and reciprocal foreign exchange were the only methods that Roosevelt suggested. The former was a rejoinder to the Hoover administration's "panic-stricken policy of delay and improvisation."[120] In its place, Roosevelt envisioned something akin to the planning agencies of World War I. His reasons went far toward forgetting the forgotten man: "I am speaking of the necessity . . . that there be a real community of interests, not only among the sections of this great country, but among its economic units and the various groups in these units. . . . I plead not for a class control but for a true concert of interests."[121] The eventual realization of Roosevelt's concert of interests was the National

Industrial Recovery Act (NIRA)—a bill that put planning power almost exclusively in the hands of the industrial elite.

But while Roosevelt tried to differentiate his methods of recovery from Hoover's, he adopted, for the first time as a presidential candidate, the chief Hooverian cause for the depression's depth and duration:

> That a great fear has swept the country few can doubt. Normal times lull us into complacency. . . . with the coming of economic stress we feel the disturbing hand of fear. This fear spreads to the entire country and with more or less unity we turn to our common government at Washington (631).

Prior to this address, the nation had been suffering from a physical, observable illness; in Minneapolis, though, Roosevelt accepted Hoover's psychogenic account of the nation's health. Unlike the president, however, he chose not to allay the nation's fears by appealing to confidence and an imminent return to prosperity. Recovery was instead contingent on structural changes and reforms (planning and reciprocal exchange). Business cycles, in other words, could be planned away; they could not merely be talked away.

Presidential Slights and Primary Angst

The nation's governors arrived in Washington, D.C. in late April for their annual conference. Hoover agreed to address the conferees at the White House, but he arrived late. As noted in chapter 3, Franklin and Eleanor were furious: they sensed that evil designs informed Hoover's tardiness. For, while the president dallied, Roosevelt stood in the sweltering heat for half an hour. As Freidel notes, "Rumors were still circulating that he was a cripple without the physical stamina to be president. He was convinced, and so was Mrs. Roosevelt . . . that Hoover's action was deliberate." [122] Roosevelt would later offer masterful testimony to the nation that he was no cripple. To Hoover's evil designs, he offered a muted response later that same day: Hoover's presidential vision was clouded "by a lazy optimism." [123]

Roosevelt's heightened sense of anger, though, may have had less to do with Hoover than with his plummeting political stock. Several months earlier Jim Farley had predicted a first ballot victory in Chicago; by late April and early May, Howe "shuddered" at the "distinct possibility that his beloved Franklin would not be nominated at all!" [124] On April 26 Roosevelt was trounced badly in Massachusetts by Smith. On May 2 Connecticut pledged its delegates to Smith. Rhode Island and New Jersey followed suit two weeks later. The coveted California delegation pledged its votes to Hearst's candidate of choice, Garner.

Despite the setbacks, the Brains Trust worked feverishly to prepare a campaign blueprint. The eleven topic memorandum was finalized on

May 19, Roosevelt approved it in Warm Springs two days later. On the following day, he delivered his final pre-convention campaign speech at Atlanta's Oglethorpe University. The speech has a rather bizarre genesis. At a mid-May picnic, Roosevelt biographer and *New York Herald Tribune* reporter Ernest K. Lindley, among others, ribbed the Governor for his noncommittal speeches. Roosevelt reportedly challenged, "if you fellows think my speeches are so bad, why don't you write one for me?"[125] Two days later Lindley handed him one, and he used the draft "practically verbatim."[126] Not surprisingly, it bore little resemblance to Roosevelt's earlier speeches, particularly his Jefferson Day address.

"Bold, Persistent Experimentation"

The theme of economic planning persisted, but the organic, cross-class unity was gone: the leaders of big business, according to Roosevelt, were culpable for the nation's miseries. Gone too was any mention of international economic alliances. The answer to stimulating industrial demand did not reside in reciprocal exchanges; rather, it involved an intra-national redistribution of purchasing power, "a wiser, more equitable distribution of the national income."[127] Such a measure required a fairly radical restructuring of the nation's tax codes, but Lindley was just as noncommittal as his predecessors. Roosevelt concluded:

> When the Nation becomes substantially united in favor of planning the broad objectives of civilization, then true leadership must unite thought behind definite methods. The country needs and, unless I mistake its temper, the country demands bold, persistent experimentation. It is common sense to take a method and try it. If it fails, admit it frankly and try another. But, above all, try something (646).

Roosevelt would apparently wait for the nation to unite on broad objectives; but he also was not tipping his hand on "definite methods" either.

Less overtly, the vernacular that Roosevelt employed was that of science, a terminology consistent with the text's master metaphor. Roosevelt referred at five different places in the relatively short address to the nation's economy as an "economic machine." The economy, in other words, could be "set into motion" if only the proper methods of adjustment were implemented. Such a thoroughly scientized vision of economic recovery bore no resemblance to a psychically disturbed populace. The "illness" inhered in a human creation, not in the human psyche. The mechanization of recovery also functioned to temper what many perceived to be a latent radicalism: the need for economic planning did not arise because the machine needed replacing. It arose because those tending to the machine had not properly retuned it from time to time (643). Man could "control what he has created," Roosevelt intoned; he did not need a new creation. Again, Lippmann's remarks obtained: he could potentially appease both the conservative and liberal factions within his own party.

Throughout May and June, Farley counted and re-counted the Democratic delegates pledged to Roosevelt. While he possessed a large majority, he was far short of the two-thirds majority. The shortage, however, did not appear to faze Roosevelt, for he had made plans weeks in advance to make a dramatic flight to Chicago to receive the party's nomination in person. He nearly had to cancel the flight. Following the third ballot, Roosevelt phoned the emerging dark-horse candidate, Ohio's Newton Baker. He said to Wilson's former Secretary of War, "It now looks as though the Chicago convention is in a jam and that they will turn to you. I will do anything I can to bring that about if you want it." [128] Baker abjured. An hour later, Roosevelt had the needed two-thirds majority. Accounts differ widely as to who or what caused the Rayburn-Garner-McAdoo forces to surrender the California and Texas delegations to Roosevelt.[129] Suffice it to say that one of America's most important presidents was nearly defeated by the leadership of his own party.

A New Deal, A New Body

Coterminous with Roosevelt's strategic rhetorical jockeying during his second gubernatorial term was the issue that continued to shadow his presidential aspirations—his poor health. With the speculation of a possible presidential bid came the predictable doubts about the fitness of Roosevelt's body. As *Time* reported, "one sure evidence of Governor Roosevelt's lead toward the nomination was the recent spread of unfavorable stories about his health." [130] Thus Roosevelt would again be forced to "call upon all his highly developed skill at cavalier deception" in order to sway a skeptical electorate.[131]

But even before Roosevelt had decided to seek the presidency, some members of his own party resurrected the health issue. In the spring of 1930 the *New York Times* reported, "Some Democrats at Washington, obviously with other candidates in mind, have hastened to express fear that Mr. Roosevelt may not be in good enough health to make the race in 1932." [132] Two months later, following a national Governor's Conference in Salt Lake City, Utah, visiting governors were reported to have "been looking him [Roosevelt] over and were weighing his fitness for the difficult task that will confront the Democrats in 1932." [133] Some Democrats, the *New York Daily News* reported, were leaning toward Maryland Governor Albert Ritchie, since he would "be better fitted than Mr. Roosevelt to bear the physical burdens of the presidency." [134] That Roosevelt was increasingly frustrated by others' perceptions of his health is illustrated by one of several letters he personally wrote to newspaper editors, even those with very small circulations. To the editor of the *Danville Register* he wrote, "This is not written to you for publication but merely as a general protest at the statement in your editorial of November 7th that my health is still poor." He continued, "My health is excellent, though as you know I still have to wear braces following infantile paralysis, but that can hardly be construed as having anything to do with politics for . . . I am spending all of my time on the duties of the Governorship."[135]

Given the limitations of such epistolary refutations, and the concerns raised by party leaders, Roosevelt engaged in the first of two very public, highly rhetorical, medical examinations. Thomas C. Wiegele states that "medical information projected into the public consciousness by an efficient and aggressive mass media can have a powerful political effect."[136] What Roosevelt projected into the public consciousness via the *New York Times*, among others, was a doctor's report that "showed him to be in excellent physical condition."[137] The medical examination was conducted so that Roosevelt could take out a $500,000 life insurance policy, the beneficiary of which would be the Warm Springs Foundation. The insurance policy and the medical report, as Gould notes, had a dual purpose: the action "not only provided security for Warm Springs; it also silenced those critics who questioned FDR's fitness to govern."[138] Yet Gould, perhaps owing to historical hindsight, overstates the case: the policy and the report did not "silence" Roosevelt's critics. The *New York Times*, for example, two days after the report, pointed out that, even when Roosevelt "has sufficiently dealt with the issue of character, he has still the issue of capacity."[139]

In fact, if anything, the "whispering campaign" seemed to gain momentum during the spring and summer of 1931. During Jim Farley's somewhat surreptitious 1931 delegate-seeking trip across the country, the candidate's health was a pivotal issue: "wherever he [Farley] went, he still had to assure politicians that Roosevelt was physically fit enough to be president."[140] Yet the whispering grew louder among some. Mrs. Jesse W. Nicholson, President of the National Women's Democratic Law Enforcement League, was quoted by *Time* as saying, "This candidate [FDR], while mentally qualified for the presidency, is utterly unfit physically."[141]

According to Kenneth R. Crispell and Carlos F. Gomez, Roosevelt and his advisors were increasingly at a loss over the health issue: "While he undeniably was a cripple, they felt constrained to show that his illness was behind him, that it now had no adverse effect other than the paralysis of his lower body."[142] Emphasis should here be given to the word "show," for to call attention explicitly to Roosevelt's crippled body was to risk evoking public sympathy. And, as Jerrold M. Post and Robert S. Robins note, "polio adds the special difficulties of public image. Pity is deadly to a politician."[143] Roy V. Peel and Thomas C. Donnelly are more specific: "The technique of arousing sympathy for a leader is one that must be handled with extreme delicacy in that the need for sympathy implies weakness, and in a crisis the people want a strong leader."[144]

The second public showing, what Freidel terms "a spectacular stunt," was contrived during the summer of 1931.[145] The event was largely the brainchild of Republican writer Earle Looker, who challenged Roosevelt to be examined by an eminent team of physicians. Additionally, Roosevelt agreed to have Looker observe him, unannounced, at his executive office in Albany. The favorable review of Roosevelt's health and stamina, published in *Liberty* magazine on July 25, 1931, proved a success, especially among skeptical Democrats. Before the article was even published, Looker boasted to Roosevelt by letter, "Well sir, we got away with the 'Liberty' article despite all obstacles. . . . I think we can be sure that at least seven and a half million readers are sure you are physically fit!"[146] Farley labeled the article "a corker," and "it answers fully the questions . . . put to me many times during the past three weeks."[147] Howe was quick to seize on the favorable medical news: he sent "a copy to every county Democratic chairman in the country, and to any correspondent who expressed doubts over Roosevelt's health."[148]

I maintain that there was a third "showing": at the 1932 Democratic National Convention, specifically on July 2. The principal reason being that, while the publicity campaigns proved largely successful among influential Democrats, the whispering campaign was still pervasive among other groups. As Gunther notes, "there was much surreptitious talk that Roosevelt was still a sick man; one rumor . . . was that infantile paralysis attacked the brain in the end, and that FDR was in danger of going crazy." Thus, he still needed "to show himself to the people, and thus dispel any lingering rumors that he was not physically fit."[149] The "show" involved making "every effort to portray the Democratic nominee as a man who had conquered polio and who could walk."[150]

The nation, if it was reading carefully, received an intimation on May 16, 1932, that Roosevelt might attempt something dramatic. The *New York Times* reported "that a whispering campaign about his physical condition was being spread throughout the Middle West in an effort to head off his nomination by the Democrats in Chicago." Furthermore, Ike Dunlap, a friend then visiting Roosevelt at Warm Springs, reportedly "suggested that it might be well for the Executive to enter into some activity which could be broadcast to demonstrate his physical fitness."[151] That broadcast, I argue, involved both Roosevelt's flight to Chicago and his acceptance speech.

Several weeks prior to the convention, Roosevelt secretly chartered a Ford Trimotor airplane. Should he win the party's nomination, he would fly to Chicago and receive it in person. Such an embodied acceptance was not part of party tradition. Prior to 1932 the winning candidate would only be informed of the nomination several weeks after the convention had concluded. He would then make an obligatory acceptance speech—usually to a small crowd. In making his travel plans, Roosevelt had several options: he could drive to the convention; he could proceed to Chicago by train; and he even kidded that he might rent a five-seat bicycle so that his sons could peddle him there,[152] Instead, he selected the most dramatic form of transportation.

Historically far-removed from the exigencies of Roosevelt's health, contemporary commentators such as Stephen Skowronek claim that the principal significance of the flight to the Democratic National Convention was its stunning repudiation of tradition—a gesture that presages, and would be the hallmark of, the Roosevelt administration. "This stunning display of independence by a nominee," Skowronek argues, "crystallized in an instant a profound change in traditional relationships between candidates and the organizations they were chosen to represent."[153]

Those a bit closer in time to the scene, while they still recognized the flight as a rhetorically charged move, offer a very different interpretation. The *Chicago Tribune* opined that "utilization of the plane for a quick jump, it is hoped, will offset any propaganda that the governor is physically unfit to meet the duties of the presidency."[154] Similarly, albeit tending toward the hagiographic, Arthur Sears Henning declared that "the man who has all but recovered from the paralysis of the legs with which he was stricken a decade ago had come to show the people that he is not physically disqualified for the exacting duties of the presidency."[155] Peel and Donnelly note, "The quick jump across the country also helped greatly to dispel any belief that the governor was physically weak or that he was not a man of action."[156] Each "reading" of the flight was confirmed nearly forty years later by an insider's account: Roosevelt's son, Elliott, who walked frequently by his side, states that his father "wanted to demonstrate by this gesture that he was a man of vigorous action, not the semi-invalid depicted without fail by his enemies in both parties."[157] The gesture, we should not forget, was also an act of no small bravery: aviation was still very much in its infancy. As Stiles summarizes, "the idea was to prove once and for all that Franklin Roosevelt was a normal man in spite of the inactivity of his legs."[158]

The expectations and drama created by the eight-hour flight seemed to necessitate an equally stirring acceptance speech, especially given that it would be broadcast live to the nation.[159] The importance of the speech, especially its masterful yet subtle emphasis on Roosevelt's health, Hoover's sickness, and the nation's impending recovery, is underscored by one of its chief architects, Raymond Moley. In painstaking detail, Moley recounts the events leading up to the speech, including the shocking revelation that the speech was almost not delivered.[160] Moley, Roosevelt, and Samuel Rosenman had worked on the speech for several weeks prior to the convention, an association that worried and angered Howe.

Howe was always protective of "the Boss," but he was particularly incensed by Rosenman's rhetorical influence. Howe was suspicious that Rosenman's hand would be clearly visible in the speech, a suspicion that was confirmed when he had the entire speech read to him over the phone immediately following Roosevelt's nomination. Despite his own physical infirmities, Howe immediately set to writing another acceptance speech. The following day, Moley's worst case scenario had become a reality: Howe greeted Roosevelt at the airport with a new speech. As the motorcade headed toward the Congress Hotel, Roosevelt alternately waved to the sweltering masses and glanced at Howe's draft. Somewhere during the ride, he reached a decision. Roosevelt walked into the boisterous convention hall with his lower half carefully hidden from view by those surrounding him.[161] As he mounted the platform, Moley, from the back of the convention hall, strained to hear the words with which he had grown familiar. To his dismay, he did not hear them. But, just a few paragraphs into the speech, the familiarity returned. Roosevelt had simply substituted Howe's first page with the first page of the earlier draft.

The five-paragraph exordium was the stuff of standard political fare: Roosevelt thanked his audience; he praised previous party leaders and expressed his commitment to the party. At closer inspection, though, Roosevelt called attention to the physical body—his own, his listeners', and the deceased body of Woodrow Wilson. In fact, the very first sentence emphasized a corporate corporeality and the physical demands endured by both speaker and listener: "I appreciate your willingness after these six arduous days to remain here, for I know well the sleepless hours which you and I have had."[162] The fact that Roosevelt experienced the ardor of six days, and yet still insisted on flying to the convention, underscored his physical stamina. Additionally, Roosevelt's late arrival—a subtle, but important, disclaimer related to his physical presence in Chicago—had nothing to do with his health, but with the unpredictable "winds of Heaven." The winds were so strong and posed such a physical threat that Roosevelt "could only be thankful for my Navy training." His reference to the Navy is intriguing, for it suggests a military presence and military leadership—images that belie any sense of sickness or enervation. By calling attention to his naval training, despite it being removed by two decades, Roosevelt thus subsumed his post-polio body within his World War I era body.

He called further attention to his physical appearance and, by implication, his physical health, by elaborating the symbolic meaning of his flight, which, he claimed, was "symbolic" of his intention to break "foolish traditions" and to "avoid all hypocrisy or sham." His "unprecedented and unusual" flight was warranted by the "unprecedented and unusual times"—what Kenneth Burke would term a scenic imperative. That the scene may have more strictly biological motivations is underscored by the corresponding imagery that Roosevelt utilized. The flight represented his unwillingness "to avoid all silly shutting of the eyes to the truth in this campaign. You have nominated me and I know it, and I am here to thank you for the honor" (648). Roosevelt, of course, could have easily acknowledged his nomination via radio, but such a disembodied gesture would not have focused the delegates' (and the nation's) collective gaze on their candidate. Roosevelt's ocular reference not only implicated his willingness to be seen, it also linked truth and reality with an ability to see clearly—a linkage, and its opposite (blindness), that recur throughout the speech.

Roosevelt then made a transition from the visual to the peripatetic, and herein did he first provide verbal testimony to his ability to walk and, by inheritance, to lead.

> Let us now and here highly resolve to resume the country's *uninter-*
> *rupted march along the path* of real progress . . . Our indomitable leader
> in that *interrupted march* is no longer with us, but there still survives
> today his spirit. Many of his captains, thank God, are still with us, to
> give us wise counsel. Let us *feel* that in everything we do there still
> lives with us, *if not the body,* the great indomitable, unquenchable,
> progressive soul of our Commander-in-Chief, Woodrow Wilson (648;
> emphasis added).

To march is not simply to walk; it is to walk with purpose, discipline, and direction. And Roosevelt, as former Assistant Secretary of the Navy under Wilson, was a qualified captain, a leader who could take over where Wilson had left off. That Roosevelt was *the* captain to lead the Wilson army is attested to by the spatio-temporal marker "now and here," a marker that not only called attention, again, to the symbolic importance of the flight, but also highlighted Roosevelt's legitimacy as a fitting heir to the body and soul of Woodrow Wilson. This latter point was certainly at issue as the convention unfolded: Wilson's former Secretary of War, Newton Baker, was rumored to be the dark-horse candidate should Roosevelt's pledged delegates prove tractable. In fact, prior to the fourth and deciding ballot, Roosevelt phoned Baker and promised him the nomination should he want it. Baker politely declined. Thus did Roosevelt inherit, perhaps by default, Wilson's bodily and ideological legacy.

Having justified his physical abilities to lead the Wilson army and "enter this new battle," Roosevelt moved to discuss the opposing views of the "Republican leaders" and the Democratic party with respect to the nation's "economic and social life" (649). But before juxtaposing those who support "blind reaction on the one *hand*" and "the party with clean *hands,*" he offered a very physical warning to members of both parties:

> Here and now I invite those nominal Republicans who *find* that their
> *conscience* cannot be squared with the *groping* and the failure of their
> party leaders to *join hands* with us; here and now, in equal measure, I
> warn those nominal Democrats who *squint* at the future with their
> *faces* turned toward the past, and who *feel* no responsibility to the de-
> mands of the new time, that they are *out of step* with their Party (649;
> emphasis added).

Not only did Roosevelt again utilize the spatio-temporal marker to underscore the flight and his physical presence, but he turned the tables on his conservative brethren. Smith, Raskob, and Jouett Shouse, the conservative triumvir, were the "real" cripples for not being able to keep up with the party's progressive movement under the leadership of its marching nominee. Roosevelt employed the imagery of hands and feet to suggest a corporeal fusion of feeling—a physical solidarity, not an unwelcome sexuality, was offered. Hoover and other Republican party leaders were guilty of unspecified sins against the body politic. That they were sins of and against the body is emphasized by the appeal to hands "groping" in the dark—a bodily invasion that has its moral expression squarely in the conscience.

The moral repugnance, though, pales in comparison to the sort of Frankenstein economic monster birthed by Hoover and his cohorts. For Roosevelt, the nation's economy was an embodied and observable phenomenon, expressed in terms of "the clear fact of our economic condition." This condition had been adversely affected by the Republicans' deformed progeny: "The people will not forget the claim made by them [Republican leaders] then [1928] that prosperity was only a domestic product *manufactured* by a Republican President and a Republican Congress. If they claim *paternity* for the one they cannot deny *paternity* for the other" (650; emphasis added). The metaphors, at first glance, seem badly mixed: birthing and building seem to entail very different sorts of correspondences. Furthermore, how could a Republican president (male) and a Republican Congress (male) give birth to offspring?

The divergent metaphors are perhaps explicable within the context of the Hoover presidency. Hoover, we should remember, was elected as "The Great Engineer," someone who could apply the rationalism and precision associated with engineering to the nation's social and economic issues. Hoover was seen by many as cold and calculating, a person who could literally "build" economic progress and prosperity. But, by making economics machine-like, Hoover had violated the very natural laws he purported to study. Not surprisingly, the deformed progeny had grown "beyond our natural and normal growth" (650). Hoover and his Republican brethren had birthed a Frankenstein monster—a deformed beast incapable of surviving in a world where "economic laws are not made by nature. They are made by human beings" (657). Thus did Roosevelt reembody economic recovery—away from a misanthropic intellectual elite to "the kind of economics that you and I and the average man and woman talk" (650).

Such talk took the form of a story in which Roosevelt "touches on" and "looks at" events that culminated in the depression. Importantly, he medicalized one of the chief causes of it, namely stock market speculation. The common folk were not fully responsible for the stock market crash since they were "under the spell of delirious speculation." Such delirium was precipitated by government policies and the unscrupulous motives of banks and corporations. Roosevelt concluded, "Those are the facts. Why blink at them?" (651). Again, he called attention to his acute vision and his ability to cast near blinding light on the dark secrets of finance.

But Roosevelt implored his audience to engage in a different type of seeing, one equally about facts and bodies. "Translate that [the depression] into human terms. *See* how the events of the past three years have *come home* to specific groups of people: first, the group dependent on industry; second, the group dependent on agriculture; third . . . the people who are called 'small investors and depositors'" (651; emphasis added). Roosevelt was quite literal with respect to the domesticity of the depression:

> *Go into* the home of the business man. He knows what the tariff has
> done for him. *Go into* the home of the factory worker. He knows why
> goods do not move. *Go into* the home of the farmer. He knows how the
> tariff has helped to ruin him. At last our *eyes are open* (657; emphasis
> added).

Roosevelt not only put a human face and body on the depression, but he also did so in a manner that emphasized his own physical prowess: he had gone into these homes to view first hand the embodied economic effects of Republican rule.

Having impugned the Hoover administration, Roosevelt shifted to his positive position on such economic topics as credit, taxation, unemployment, agriculture, and tariffs—each of which was articulated, to varying degrees, in physical terms. Nearly four months earlier, on April 7, Roosevelt had delivered a controversial ten-minute radio address in which he called for economic policies "that put their faith once more in the forgotten man at the bottom of the economic pyramid." Many, including Smith, reacted virulently to Roosevelt's blatant class appeal. By July, Roosevelt had changed his position considerably, and again he linked a policy issue (credit) with a physical ability: "all of these groups, each and every one, the top of the pyramid and the bottom of the pyramid, must be considered together. . . . Statesmanship and vision, my friends, require relief to all at the same time" (652). Vision, of course, was occluded by sitting down. By standing tall, perhaps taller than any of his contemporaries, Roosevelt could see the entire class spectrum. Such acute vision was vital to relieving the ills that afflicted the entire body politic.

That Roosevelt was literal about his role as national doctor, as Suzanne Daughton details, is attested to by his frequent use of medical terminology to describe the New Deal.[163] But even before becoming president Roosevelt spoke of his willingness to make housecalls and the physical intimacy such visits would entail:

> I shall be able to make a number of short visits to several parts of the
> Nation. My trips will have as their first objective the study at first *hand,*
> from the *lips* of men and women of all parties and all occupations, of

the actual conditions and needs of every part of an interdependent
country (658; emphasis added).

In the span of eleven years, the roles had been reversed: the physically crippled had come to "take care of" a sick nation.

But Roosevelt could walk, or so he implied as he spoke about taxation. "I
know something of taxes. For three long years I have been *going up and down*
this country preaching that Government—Federal and State and local—
costs too much. I shall not stop that preaching" (652; emphasis added). This
admission is curious. Why not use instead, "I have been traveling across this
country"—a much more standard locution? One explanation is that "going
up and down" the country suggests a much more strenuous physical activity. Roosevelt had climbed steep hills and descended deep valleys, a perilous
journey for anyone, and yet he had been doing it for "three long years." Roosevelt, the peripatetic preacher, may have been longsuffering, but he was no
sedentary cripple.

Roosevelt returned to a familiar set of physical images as he moved to discuss the problem of unemployment. He first proposed to "take *definite steps*
to shorten the working day and the working week" (654; emphasis added).
He also suggested a massive reforestation plan—a plan that would eventually materialize into the Civilian Conservation Corps (ccc) on March 19,
1933. The plan was necessary since "we *face* a future of soil erosion and tim-
ber famine. It is *clear* that economic *foresight* and immediate employment
march hand in hand in the call for the reforestation of these vast areas" (654;
emphasis added). Here, Roosevelt and the unemployed marched (not
walked) in unison toward the vision that he saw so clearly.

His physical rhetoric extended into the realm of agriculture, where he
hoped to lighten "some of the impoverishing burdens from his [the farmer's]
back" (654). One of the means to accomplish this involved what was known
as Domestic Allotment, a measure that promoted planning of agricultural
production. Such a relatively drastic measure, Roosevelt reassured, would
be "a desirable *first step* in the reconstruction of agriculture. . . . it will serve
in great measure in the *long run* to remove the pall of a surplus" (655; emphasis added). As for the wording of a bill, "the Democratic Party *stands*
ready to be guided by whatever the responsible farm groups themselves
agree on" (655; emphasis added). Roosevelt, in other words, would not take
the emergency lying down; instead, he would offer farmers the same sort of
visible and active leadership as with credit, taxation, and unemployment.

In June, 1930, fifteen months after proposing some protectionist agricultural legislation, Hoover signed into law the Smoot-Hawley Tariff Act. As
Richard Hofstadter notes, the autarkic legislation "was a virtual declaration
of economic war on the rest of the world."[164] Though he refused to call it by
name, Roosevelt alluded to the putatively Republican measure toward the
close of the address, and, perhaps predictably, the imagery again suggested

sexual deviance. Roosevelt chronicled the "one great, simple, crystal-pure fact" that the nation "has been led by the Republican leaders to erect an impregnable barbed wire entanglement around its borders through the instrumentality of tariffs" (656). "Erect" and "impregnable" are too close for metaphorical comfort. The ultimate effect seemed to involve a sublimation of the sexual urge, resulting in a hostile economic response that has "isolated us from all other human beings in all the rest of the round world" (656). Physical and economic isolation and repression were the tangible results, a situation inimical to "the restoration of the trade of the world" (657).

Roosevelt's peroration includes perhaps the best-remembered political label in the history of twentieth-century American public address. In what was considered a throw-away line by his advisors, Roosevelt stated, "I pledge you, I pledge myself, to a new deal for the American people" (659). Thus was born the Rooseveltian New Deal—despite the fact that Roosevelt never offered a consistent, systematic set of policy objectives. But to remember the peroration only for this contractual promise misses the physical culmination of the address, in which Roosevelt's listeners rise, walk, and view tomorrow's landscape with their new leader. In keeping with the text's emphasis on standing, seeing, and walking, Roosevelt ended most appropriately:

> Never before in modern history have the essential differences between the two major American political parties *stood out* in such *striking contrast* as they do today. Republican leaders not only have failed in material things, they have failed in *national vision* . . . they have pointed out *no path* for the people below to *climb back to* places of security and safety in our American life (658–59; emphasis added).

They were thus the "false prophets" of prosperity, the reprobates responsible for leading the American people along "the easy road without toil" (658). Economic recovery for Roosevelt was premised on an ability to see the future and a visceral physicality in which walking without toil simply would not suffice; recovery involved using all of one's limbs. Roosevelt was not merely being figural: the political campaign was indeed "a call to arms" (659).

Summary

Herbert Hoover could not have been happier with the outcome of the Democratic National Convention. Some of that happiness can be attributed to his perception of Roosevelt's health. On April 27, 1932, Theodore Joslin recorded in his diary, "Back in the office tonight, we discussed the elections in Mass[achusetts] and Pennsylvania, with the President strongly of the opinion the results mean the elimination of Roosevelt. He shouldn't think of running. He is a sick man. He wouldn't live a year in the White House."[165]

Hoover's happiness also stemmed from a fear of running against Newton Baker. On June 9, 1932, Hoover stated to Joslin, "Well I hope you are right [that Roosevelt will win the nomination] . . . but I think you are wrong. I hate to think it, but I believe they will nominate Newton Baker." [166] Nearly three weeks later, the dialogue continued: " 'Do you still think Roosevelt will be nominated,' he asked me. 'Absolutely,' I replied. 'He'll get it on the second or third ballot.' 'I hope so,' the President continued. 'Our salvation lies largely in his nomination.' " [167] Thus, after hearing the news of Roosevelt's nomination, Hoover reportedly "smiled more broadly than he had in months." [168]

With the allusion of clarity and certainty that the past provides, it seems inconceivable that Roosevelt came within a few hours of not receiving his party's nomination. It also seems inconceivable that many of his economic beliefs mirrored Hoover's. Not only were the policy measures similar, but the rhetorical strategies contained similarities as well: the metaphors of war and health and sickness were Hooverian staples. More importantly, Roosevelt, like Hoover, believed that collective confidence was essential to economic recovery. The similarities were such that the inimical Oswald G. Villard declared there to be "no hope" that the nation would "have a really different Administration in Washington from that which we are now afflicted." [169]

Villard's characterization, though, was premature. We should not forget that Roosevelt was still in the process of selling himself to a party that was top heavy with conservatives—a party still very much dominated and controlled by its leaders. Roosevelt, in other words, could not appear too radical, lest he ostracize himself from those controlling large blocs of delegates. Yet he was not content to kowtow only to conservatives; he also sought the western Progressive vote within his party. Not surprisingly, then, his preconvention speeches often lacked consistency.

What remained to be seen once he had secured his party's nomination was which Roosevelt would emerge during the head-to-head campaign against Hoover. Would it be the radical Roosevelt, characterized by militant class appeals to the "Forgotten Man?" Or would it be the conservative Roosevelt, one who simply tinkered with or healed the existing economic machine/body? Was there a need for revolution and war, or did the nation simply need more time to heal its economic wounds? The answer, as I will attempt to show in the next two chapters, was not insignificant.

Notes

1. Franklin D. Roosevelt, "Address of Governor Roosevelt" [final draft], November 7, 1932, FDR Speech Files, Box 12, Franklin D. Roosevelt Presidential Library, Hyde Park, New York (hereafter, FRPL).

2. See, for example, Geoffrey C. Ward, *A First-Class Temperament*, p. 750.

3. Laura Crowell, "Roosevelt the Grotonian," *Quarterly Journal of Speech* 38 (1952): 33, 36. For an examination of Biblical influences on Roosevelt's rhetoric, see Joseph Schiffman, "Observations on Roosevelt's Literary Style," *Quarterly Journal of Speech* 35 (1949): 222–26.

4. Quoted in James MacGregor Burns, *Roosevelt: The Lion and the Fox*, p. 14. The school's other distinguished alumni included Averell Harriman and Dean Acheson.

5. Ibid., p. 25.

6. Elliott Roosevelt, ed., *F.D.R: His Personal Letters, 1905–1928*, p. 66.

7. Cowperthwaite claims that this post had important effects on Roosevelt; see L. LeRoy Cowperthwaite, "Franklin D. Roosevelt at Harvard," *Quarterly Journal of Speech* 38 (1952): 37–41.

8. Frank Freidel, *Franklin D. Roosevelt: A Rendezvous with Destiny*, p. 14.

9. Ibid., p. 15.

10. Burns, *Roosevelt: The Lion and the Fox*, p. 25.

11. Ibid., p. 32.

12. The final tally was 15,708 to 14,568.

13. For an account of Howe's work for Roosevelt, see Lela Stiles, *The Man Behind Roosevelt: The Story of Louis McHenry Howe*. As for the relationship between Howe and Roosevelt, see Alfred B. Rollins, Jr., *Roosevelt and Howe*.

14. Quoted in Burns, *Roosevelt: The Lion and the Fox*, p. 50.

15. Freidel, *Franklin D. Roosevelt: A Rendezvous with Destiny*, p. 29.

16. Freidel, *Franklin D. Roosevelt: A Rendezvous with Destiny*, p. 31.

17. Ibid., 33. For a good discussion of the Mercer relationship and its effect on Eleanor, see Joseph P. Lash, *Eleanor and Franklin*, pp. 220–27.

18. Roosevelt's first electoral defeat came in 1914, when he ran for the U.S. Senate.

19. Quoted in Burns, *Roosevelt: The Lion and the Fox*, p. 76. For an extensive examination of Roosevelt's rhetoric in the 1920 presidential campaign, see G. Jack Gravlee, "Franklin D. Roosevelt's Speech Preparation During His First National Campaign," *Speech Monographs* 31 (1964): 437–60.

20. Burns, *Roosevelt: The Lion and the Fox*, p. 76.

21. Roosevelt, ed., *F.D.R.: His Personal Letters, 1905–1928, Volume One*, p. 525.

22. Quoted in Jean Gould, *A Good Fight*, p. 24.

23. Tony Gould, *A Summer Plague: Polio and Its Survivors*.

24. Naomi Rogers, *Dirt and Disease: Polio Before FDR*, p. 29.

25. Theo Lippman, Jr., *The Squire of Warm Springs*, p. 65.

26. John Duffy, "Franklin Roosevelt: Ambiguous Symbol for Disabled Americans," *Midwest Quarterly* 29 (1987): 120.

27. "Franklin D. Roosevelt Ill," *New York Times*, August 27, 1921, p. 9.

28. "Franklin D. Roosevelt Better," *New York Times*, August 29, 1921, p. 11.

29. "Franklin D. Roosevelt Improving," *New York Times*, September 10, 1921, p. 4.

30. "F. D. Roosevelt Ill of Poliomyelitis," *New York Times*, September 16, 1921, p.1.

31. John Gunther, *Roosevelt in Retrospect*, p. 225.

32. Ibid., p. 226; emphasis in original.

33. Roosevelt, ed., *F.D.R.: His Personal Letters, 1905–1928, Volume One*, p. 530.

34. Ward, *A First-Class Temperament*, p. 704.

35. Quoted in Hugh Gregory Gallagher, *FDR's Splendid Deception*, p. 63.

36. Kenneth S. Davis, *Invincible Summer*, p. 29.

37. Lawrence + Roosevelt + Company = "Larooco."

38. *FDR: A Documentary*, PBS, 1994, written and directed by David Grubin.

39. Robert T. Goldberg, *The Making of Franklin D. Roosevelt*, p. 71.

40. Ralph E. Renaud, "Mac Slips on Sidewalks of N.Y.; Bang! Away Goes His Majority," *New York Herald Tribune*, June 27, 1924, p. 5.

41. "Roosevelt Boom Grows Despite His Reticence," *New York Herald Tribune*, June 28, 1924, p. 6.

42. Kyle D. Palmer, "Ku Klux Hood and Gown Foil Democratic Craft," *Los Angeles Times*, June 27, 1924, pp. 1, 5.

43. Robert M. Lee, "Nothing But Smith as Gentlemen from Bowery Pack Gallery," *Los Angeles Times*, June 27, 1924, p. 3.

44. Oswald Garrison Villard, "An Unconventional Convention," *Nation*, July 9, 1924, pp. 35–36.

45. "Roosevelt Boom Grows Despite His Reticence," *New York Herald Tribune*, June 28, 1924, p. 6.

46. Frank Freidel, *Franklin D. Roosevelt: The Ordeal*, p. 184.

47. For a good account of Roosevelt's 21 year affiliation with Warm Springs, see Lippman, *The Squire of Warm Springs*.

48. He reportedly invested two-thirds of his fortune—$190,000—in the initial construction.

49. Roosevelt, ed., *FDR: His Personal Letters, 1905–1928*, p. 566.

50. Ibid., p. 568.

51. Freidel, *Franklin D. Roosevelt: A Rendezvous with Destiny*, p. 52.

52. Raskob pledged $100,000 to the foundation, according to Elliott A. Rosen, *Hoover, Roosevelt and the Brains Trust: From Depression to New Deal*, p. 29.

53. Finis Farr, *FDR*, p. 152.

54. Freidel, *Franklin D. Roosevelt: The Ordeal*, p. 257.

55. "An Unfair Sacrifice," *New York Herald Tribune*, October 3, 1928, p. 26.

56. H. D. Kingsbury, "Roosevelt to be Freed of Heavy Campaign Work," *New York Herald Tribune*, October 3, 1928, p. 16.

57. Freidel, *Franklin D. Roosevelt: The Ordeal*, p. 259.

58. "Roosevelt Stands Campaigning Well," *New York Times*, October 22, 1928, p. 2.

59. "In Brown-Derbyland," *Time*, October 15, 1928, p. 12.

60. "A 'Flattering' Campaign," *New York Times*, October 17, 1928, p. 28.

61. Freidel, *Franklin D. Roosevelt: The Ordeal*, p. 266. For a rhetorical reading of Roosevelt's attempts to disguise his disability in 1928, see Amos Kiewe, "A Dress Rehearsal for a Presidential Campaign: FDR's Embodied 'Run' for the 1928 New York Governorship," *Southern Communication Journal* 64 (1999): 155–67.

62. Smith lost New York by more than 100,000 votes. Out of 4.2 million votes cast, Roosevelt won by only 25,000.

63. For a rhetorical perspective on the fireside chats, see Waldo W. Braden and Earnest Brandenburg, "Roosevelt's Fireside Chats," *Speech Monographs* 19 (1955): 290–302.

64. Elliott Roosevelt, ed., *F.D.R.: His Personal Letters 1928–1945, Volume Two*, p. 98.

65. See James A. Farley, *Behind the Ballots: The Personal History of a Politician*, pp. 80–88.

66. Franklin D. Roosevelt, "At Luncheon Meeting of Bond Club, New York City, January 16, 1930," in *Public Papers of Franklin D. Roosevelt: Forty-Eighth Governor of the State of New York, 1930*, p. 684. Subsequent references are noted in the text.

67. Franklin D. Roosevelt, "Before the State Federation of Labor, Buffalo, August 27, 1930," in *Public Papers of Franklin D. Roosevelt, 1930*, p. 752.

68. Franklin D. Roosevelt, "Radio Address at Knights of Columbus Convention, Schenectady, May 31, 1930," in *Public Papers of*

Franklin D. Roosevelt, 1930, p. 740, Subsequent references are noted in the text.

69. Franklin D. Roosevelt, "Before the Advertising Club, New York City, October 28, 1930," in *Public Papers of Franklin D. Roosevelt, 1930,* p. 811.

70. Roosevelt made much the same claims four days later; see Franklin D. Roosevelt, "The Governor Outlines the Democratic Proposals for Next Two Years," in *Public Papers of Franklin D. Roosevelt, 1930,* p. 827.

71. Franklin D. Roosevelt, "Radio Address by Governor—Collier's Hour—March 2, 1930," in *Public Papers of Franklin D. Roosevelt, 1930,* p. 711. Subsequent references are noted in the text.

72. Roosevelt, ed., *F.D.R.: His Personal Letters, 1928–1945, Volume Two,* p. 201.

73. Franklin D. Roosevelt, "Inaugural Address," in *Public Papers of Franklin D. Roosevelt: Forty-Eighth Governor of the State of New York, 1931,* p. 15.

74. Franklin D. Roosevelt, "Inaugural Address," p. 12. He also mentioned in this address that his anti-centralization response was prompted by a letter from "an eminent editor." The editor in question was Henry Goddard Leach, who had warned Roosevelt that the cities had broken down, and therefore the state or federal government should intervene. Roosevelt wrote back to Goddard on December 11, 1930: "I go along with you 100% in the thought that something must be done, but the answer is not State control or Federal control. That is moral cowardice and heads the country for the type of government now in effect in Russia and Italy (Roosevelt, ed., *F.D.R.: His Personal Letters, 1928–1945, Volume Two,* p. 163).

75. Franklin D. Roosevelt, "Before Conference of Governors, French Lick, Indiana, June 2, 1931," in *Public Papers of Franklin D. Roosevelt, 1931,* p. 738.

76. In a letter to Mrs. Caspar Whitney dated December 8, 1930, Roosevelt said that "while I am very much opposed to the extension of federal action in most economic social problems, nevertheless the Federal Government has a very distinct function as a fact gatherer for the whole Nation" (Roosevelt, ed., *F.D.R.:*

His Personal Letters, 1928–1945, Volume Two, p. 161).

77. Franklin D. Roosevelt, "Before Round Table, University of Virginia, Charlottesville, Virginia, July 6, 1931," in *Public Papers of Franklin D. Roosevelt, 1931,* p. 749. Subsequent references are noted in the text.

78. Franklin D. Roosevelt, "Radio Address from Albany to Cheraw, South Carolina, September 17, 1931," in *Public Papers of Franklin D. Roosevelt, 1931,* p. 769.

79. Freidel, *Franklin D. Roosevelt: A Rendezvous with Destiny,* p. 11.

80. Franklin D. Roosevelt, "At State College of Agriculture, Cornell University, February 14, 1930," in *Public Papers of Franklin D. Roosevelt, 1930,* p. 701.

81. Franklin D. Roosevelt, "Before Conference of Governors, French Lick, Indiana, June 2, 1931," in *Public Papers of Franklin D. Roosevelt, 1931,* p. 734.

82. Franklin D. Roosevelt, "At Van Hornesville School Commencement, Van Hornesville, June 22, 1931," in *Public Papers of Franklin D. Roosevelt, 1931,* p. 740.

83. Franklin D. Roosevelt, "Before the American Country Life Conference, Ithaca, August 19, 1931," in *Public Papers of Franklin D. Roosevelt, 1931,* p. 755. Subsequent references are noted in the text.

84. Franklin D. Roosevelt, "Radio Address, Albany, November 13, 1931," in *Public Papers of Franklin D. Roosevelt, 1931,* p. 782.

85. Franklin D. Roosevelt, "Economic Conditions—Local Tax Burdens—Labor Legislation, October 20, 1930," in *Public Papers of Franklin D. Roosevelt, 1930,* p. 781.

86. Franklin D. Roosevelt, "Before the Advertising Club, New York City, October 28, 1930," in *Public Papers of Franklin D. Roosevelt, 1930,* p. 812. Subsequent references are noted in the text.

87. Kenneth S. Davis, *FDR: The New York Years, 1928–1933,* p. 191.

88. Ibid., p. 126.

89. Ibid., p. 18; Rosen, *Hoover, Roosevelt and the Brains Trust,* p. 28.

90. Davis, *FDR: The New York Years*, p. 126.

91. Roosevelt, ed., *F.D.R.: His Personal Letters, 1928–1945, Volume Two*, pp. 230–31.

92. Quoted in Davis, *FDR: The New York Years*, p. 256.

93. Rosen, *Hoover, Roosevelt and the Brains Trust*, p. 96.

94. Franklin D. Roosevelt, "American System of Party Government, at Democratic Victory Dinner, Hotel Astor, New York City, January 14, 1932," in *Public Papers of Franklin D. Roosevelt: Forty-Eighth Governor of the State of New York, 1932*, p. 541. Subsequent references are noted in the text.

95. The letter contained no mention of unemployment, farm relief, public power development or labor reform; it did, however, emphasize tariff protection. See Davis, *FDR: The New York Years*, p. 201.

96. Ibid., p. 205.

97. Rosen, *Hoover, Roosevelt and the Brains Trust*, p. 13. At this time, Roosevelt's advisors included Howe, House, Farley, Flynn, and O'Connor.

98. Quoted in Davis, *FDR: The New York Years*, p. 259.

99. Richard Oulahan, *The Man Who . . . : The Story of the Democratic National Convention of 1932*, p. 42.

100. For other analyses of Roosevelt's international rhetoric, see Earnest Brandenburg, "Franklin D. Roosevelt's International Speeches, 1939–41," *Speech Monographs* 16 (1949): 21–40; and Earnest Brandenburg, "The Preparation of Franklin D. Roosevelt's Speeches," *Quarterly Journal of Speech* 35 (1949): 214–21.

101. Franklin D. Roosevelt, "Problem of Adequate Markets for American Industry and Agriculture, before the Members of the New York State Grange, State Armory, Albany, February 2, 1932," in *Public Papers of Franklin D. Roosevelt, 1932*, p. 550. Subsequent references are noted in the text.

102. In 1932 Roosevelt never publicly stated his willingness to change the tariff rates or abolish Smoot-Hawley altogether.

103. Davis, *FDR: The New York Years*, p. 257.

104. Ibid., p. 259.

105. Nor did Roosevelt see his own affliction as permanent. Until he died, he believed that recovery was possible.

106. Walter Lippmann suggested as much in a column written shortly after the speech: "Governor Roosevelt does not have a wide national popularity. He does not have the affection of the masses in the pivotal sections of the country. He does not have the confidence of the national Democratic leaders. . . . Governor Roosevelt has been definite about no great issue except his repudiation of the league"; see Lippmann, "Today and Tomorrow," *New York Herald Tribune*, February 12, 1932. Located in President's Secretary File, Box 694, "Walter Lippmann, 1929–1933," HHPL.

107. Beginning in the fall of 1930 Moley worked as a member of the Seabury investigations (Rosen, *Hoover, Roosevelt and the Brains Trust*, p. 128).

108. Davis, *FDR: The New York Years*, p. 263.

109. Raymond Moley to Nell Moley, April 12, 1932; Raymond Moley Papers, "Indexed Correspondence," Box 38–43, Hoover Institution on War, Revolution, and Peace, Stanford University, Stanford, California.

110. Samuel I. Rosenman, *Working with Roosevelt*, p. 57; Rosen, *Hoover, Roosevelt and the Brains Trust*, p. 129.

111. Rosen, *Hoover, Roosevelt and the Brains Trust*, p. 114.

112. Franklin D. Roosevelt, "Scientific Planning as a Fundamental for Improvement of Agriculture, at Annual Meeting of the New York State Agricultural Society, Albany, January 20, 1932," in *Public Papers of Franklin D. Roosevelt, 1932, p. 546*.

113. The permanent chairman position would be decided at the convention.

114. Franklin D. Roosevelt, *The Public Papers and Addresses of Franklin D. Roosevelt, volume one: The Genesis of the New Deal, 1928–1932*, ed. Samuel I. Rosenman, p. 625.

115. Oulahan, *The Man Who . . .*, p. 43.

116. Quoted in ibid., p. 43.

117. Franklin D. Roosevelt, "Campaign for Financial Aid to Catholic Charities' Agencies in New York City, as Catholic Charities' Luncheon, New York City, April 9, 1932," in

Public Papers of Franklin D. Roosevelt 1932, p. 575.

118. Rexford G. Tugwell, *The Brains Trust*, p. 50.

119. Quoted in Davis, *FDR: The New York Years*, 276. Similarly, the editor of the *Illinois State Register*, Vincent Y. Dallman, declared that the speech "was a sockdolager. It has given impetus to the irresistible movement to make you the next president of the United States" (Vincent Y. Dallman to Franklin D. Roosevelt, President's Personal File 658, "Vincent Y. Dallman," FRPL).

120. Franklin D. Roosevelt, "Address at Jefferson Day Dinner, St. Paul, Minn. April 18 1932," in *The Public Papers and Addresses of Franklin D. Roosevelt, 1928–1932*, p. 632. Subsequent references are noted in the text.

121. The *New Republic* claimed that the speech was "meant to heal the breach [created by the Forgotten Man speech] rather than to clarify it" ("Demagogues and Plutogogues," *New Republic*, April 27, 1932, p. 286).

122. Freidel, *Franklin D. Roosevelt: A Rendezvous with Destiny*, p. 82. Freidel notes that "other Democratic contenders for the nomination were whispering that Roosevelt did not have the physical stamina to be president" (Frank Freidel, "The Interregnum Struggle Between Hoover and Roosevelt," in *The Hoover Presidency: A Reappraisal*, ed. Martin L. Fausold and George T. Mazuzan, p. 137).

123. Franklin D. Roosevelt, "Washington as the Symbol and Inspiration for Present Day America, before the Conference of Governors, Richmond, Virginia, Wednesday, April 27, 1932," in *Public Papers of Franklin D. Roosevelt, 1932*, p. 587.

124. Davis, *FDR: The New York Years*, p. 300.

125. Quoted in ibid., p. 292.

126. Ibid., p. 292.

127. Franklin D. Roosevelt, "Address at Oglethorpe University, May 22, 1932," in *The Public Papers and Addresses of Franklin D. Roosevelt, 1928–1932*, p. 645. Subsequent references are noted in the text.

128. Quoted in C. H. Cramer, *Newton D. Baker: A Biography* (Cleveland: World, 1961), p. 252.

129. According to Davis, Joe Kennedy called Hearst to persuade him to have Garner withdraw (*FDR: The New York Years*, p. 326). According to Rosen, the major players were Daniel C. Roper and McAdoo, and that the latter requested veto power of certain cabinet appointments, p. 260. And, according to William Thiemann, movie mogul Louis B. Mayer intervened with Hearst, telling him that a developing wave was behind the internationalist Baker ("President Hoover's Efforts on Behalf of FDR's 1932 Nomination," *Presidential Studies Quarterly* 24 [1994]: 89).

130. "Political Notes," *Time*, June 15, 1931, pp. 16–17.

131. Ward, *A First-Class Temperament*, p. 624.

132. "Exposed to Frost," *New York Times*, April 29, 1930, p. 26.

133. W. A. Warn, "Roosevelt in Line for 1932 After Trip," *New York Times*, July 6, 1930, sec. 2, p. 1.

134. "The Democratic Landslide," *Literary Digest*, November 15, 1930, p. 7.

135. Franklin Roosevelt to *Danville Register*, December 18, 1930, FDR Governorship Papers, Series 1, "Newspaper Attacks on Governor," FRPL.

136. Thomas C. Wiegele, "Presidential Physicians and Presidential Health Care: Some Theoretical and Operational Considerations Related to Political Decision Making," *Presidential Studies Quarterly* 20 (1990): 82.

137. "Roosevelt's Life Insured for $500,000 by Warm Springs," *New York Times*, October 18, 1930, p. 1.

138. Gould, *A Summer Plague*, p. 55; see also, Gould, *A Good Fight*, p. 219.

139. "The Governor's Campaign," *New York Times*, October 20, 1930, p. 20.

140. Frank Freidel, *Franklin D. Roosevelt: The Triumph*, p. 210.

141. "Prohibition," *Time*, April 27, 1931, p. 18.

142. Kenneth R. Crispell and Carlos F. Gomez, *Hidden Illness in the White House*, p. 92.

143. Jerrold M. Post and Robert S. Robins, *When Illness Strikes the Leader*, p. 25.

144. Roy V. Peel and Thomas C. Donnelly, *The 1932 Campaign: An Analysis*, p. 168, n. 44.

145. Freidel, *Franklin D. Roosevelt: The Triumph*, p. 210.

146. Earle Looker to Franklin Roosevelt, July 16, 1931, FDR Governorship Papers, Series 1, "Earle Looker," FRPL. Looker later penned a fairly obscure election-year biography on Roosevelt; see Earle Looker, *The American Way: Franklin Roosevelt in Action.* For a fascinating look at the Looker/Roosevelt connection, see Amos Kiewe, "The Body as Proof: Franklin D. Roosevelt's Preparations for the 1932 Presidential Race," *Argumentation & Advocacy* 36 (1999): 88–100.

147. Quoted in Freidel, *Franklin D. Roosevelt: The Triumph*, p. 211.

148. Ibid., p. 211.

149. Gunther, *Roosevelt in Retrospect*, pp. 266, 272.

150. R. E. Gilbert, "Disability, Illness, and the Presidency: The Case of Franklin D. Roosevelt," *Politics and the Life Sciences* 7 (1988): 35.

151. "Roosevelt Hears of Whispering Plot," *New York Times*, May 16, 1932, p. 8.

152. Elliott Roosevelt and James Brough, *The Roosevelts of Hyde Park: An Untold Story* (New York: G.P. Putnam's Sons, 1973), p. 303.

153. Stephen Skowronek, "Franklin Roosevelt and the Modern Presidency," *Studies in American Political Development* 6 (1992): 327.

154. "F. D. Roosevelt Will Fly Here to Accept Today," *Chicago Tribune*, July 2, 1932, p. 3.

155. Arthur Sears Henning, "Nominee Flies to Convention; Speaks; Asks for a 'New Deal,'" *Chicago Tribune*, July 3, 1932, p. 1.

156. Peel and Donnelly, *The 1932 Campaign*, pp. 103–104.

157. Roosevelt and Brough, *The Roosevelts of Hyde Park*, p. 303.

158. Stiles, *The Man Behind Roosevelt*, p. 191.

159. Despite the notoriety of the New Deal speech, only one scholar has given its rhetorical content much consideration; see Robert T. Oliver, "The Speech that Established Roosevelt's Reputation," *Quarterly Journal of Speech* 31 (1945): 274–82.

160. Raymond Moley, *After Seven Years*.

161. Gould, *A Good Fight*, p. 232.

162. Franklin D. Roosevelt, "The Governor Accepts the Nomination for the Presidency, Chicago, Ill. July 2, 1932," in *The Public Papers and Addresses of Franklin D. Roosevelt, 1928–1932*, p. 647. Subsequent references are noted in the text.

163. Suzanne M. Daughton, "FDR as Family Doctor: Medical Metaphors and the Role of Physician in the Domestic Fireside Chats" (paper presented at the Speech Communication Association convention, New Orleans, La., November, 1994).

164. Richard Hofstadter, *The American Political Tradition*, p. 398.

165. Diary entry, April 27, 1932, Theodore G. Joslin Papers, Box 10, Herbert Hoover Presidential Library, West Branch, Iowa (hereafter, HHPL).

166. Diary entry, June 9, 1932, Theodore G. Joslin Papers, Box 10, HHPL.

167. Diary entry, June 28, 1932, Theodore G. Joslin Papers, Box 10, HHPL.

168. Diary entry, July 1, 1932, Theodore G. Joslin Papers, Box 10, HHPL.

169. Oswald G. Villard, "The Roosevelt Candidacy," *Nation*, June 1, 1932, p. 612.

Chapter Five

Making House Calls
Health, Sickness, and the "Body" Economic

According to at least two important sources, Franklin Roosevelt's dramatic
flight and speech to the Democratic National Convention achieved the desired effect. On July 4, the *New York Times* editorialized:

> Governor Roosevelt put into his appearance and address before the
> Chicago Convention something of the breeziness that went naturally
> with his flight through the air. The dash and vigor which he had
> shown by setting out for Chicago in an airplane also marked his
> speech. . . . The Democratic candidate for the Presidency is bringing
> a fresh and eager mind and an ardent spirit to the work which his
> party has placed in his hands.[1]

The following day, Claude G. Bowers opined, "the speech of Roosevelt was a
triumph. The delegates found before them a virile figure, physically
strong . . . a militant figure with an eagerness to fight."[2] Given the crystal-
lizing effects of the flight and speech, coupled with Hoover's plummeting
electoral prospects, many of Roosevelt's closest advisors urged him to wage
a front-porch campaign. He could win easily simply by staying at home in
either Albany or Hyde Park and periodically addressing the nation by radio.

Having worked so hard in his eleven-year political comeback, Roosevelt
opted for the more difficult route: he would criss-cross the nation via train to
redeem his pledge of "observing at first hand" the "actual conditions and
needs of every part of an interdependent country."[3] And so, precisely at
11:00 P.M. on September 12, the *Roosevelt Special* departed from Albany. Yet
the trip must be viewed as more than mere pledge redeeming, as more than
Roosevelt conducting fact gathering work at train depots across the country. That something more was stated explicitly by Roosevelt during an extemporaneous speech from the train's rear platform, just three days into the
trip, in Goodland, Kansas. Roosevelt greeted the approximately 1,000
people assembled: "It's fine to see you! We are going through the country doing a very simply thing: *we are showing ourselves to you,* and we are talking very simply and plainly to the voters in most of the United States."[4]

Raymond Moley and Louis Howe must have winced at Roosevelt's blatant admission of motive: the governor was supposed to stray from such overt references to his body. Perhaps not surprisingly, in the dozens of speeches Roosevelt would make in the coming days, none of them contained this admission; instead, Roosevelt's apparent good health would be a byproduct of his active presence on the campaign trail.[5]

While Roosevelt was indeed showing himself to his audience, his claim of "talking very simply and plainly" is much more debatable. As many commentators have accurately noted, Roosevelt's campaign rhetoric was rife with contradictions, ambiguities, and inconsistencies. Yet a careful reading of the speeches reveals several recurring themes concerning how Roosevelt envisaged economic recovery. First, recovery could be engendered by confidence, but a confidence that Roosevelt attempted to distinguish from the Hooverian idea. Second, he rendered the Great Depression explicable by translating complex economic problems into bodily terms. Third, and related to the preceding two, Roosevelt elevated himself to the role of national doctor by employing metaphors of health and sickness—a role for which he was uniquely qualified, given his eleven year battle with infantile paralysis.

"A Chameleon on Scotch Plaid"

Scholars of many stripes have largely ignored the rhetorical intricacies and nuances of Roosevelt's post-Chicago presidential campaign. Many, with the clarity that hindsight provides, claim that Roosevelt's victory over Herbert Hoover was assured with William Gibbs McAdoo's July 1 declaration. They then give an approving nod to the high-minded principles that Roosevelt sounded at San Francisco's Commonwealth Club, and they note his lack of perspicacity four weeks later in Pittsburgh. The November 8 election results are next tallied, followed by a bleak description of the interregnum period. The "good stuff" begins only on March 4, 1933.

It is tempting to fast-forward to the "good stuff" for two interrelated reasons. Roosevelt delivered more than one hundred speeches during the campaign, most of which were given to predominantly partisan audiences. The speeches, therefore, are often only too predictable: Hoover is blamed for everything save the Lindbergh kidnapping,[6] while Roosevelt fashions himself as the nation's reluctant savior. To examine closely more than one hundred iterations of this basic theme can be daunting. But even in those instances when Roosevelt strayed into the world of policy, his pronouncements were often vague, contradictory, or inconsistent. Gene Smith, for example, notes that "the governor's [campaign] speeches were entirely contradictory."[7] Early in the campaign, Henry F. Pringle anticipated Hoover's claim that Roosevelt was a chameleon on scotch plaid: "The truth is that Franklin Roosevelt hauls down banners under which he has marched in the past and unfurls no new ones to the skies."[8] As the campaign unfolded, several political pundits were in lockstep with Lippmann: Roosevelt's speeches "beautifully illustrate the Democratic attempt to win the radically inclined and the conservatively inclined at the same time."[9] The exasperated editors of the liberal weekly, the *Nation,* concluded in November that "if anybody can get a clear-cut view of Governor Roosevelt's fundamental principles, his deep and underlying beliefs, he is much cleverer than we."[10] The ambiguities and contradictions were exacerbated by the minibureaucracy of speech writers that Roosevelt employed—many of whom did not know where he stood on various issues.[11] Gone were the relatively uncomplicated days when Moley, Rosenman, Berle, and Tugwell would help craft the governor's messages. Moley notes with chagrin that Roosevelt's first major post-convention policy speech was composed by twenty-five different contributors.[12]

In sum, Roosevelt's 1932 presidential campaign is critically challenging: coherence, clarity, and consistency are not part of the rhetorical landscape. But, as I will try to establish, there is a payoff for a careful reading, especially in light of the issues and questions that we are pursuing. I will not comment on every speech that Roosevelt delivered; a large part of the campaign corpus is comprised of merely extemporaneous attempts at *ingratio.* But many speeches make extensive comment on a broad range of economic issues, from rhetoric's role in facilitating economic recovery to hydroelectric power, the nation's credit system, and the philosophical principles supposedly guiding Roosevelt's envisioned "New Deal."

Health, Sickness, and Confidence

Though some date the campaign's inception to August 20, Roosevelt delivered his first major statement on July 30 in a nationwide radio address. It is clear from an earlier draft of the speech that he initially wanted to put his own distinctive stamp on the campaign. But such a move, so soon after the fracas in Chicago, might have further ostracized conservative factions within the party.[13] So instead, Roosevelt towed the party line: he read portions of the entire Democratic platform at various points in the speech. Excised from the speech were specific measures pertaining to agriculture, tariffs, and international debt obligations.[14]

Although the platform called for "a drastic change in economic and governmental policies," Herbert Hoover would likely have been right at home with most of its prescriptions: reduced government expenditures, a balanced budget, graduated taxes on those most able to pay, sound currency, unemployment relief through public works, and protective tariffs were all measures that Hoover supported.[15] Roosevelt even adopted a distinctly Hooverian approach to presidential rhetoric: "mere oratory and mere emotion are having less to do with the determination of public questions. . . . Today, common sense plays the greater part and final opinions are arrived at in the quiet of the home" (659). Roosevelt traded in the "quiet of the home" and the subordination of his own political agenda for the rancor of the campaign trail three weeks later in Columbus, Ohio.

Columbus seems to have been an odd place for Roosevelt to "begin" his campaign. He had no special ties to the state or city save one: cousin Teddy launched his 1912 presidential campaign in the same place. His cousin hoped that the results would be different twenty years later. The speech differs radically in content and style from his dutiful radio address, and instead of denigrating "oratory," Roosevelt gave it an honored place.

George Bush was not the first presidential candidate to be labeled weak and ineffectual; in 1932 Roosevelt was seen by many, particularly intellectuals, in much the same manner. It is not surprising, then, that Roosevelt officially began his presidential campaign with a fierce assault on the "Great Engineer." What is somewhat surprising is how Roosevelt defined Hoover and his administration. Instead of attacking him as a conservative "do-nothing," Roosevelt called him a dangerous radical, someone who espoused the "dangerous doctrine" of the "new economics."[16] Hoover, Roosevelt alleged, sponsored the sordid doctrine of "high-pressure selling, lavish extravagance, [and] head-on plunges into debt and yet more debt." He had essentially forced "the old economics . . . out of business" (672).

Yet the new economics, according to Roosevelt, was not simply about people going into debt on their own accord; rather, such consequences had important rhetorical antecedents. Through his public promises of prosperity and the abolition of poverty, Hoover had created a fairy-tale economic world—a world that cast the American public in "the role of our old friend, Alice in Wonderland." Roosevelt related the tale:

> Alice was peering into a wonderful looking-glass of the wonderful economics. White Knights had great schemes of unlimited sales in foreign markets and discounted the future ten years ahead. The poorhouse was to vanish like the cheshire cat. A mad hatter invited everyone to "have some profits." . . . A cynical Father William in the lower district of Manhattan balanced the sinuous evil of a pool-ridden stock market on the end of his nose (674).

Hoover had persuaded by alluring deceptions and Roosevelt was careful to point out that his listeners were not accomplices, but victims of his seductive inartistic proofs. "Under the spell of this fable, [the people] sacrificed on the altar of the stock market the frugal savings of a lifetime." Even the omniscient barons of big business fell victim: "Business men sincerely believed that they had heard expert advice and risked their solvency by a new burst of expansion. Common sense was hushed before the spell of an economic necromancy sponsored by Washington itself" (675). The crash, Roosevelt insinuated, was not caused by a greedy populace or a misanthropic business community; it was the result of Hoover's unethical rhetorical practices.

But the administration had compounded its rhetorical crimes in the aftermath of the crash. The "real crime of the Republican Administration" was that it "did not tell the truth"; it had simply maintained that economic conditions were sound and that prosperity would soon return (675–76). Like a doctor who had prescribed the wrong medication or who had misdiagnosed the ailment, Hoover's "new economics" had greatly imperiled the nation's economic health. Hoover had poisoned the economic body, and Roosevelt inquired, "has this party, I ask, under this leader, suddenly become the Heaven-sent healer of the country who will now make well all that has been ill?" (678).

In contrast, Roosevelt proposed a "practical group of fundamental remedies" that were "based on telling the truth" (681–82). They included, among others, federal regulation of holding companies, federal supervision of national banks, federal regulation of the securities industry, and greater restrictions on Federal Reserve funds. All were put forward toward the end of inspiring "truth telling" (682). Roosevelt made the crucial link between truth telling and a successful recovery in his conclusion:

> these assurances . . . are to my mind greatly important in the long list of remedies that we propose. Restored confidence in the actions and statements of Executive authority is indispensable. . . . It is no wonder that stagnation has resulted—a stagnation born of fear. But this is a distrust not of ourselves, not in our fundamental soundness, not in our innate ability to work out our future. It is a distrust in our leaders, in the things they say and the things they do. Therefore, the confidence that the administration has asked us as individual citizens to have in ourselves is not enough. The kind of confidence we most need is confidence in the integrity, the soundness, the liberalism, the vision, and the old-fashioned horse sense of our national leadership. Without that kind of confidence we are forever insecure (683–84).

Roosevelt was clearly in agreement with Hoover's resolute belief that confidence was vital to recovery. But the healing that confidence inspired had to come from a credible, truthful external agent; the illness was not psychosomatic since it could not be cured by a blind faith in oneself. Yet, importantly, Roosevelt expressed his belief in a verbal cure, one in which faith had to be put in Roosevelt's hands. Recovery was simply impossible under Herbert Hoover: the sacred doctor-patient trust had been badly fractured by four years of lies, half-truths, and deceptions.

Words and Things

One week later at Sea Girt, New Jersey, Roosevelt turned his attack to prohibition specifically and the Republican platform generally. Like his assault on the "new economics," Roosevelt trained his focus on Hoover's rhetoric and the words of Republican leaders. The stated reason for his investigatory hermeneutics again implied confidence: at base, the campaign was about "faith and confidence in leadership and in the words of leaders. . . . I emphasize that the deep question in this campaign is one of confidence in leadership—in leaders."[17] Not surprisingly, the different rhetorical approaches of the Democratic and Republican parties were central to the speech. In outlining the two different rhetorical approaches, Roosevelt disclosed his belief about the materiality of words.

The campaign amounted to a "battle with words," and the combatants had bipolar methods of employing them: "as a flaming sword" used to cut through to the truth of the matter; or as a "shield" that worked to deflect, evade, and obstruct an adversary (687). To this functional approach to language, Roosevelt also articulated the relationship between words and things. The Republican platform amounted to

> words upon words. Evasions upon evasions. Insincerity upon insincerity. A dense cloud of words. We rush into the clouds to find whether there is meaning and substance at the bottom of it all, and we find nothing. When we emerge from the cloud, we see another in the distance and we rush over to that. And again we find nothing. And so we rush from cloud to cloud and find at the bottom of each, nothing but dust, meaningless, worthless dust, at the bottom of a cloud of words (687).

From the outset of the campaign, Roosevelt had frequently employed ocular terminology, but here for the first time he linked the visual with the discursive. Words, although they might only produce "clouds" and "worthless dust," could nonetheless create a material reality—a reality that could be seen, examined, and judged based on its correspondence to the words employed. Words, as Roosevelt mentioned, insofar as they were "plain and clear," could also create confidence, a requisite to overcoming economic stagnation (688). This view of language and its emphasis on simplicity and clarity would recur frequently, especially as the campaign began in earnest.

While Roosevelt had hit Hoover hard in the early days of the campaign, at least one very influential member of the party sounded a note of alarm. On August 30, Colonel Edward M. House wrote to the candidate: "Two weeks ago I felt that your election was assured; today I feel that it is debatable. I may be wrong, I hope I am, but I sense a change in sentiment throughout the country which, if not counteracted, may lead to your defeat."[18]

Health and Interdependence

To the dismay of many party regulars and even some on his staff, Roosevelt decided against a front-porch campaign à la Warren G. Harding. Instead, he waged a vigorous campaign by train through the Midwest, West, and Northwest. Many, like Frank R. Kent of the *Baltimore Sun*, believed that "no argument [was] needed, no appeal [was] necessary" for Roosevelt to defeat

Hoover.[19] But according to Hugh Gallagher, one of Roosevelt's western advisors argued for a cross-country trip "so that the voters could see in person that the rumors about FDR's feeble condition were false."[20] Gallagher also contends that "Roosevelt's handicap played little direct role in his candidacy or the campaign he waged,"[21] but the historical evidence suggests otherwise.

First, campaign materials created and distributed by the Democratic National Campaign Committee (DNCC) suggest that Roosevelt's health was not just an issue, but perhaps *the* issue. For example, the "Speaker's Kit" published by the Women's Division of the party was a lengthy guide to "suggested answers to Republican assertions." Republican assertion number one was, "Franklin D. Roosevelt is unfit physically to assume the trying duties of the presidency."[22] The suggested answer? "Twelve years ago Franklin D. Roosevelt was crippled by infantile paralysis and still walks with the help of a cane and a friendly arm. In spite of this disability of the legs, Mr. Roosevelt is in topnotch physical condition." Proof of Roosevelt's good health dated to the two "showings" of his governorship:

> As recently as 1930 he was insured for half a million dollars . . .
> Furthermore, a year ago, at the request of Liberty Magazine, Governor Roosevelt was examined by three of the most eminent medical practitioners in the country. . . . They certified under oath that the health of Governor Roosevelt was such as allowed him to meet "any demand of private or public life."

The hefty insurance policy was privileged further by the DNCC. In a one-page circular with the caption, "Half a Million Life Insurance," Roosevelt is said to be "sound, healthy and physically fit."[23] Moreover, "Twelve years ago Franklin D. Roosevelt suffered an attack of infantile paralysis. Today he is fully recovered except that his legs are partially disabled. For four years, as Governor of New York, he has worked tirelessly, early and late, for the people of his state." The circular concludes by urging readers to "Stop the Whispering Campaign. Elect a Strong Leader—FRANKLIN D. ROOSEVELT."

Similarly, in the "Campaign Book of the Democratic Party: Candidates and Issues, 1932," created and distributed by the DNCC, Roosevelt's recovery from infantile paralysis is again front and center. The document notes that Roosevelt "is altogether fitted for the presidency. This is shown not only by the testimony of the most eminent physicians but by his actual record."[24] Furthermore, under the heading "A Real Governor," the booklet continues, "The story of his governorship is one of a man steadily growing in mental, physical and spiritual strength." Under the heading "A Glutton for Hard Work," we read that "Governor Roosevelt's week in and week out program is even stronger witness to his physical fitness." Finally, under the caption, "Radiant with Health," Roosevelt's appearance before the assembled delegates in Chicago is revisited:

Radiant with health, forceful in manner, vigorous in speech, and with the same disregard for outworn political theories that he demonstrated by eliminating the farce of being officially informed of his nomination a month later, Roosevelt thrilled the great audience which tested the 35,000 capacity of the Chicago stadium. . . . Roosevelt electrified the convention and bewildered the whisperers who charged he was a sick man by his spectacular flight from Albany to Chicago.

Most if not all of these claims are repeated verbatim in another booklet created and distributed by the DNCC, "Franklin D. Roosevelt: Who He Is. What He Has Done."[25]

Second, two of Roosevelt's closest advisors, Howe and Moley, both acknowledged the importance of the train trips vis-à-vis perceptions of the candidate's health. In an article written after the election, Howe recounted:

We at headquarters watched the progress of the Governor's train with perhaps a little apprehension at first but with tremendous interest and supreme confidence as the campaign wore on, for in the beginning a great majority of the Governor's advisors [including Howe] were strongly opposed to his making a tour to the coast and back, and in fact, a delegation of men who were a real power in the party councils waited on him in Albany, to persuade him from such a course. Their objections were founded to a great extent on the belief that the carefully disseminated propaganda as to the Governor's health must have some foundation, and that he would be unable to stand the rigors of a grueling campaign. This fear, however, never entered the minds of the Governor's intimate friends, least of all, the Governor himself. . . . The Governor realized that the best answer to the question as to his health was himself.[26]

Additionally, the chief architect of Roosevelt's 1932 campaign, Moley, claimed that "at no time did Roosevelt, nor did I, take the election for granted. It would have been a great mistake because the exposure of Roosevelt to the people across the country was exceptionally important, and as it proved, exceptionally favorable to his chances."[27] As to the question of whether Roosevelt "made the Western tour to prove to the people that he was physically able," Moley notes,

Oh, yes, there is no doubt about that, although I don't remember that it was specifically mentioned by him, but he wanted to show himself as being a man of vigor and vitality and wasn't hampered in any way by his physical infirmity. He did it very well because he stopped at many whistle stops and talked to people off the back platform and showed his enthusiasm and his exuberant personality and his friendliness, and this was a great psychological factor in the campaign.

It should be added that it was a great rhetorical factor as well. As I will at tempt to illustrate, Roosevelt made frequent reference to his own body and health. Perhaps more importantly, he also talked frequently of the nation's enfeebled economic health and, in the process, elevated himself to the role of national healer.[28] So, carrying political friends, family members, and the press, the *Roosevelt Special* chugged out of Albany on September 12, 1932, headed for Kansas.[29]

Roosevelt's first major policy address took place two days later in Topeka. Nearly 20,000 people, mostly farmers, braved the sweltering heat to hear the self-declared farmer talk about agriculture. Stylistically speaking the speech is inconsistent and sometimes confusing—an occurrence not the least bit surprising given the numerous hands that touched the manuscript. The confusion also spilled over into Roosevelt's specific policy proposals, and the press was quick to pounce. The *World Tomorrow* called it "plain non-sense."[30] The Tulsa *Tribune* termed it "a masterpiece of demagogic appeal, evasion, and generalization."[31] The *Nation* characterized Roosevelt's agri-cultural program as "the veriest nonsense" and added that the speech "leaves us gasping."[32]

The hostile response was engendered, in part, by Roosevelt's contradic-tory position on agricultural tariffs. On the one hand, he blasted Hoover for destroying "the foreign markets for our exportable farm surplus."[33] On the other hand, he promised to increase agriculture prices by "making the tariff effective," in other words, to impose a tariff equivalent to that enjoyed by in-dustry. Roosevelt made a bad situation worse by detailing just how agricul-tural prices would be reflated. The tariff would not be imposed by the federal government; rather, Roosevelt emphasized that the plan would be decen-tralized and "in so far as possible, voluntary" (704). Roosevelt was suggest-ing, with "studied vagueness," a controversial plan known in academic circles as Domestic Allotment—a plan whereby farmers would "voluntar-ily" agree to reduce the size of certain crops so as to bring supply into closer proximity with demand.[34] Roosevelt dared not name it as such for fear of an agricultural backlash: voluntary cooperation had not worked with Hoover's Federal Farm Board, many reasoned, so why would it work now?

Roosevelt advanced his agricultural program with the interrelated imag-ery of unity and health. Agriculture, he argued, could not be segregated from the rest of the nation's economy, particularly industry. As in his "con-cert of interests" speech of April 18, Roosevelt claimed that "our economic life today is a seamless web." Notice that Roosevelt did not use the more commonplace construction of "economy," choosing instead "economic life." Economic interdependence was inextricably tied to the nation's collec-tive life and health: "We cannot have independence in its true sense unless we take full account of our interdependence in order to provide a balanced economic well being for every citizen of the country" (697). Economic health, "balance," and interdependence would be achieved by a "unity of planning," as opposed to the Hoover administration's "scattering of efforts." Such all-encompassing planning measures would provide a "cure" or "remedy," whereas Hoover had merely prescribed "drugs" as a short-term economic palliative (699). Roosevelt's program would thus eradicate the illness altogether.

Perhaps the most important first step toward economic well-being, though, was a belief that one's health was impending. Roosevelt advised that "the farmer's hope for the future must rest upon *the policy and the spirit* in which his case is considered. The essence of this question [of agricultural relief] comes down to a matter of keeping faith with American agriculture" (705; emphasis added). But Roosevelt went one step further: he invited his farming listeners to join him in a "profession of faith" (711). Their faith and, hence, future health were partially ensured through the incantatory powers of language.

Three days later, Roosevelt further elaborated the relationship between interdependence and health as it related to the railroad industry. As he did at Topeka, Roosevelt made a complex topic comprehensible largely by attributing to it human characteristics. His stated goal was to improve "the health of these great arteries of commerce" to the point where they could "stand on their own feet."[35] Presently, the railroad industry suffered from an "epidemic" of illnesses and was being "strangled half to death" by a lack of planning. Like the situation in agriculture, the lack of concerted planning had "unbalanc[ed] the system of things" (715). The remedy was simply one of "reordering" and "coordination": "The individual railroads should be regarded as points of a national transportation system. . . . each rail service should fit into and be coordinated with other rail services and with other forms of transportation" (717).

But Roosevelt noted again that revitalized economic health was not premised solely on the policies that his administration would pursue; recovery was also contingent on belief. "We still have before us, as had those who settled this great West, battles with hunger, battles with human selfishness and, what is more important, the battle with our own spirits, seeking, in the face of discouragement, the means of restoration and relief" (712). Roosevelt's call for people to battle themselves appears to fly in the face of his pronouncement at Columbus, namely, that confidence came from without, not solely from within. Unlike his message at Topeka, however, Roosevelt did not explicitly offer an external agent to nurse the sick patient back to health; instead, people could turn inward for strength by drawing on "the hardihood of the pioneer."

Horse Sense, Neighborliness, and Poison

One of Roosevelt's principal rhetorical legacies involves his seemingly instinctual ability to humanize complex problems. We can witness this ability throughout the 1932 campaign, but perhaps its most striking manifestation occurred in Seattle on September 20. Roosevelt took an extremely complex topic—international trade and its relationship to the U.S. economy—and reduced it to the lowest common denominator. He contextualized the complex, bipartisan Smoot-Hawley tariff bill as an act of economic selfishness designed to protect "certain types of Republicans."[36] More important than the cause for the bill was its effect—an effect that made perfect sense given a simplistic understanding of human nature: "The tariff, as you in the State of Washington well know, had the inevitable result of bringing about the retaliations by the other nations of the world. Forty of them set up, *just as you and I would have done,* their own tariff defenses against us" (emphasis added). The Hoover administration had inaugurated a game of economic tit-for-tat, one in which the results were a foregone conclusion. The game was, therefore, explicable only in light of the "special protection" it offered to American businesses.

Roosevelt's solution to Smoot-Hawley was a complex game of international economic diplomacy known as reciprocal tariff agreements, wherein the United States negotiated trade agreements on a country-by-country basis. But to his listeners, Roosevelt reduced reciprocal tariff agreements to neighborly sharing: "I have advocated . . . a tariff policy based on reason, on the same good old-fashioned horse sense that you and I would use in dealing in our own business with our own neighbor."[37] Roosevelt simplified the issue further: "if it has something we need, and we have something it needs, a tariff agreement can and should be made that is satisfactory to both countries" (725). "Reason," "horse sense," "need," and "neighbors"—these were the idioms of barber-shop chatter and bridge-club conversations, not high level international diplomacy, and herein Roosevelt differed greatly from his opponent. Hoover at times seemed to revel in the minutae of technocratic jargon associated with the highest levels of government. He was elected as the "Great Engineer," and many of his speeches, briefings, and press conferences were animated by his technical expertise and understanding. Thus, in some respects it was "natural" for Hoover to implore the press to do the requisite translating. To laypersons, Roosevelt took just the opposite approach: he invoked the most common forms of identification in order to induce his listeners to accept his views.

But he was not above employing status distinctions—however subtle. At Seattle, he continued to invoke the role of omniscient country doctor to assuage fears that economic health might not return. Hoover, not by deliberate intent but through insufficient understanding, had unleashed a deadly "poison" in the economic bloodstream with the imposition of high tariffs (725). Roosevelt's "remedy" was simply to "barter" or talk with each country and, thereby, to eliminate barriers to trade.

Roosevelt's "poison" metaphor had two very important entailments. First, the people were not responsible for spreading the poison; it had been loosed by an out-of-touch president. Second, given that Roosevelt labeled

the Smoot-Hawley tariff act as poisonous, it would seem logical for him to re-
nounce it altogether. Yet, Roosevelt's proposed solution—reciprocal tariff
agreements—would only lessen the poison's toxicity; it would not remove it
from the bloodstream. The apparent contradiction was not lost on Roosevelt's critics. The *Nation* called Roosevelt's tariff policy an "incredible non-
sequitur. . . . What utter nonsense."[38] The editors complained that, given his
attack on Smoot-Hawley, he should attack the whole tariff principle.[39]

More than sixty years have largely elided the fact that Smoot-Hawley was
a bipartisan bill—an elision poignantly captured in Vice-President Al Gore's
"goodwill" offering to H. Ross Perot. Had the Texas billionaire been conver-
sant in recent U.S. history, he might have graciously declined the portrait of
Smoot and Hawley on the grounds that it was not a purely pro-big-business
Republican act. Like the North Atlantic Free Trade Agreement (NAFTA),
Smoot- Hawley passed the House and Senate with bipartisan support, not to
mention broad support from agriculture and industry. In 1932 Roosevelt
knew the bipartisan history of Smoot-Hawley, and unless he was willing to
risk great political capital, he could not align himself with the small block of
free-traders led by Tennessee's Cordell Hull. Thus was the tariff's "poison"
consigned, at least in the short run, to the nation's economic bloodstream.

The Lusty Child and the Punitive Parent

The following night in Portland, Oregon, Roosevelt faced another daunting
rhetorical task: to simplify the complexities associated with public ownership of hydro-electric power. He acknowledged the task at the outset: "This
subject has been discussed so much in complex language . . . that there is
need for bringing it back into the realm of simple, honest terms understood
by millions of our citizens."[40] The speech was uncharacteristically bold, perhaps even threatening to some. Roosevelt no doubt drew some measure of
strength from his frequent donneybrooks with New York's Legislature regarding control of the St. Lawrence River. This was one of the few issues for
which Roosevelt swore off his pledge to "bold, persistent experimentation,"
which he had articulated at Oglethorpe University. He would be guided
solely by principle:

> I want at the outset of the discussion to take my bearings, to know my
> destination, to chart my course. In discussing electrical power, the
> speaker, like a ship sailing in dangerous waters, must avoid not only
> unseen shoals and rocky reefs, he must also be on his guard against
> false lights on the shore. His only protection against all of these dan-
> gers is to set squarely and fairly before him the course that he must
> steer (727).

Roosevelt simplified the complexities of public power by again humanizing his proposals: public versus private power was analogized as a child-
adult relationship. The latter was depicted as the "lusty younger child" who

needed "to be kept very closely under the watchful eye of its parent, the people of the United States" (733). The watchful eye, a Rooseveltian staple, was not the eye of the federal government, but the eye of the people. But a watchful eye was not enough; there was need, when the lusty child got out of line (that is, when utility companies charged exorbitant rates) for more punitive measures. "I might call the right of the people to own and operate their own utility something like this: a 'birch rod' in the cupboard to be taken out and used only when the 'child' gets beyond the point where a mere scolding does no good" (739).[41]

The analogy cast big business in an unfamiliar and an unflattering role: in less than three years its social status had gone from near divine seers of mysterious market forces to an unruly and inattentive child. Concomitantly, Roosevelt cast the average citizen as the wise, all-knowing parent. The "Forgotten Man" was thus an integral factor in the development of public power. In contrast to his April 7 speech, however, Roosevelt was quick to add an important disclaimer: his power policies were not radical: "My friends, my policy is as radical as American liberty. My policy is as radical as the Constitution of the United States" (742).

The Commonwealth Club Address

On August 15, Adolf Berle sent a three-page, single-spaced memorandum to Roosevelt. In it, Berle expressed his concern for Roosevelt's place in American history. Should he lose the campaign, the loss "would probably end your career, as it did the careers of Cox, Davis, and even Al Smith."[42] But if he won, and if he became "the protagonist of an outstanding policy," he would need to articulate a guiding philosophical statement, a statement "analogous [*sic*] to Woodrow Wilson's 'new freedom' speech." Historical greatness beckoned if only Roosevelt seized the rhetorical opportunity: "I feel that appropriately phrased, some such pronouncement would probably make at once your place in history; and a political significance vastly beyond the significance of this campaign." Roosevelt implored Berle—a man, bear in mind, who did not even favor Roosevelt's nomination—to work on some such "pronouncement."[43] The result was the campaign's most remembered and revered speech, the Commonwealth Club address, which has since entered the "canon" of American public address.[44] It was also "the least characteristically Rooseveltian of all his 1932 campaign utterances."[45] And, as Rexford Tugwell later recounted, the speech "did not come, as so many seemed to think it did, straight out of Franklin's head."[46]

The speech was anomalous on at least two counts. First, it veered radically from Roosevelt's expressed goal of experimentation. Roosevelt was a pragmatist, not a political philosopher—a role for which he "had little natural inclination or attraction."[47] Second, the thesis that he advanced at the Commonwealth Club ran afoul of his earlier policy recommendations.[48] Recall that economic recovery, in large measure, was contingent on a freer flow of economic trade. At San Francisco, though, Roosevelt spurned his earlier emphasis on international trade and opted instead for an intra-national solution to the Great Depression. In his words, the "day of enlight-ened administration has come."[49] Given the confusion and contradiction associated with this canonical text, it is worth quoting Moley at some length as to its origination and delivery:

> The history of that speech is this. I was approached by Berle who made the suggestion that a speech should be delivered which would deline-ate something of the progressive theories contained in Herbert Croly's books, which had been published twenty years earlier. He did so and submitted to me a file to be carried on the train on our trip. The Berle draft remained in my briefcase during the trip across the country, but when we left Portland and were approaching San Francisco on the train going down, it became apparent to me from conversations with newspapermen and others that the San Francisco speech, which was to be delivered at the Commonwealth Club, should be a major speech. Up to that time, Roosevelt had believed that all he needed to do in San Francisco was to greet the people and congratulate them on the Golden Gate and other trivialities. But since the Commonwealth Club would have an audience of very serious people and wide publicity, I decided that this was the place to use the Berle draft. . . . I didn't have time enough to revise it as I should have, especially the unfortunate break in there which asserted that the industrial plant was built and that it need not be rebuilt. This was obviously an error and a blunder. . . . with my changes I got the speech copied and took it to Roosevelt that night in the Palace Hotel. He read it over, made a few slight corrections, and that was that. The speech was very largely de-livered as it had been written by Berle and slightly amended by me.[50]

Returning to the text: the day of enlightened administration had been prepared by the closing of the western frontier—a direct reference to Fred-erick Jackson Turner's frontier thesis. There was, quite literally, no more space for the displaced worker. "Our last frontier has long since been reached, and there is practically no more free land. . . . There is no safety valve in the form of a Western prairie to which those thrown out of work by the Eastern economic machine can go for a new start" (750). That the phys-ical landscape had indeed grown beyond capacity was accentuated by a subtle claustrophobia. Roosevelt mentioned, for example, the "concentra-tion" of "growing corporations"; industrial "growth" had "narrowed and stiffened"; the small businessman had been "squeezed out" or "absorbed" by large combinations; the independent businessman had been "forced to the wall" and "squeezed out" by corporate competitors; and "tariff walls" had isolated the United States from its trading partners. In sum, unbridled eco-nomic development had resulted in a "closer economic system" in which large economic units quite literally crowded out the little guy. Moley later noted, "I regret that I did not very carefully edit this speech, because the expression that was used, that 'our industrial plant is built,' was obviously silly and has been commented on critically since."[51]

The displaced and dislocated needed safe dwellings—dwellings, Roosevelt promised, that would be erected under a new social contract between private business and the federal government. The contract would provide a haven "within which every individual may have a place if he will take it; in which every individual may find safety if he wishes it" (755). Terms of the contract were characteristically vague, as Roosevelt chose not to elaborate the specifics of the "new" contract. But it was evident that the contract was neither radical nor subversive. It would simply provide "safety for our economic structures" (752).

Berle proved to be prescient: the speech's political significance did indeed outlive the 1932 campaign. It survives as a classic in the Rooseveltian ouevre, even though the speech and its high-minded ideals were Berle's, not Roosevelt's.[52] Even the language was Berle's, as an earlier draft reveals.[53] Interdependence, organicism, health and sickness, and confidence were conspicuously missing—as was any mention of reciprocal tariff agreements. As it turned out, the "new social contract" provided no stable, safe dwelling place for the dislocated masses—save a discursive place. But the speech, as Berle's memorandum makes acutely clear, was not intended for policy; it was designed to galvanize and sustain Roosevelt's rhetorical-historical legacy—and within that frame of reference, the speech was and is an unequivocal success.

Embodied Recovery

The Commonwealth Club address is even more deviant in the context of Roosevelt's next major campaign speech, a September 29 address on agriculture and tariffs in Sioux City, Iowa. At San Francisco, Roosevelt inaugurated the new day of "enlightened administration"; six days later the sun appeared to have already set.[54] First, Roosevelt heaped scorn on the Hoover administration for "being the greatest spending administration in peace times in all our history. It is an Administration that has piled bureau on bureau, commission on commission."[55] He concluded summarily that the federal government was "attempting too many functions." It goes almost without saying that "enlightened administration" would need bureaus, commissions, and greater tax revenues. Even more incriminating was Roosevelt's claim that Hoover was attempting too much, but doing more was precisely the message that Roosevelt had espoused six days earlier.

Second, Roosevelt returned to his pre–Commonwealth Club belief that economic recovery was premised, in part, on negotiating lower tariffs instead of reordering a mature, closed system. He was adamant: "no substantial progress toward recovery from this depression, either here or abroad, can be had without a forthright recognition of those [Smoot-Hawley tariffs] errors" (762). He continued: "I say to you, in all earnestness and sincerity, that unless and until this process [trade contraction caused by Smoot-Hawley] is reversed throughout the world there is no hope for full economic recovery, or for true prosperity in this beloved country of ours" (765–66).

As I have indicated elsewhere, Roosevelt's proposed tariff policy was not a reversal of Smoot-Hawley; in fact, he conceded that it was "not widely different from that preached by Republican statesmen and politicians." More specifically, he said that "we should not lower them [tariff rates] beyond a reasonable point, a point indicated by common sense and facts. Such revision of the tariff will injure no legitimate interests" (767). Roosevelt was decidedly in favor of "giving the American producer an advantage over his foreign competitor" (769).

Roosevelt also attempted to counter accusations that he would be bested at the international bargaining table. Not surprisingly, he contextualized the charges within the sphere of health and sickness:

> Do you believe that our early instincts for successful barter have degenerated or atrophied? I do not think so. I have confidence . . . that the red blood of the men who sailed our Yankee clipper ships . . . still courses in our veins. I cannot picture Uncle Sam as a supine, white-livered, flabby-muscled old man cooling his heels in the shade of our tariff walls (767–68).

The image of a prostrate man, someone whose once strong legs had "degenerated or atrophied" was one that Roosevelt "could not picture"—despite the reservations of many and despite the fact that he drew a most convincing picture. The implication was clear: Roosevelt was blind to his own handicap; he was strong enough to take on "our more experienced friends" at the bargaining table (768). Thus did Roosevelt embody the very possibility of America's renewed economic health; it was nascent within his own crippled body.[56]

Roosevelt not only overturned the policy implications of his Commonwealth Club address, but on October 1 in Chicago he even contravened its dominant image. He stated that "if we as a Nation can retain the spirit of the pioneers we shall conquer even the wilderness of depression."[57] But perhaps more important than the apparent contradiction was an admission of rhetorical strategy. As his whirlwind tour of the West and Midwest neared its end, Roosevelt confessed to the relatively small crowd of Democratic well-wishers, "I have stated my position, my friends, in simple terms. . . . I have spoken of saving the railroads from receivership; I have spoken of the tariff in words, I think, that laymen like myself can understand." He added that his rhetoric of economics was based on the simple idea that "economic policies and attitudes towards economic life" were firmly grounded in "the life of human beings." At the most obvious level, Roosevelt's inventional heuristic simplified complex economic phenomena for common people. On a more subtle plane, Roosevelt had also humanized the depression itself and thereby rendered it explicable, familiar, and, most importantly, solvable.[58] In contrast, the Republican leadership had engaged in a campaign of deliberate mystification: their economic program could not be understood by the common person. Roosevelt's accusation went to the heart of the oft-expressed sentiment that Herbert Hoover was badly out of touch with the American people.

Poverty as Disease

Roosevelt gave his last major address of the trip on October 2 in Detroit. In it, he chronicled how progressive measures such as better public health, workman's compensation, old age insurance, and mental hygiene had prevented the spread of poverty. But poverty, he added, was not unlike a disease: "We have got beyond the point in modern civilization of merely trying to fight an epidemic of disease by taking care of the victims after they are stricken. . . . We seek to prevent it and the attack on poverty is not very unlike the attack on disease."[59] Medicalizing poverty served at least three important rhetorical functions. First, it reduced the complex social forces associated with poverty to a universal locus of causality, one in which science held potential "remedies." Second, poverty, like certain diseases, came from without: people were indiscriminately infected with poverty; they were not, therefore, culpable for something beyond their immediate control. Roosevelt noted that "the causes of poverty in the main are beyond the control of any one individual." Third, medicalizing poverty thrust the unwitting victims into an extremely acquiescent role. Without supervision and treatment, they could not exorcize their symptoms.[60] They were essentially forced to follow the omniscient doctor's prescriptions, and then allow nature to run its course.

Roosevelt contextualized progressive cures for poverty as a movement forward—as a "path of faith," a "path of hope" and a "path of love" that culminated in "the path of social justice"—and, as he indicated in his July 2 acceptance speech, he would lead the way. After repeating "we cannot go back" six times in one paragraph, he concluded: "there are a lot of new steps to take. It is not a question of just not going back. It is a question also of not standing still. . . . the problem of unemployment in the long run can be and shall be solved by the human race."

A Retreat to Conservatism

By the time "the Boss" arrived back in Albany, Louis Howe was apoplectic: he was convinced that Roosevelt had alienated the powerful business community with talk of lower tariffs, economic interdependence, closed frontiers, and enlightened administration. It was long past time for him to return to the fiscal conservatism he had preached at Columbus—so felt Howe and

Bernard Baruch's appointed rhetorician, Hugh Johnson. Roosevelt and Moley must not have disagreed too vehemently, for beginning on October 13 the governor's economic rhetoric took a decided thematic shift, even though many of the stylistic elements remained in place.

Before a nationwide radio audience, Roosevelt opened his conservative campaign by talking about unemployment relief and who was responsible for it. Outwardly, he seemed to be in lockstep with Hoover: "The first principle I would lay down is that the primary duty [for relief] rests on the community, through local government and private agencies."[61] If local funds proved insufficient, "the State comes into the picture." When the state was unable to fulfill its obligations, then it "becomes the positive duty of the Federal Government to step in to help" (789). Centralized relief was thus the last link in the governmental chain, something to be tried only as a last-ditch effort. This effort, moreover, needed to be tempered by fiscal caution: "I have constantly reiterated my conviction that the expenditures of cities, States and the Federal Government must be reduced in the interest of the Nation as a whole."

But while Roosevelt pledged that economy should never "be practiced at the expense of starving people," he attacked the Hoover administration for its fiscal excess. Its spending on relief efforts, principally its public work programs, even threatened the nation's future economic stability. In contrast, he promised that his administration's public works programs would "be considered from the point of view of the ability of the Government treasury to pay for them" (790). Roosevelt was subtly intimating that relief was subservient to a balanced federal budget—the sine qua non of fiscal conservatism. And a balanced federal budget was precisely what Roosevelt promised less than a week later in Pittsburgh.

Of the scores of speeches that Roosevelt delivered during the 1932 presidential campaign, only one would later haunt him. Ironically, it was the only speech of the entire campaign, claims biographer Kenneth S. Davis, in which he spoke from his own personal convictions and beliefs.[62] Though Roosevelt acolytes later dismissed the speech as an aberration and as a Johnson/Howe brainchild, Moley claimed that "so far as it is possible for anyone to be positive of anything, I am sure that the speech, as delivered, represented Roosevelt's wholehearted views on government finance."[63] Roosevelt's views seemed to mirror several Democratic senators. In a letter to Moley, Johnson proclaimed that several senators thought the revised budget speech was "a knockout and exactly what is necessary just now in this part of the country."[64]

Roosevelt's views were put forth primarily in a negative manner; that is, they were broadly discernable through his attacks on Herbert Hoover. The principal problem with the Hoover administration's economic policies was its "extravagant" spending proposals—proposals that Roosevelt claimed were "economic heresies" and "radical economic theories."[65] That Roosevelt characterized them in such hyperbolic terms is explicable given his master metaphor associated with fiscal policy. Specifically, the federal government's credit—a direct correlate of its revenue and spending totals—was the core "foundation," the essential "financial structure" upon which economic recovery rested. Federal deficits only imperiled the "stability" of such foundations. Thus, the $3.75 billion federal debt that had accumulated over the preceding three years threatened to undermine and ultimately "collapse" the nation's tottering financial structure.

Given the vital significance of a federally balanced budget, Roosevelt's views on "the income side of the ledger" (taxation) come into sharper relief. Despite the fact that in June, Hoover had signed into law the largest peacetime tax increase in the nation's history, Roosevelt suggested that it was not enough. "A Government charged with maintaining the financial stability not only of the U.S. itself, but of the whole American nation under all conditions, is under a very solemn duty . . . to take immediate steps to avoid a deficit" (800). Furthermore, Roosevelt mocked the Hoover administration for decreasing taxes immediately following the stock market crash—a move that would later draw praise from John Maynard Keynes's followers. In sum, given the primary importance of a federally balanced budget, Roosevelt concluded that the administration deserved "retribution" for "chasing after strange economic gods" (804).

Later in the speech, however, Roosevelt revealed that orthodox fiscal policy, while important, was only part of the calculus for economic recovery. In two different places, he made reference to the other "part":

> The president appeared with his December 1931 Budget Message. It was a fateful moment. That was the time . . . for an honest demonstration to the world that might have set the whole world trend of economic events in an upward direction or at least checked the decline. All that it was necessary to do was finally to end once and for all the two years of vacillation and secretiveness, to tell the truth to the Congress of the United States (804–805).

He added that "a powerful cause contributing to economic disaster has been this inexcusable fiscal policy and the obscurity and uncertainty that have attended and grown out of it" (811). The other "part" was thus honest and clear presidential rhetoric. Unlike the pre-1932 Hoover, Roosevelt was unwilling to place all of his hopes for economic recovery on presidential rhetoric, but it was, nonetheless, a "powerful cause" both in prolonging the depression and in expediting recovery.

Ambivalence

On the same day that he excoriated the Hoover administration for its economic heresies, Roosevelt made very different overtures to his audience at Wheeling, West Virginia—overtures that may have further appeased big business. For the first time in the campaign, Roosevelt "Democratized" two major Hooverian instrumentalities for recovery. He first praised the Wilson administration and Senator Carter Glass for creating the Federal Reserve System. He added, "Had there been no Federal Reserve System, the collapse would indeed have been complete."[66] This strongly suggested that Roosevelt would continue the Hoover administration's policy of an expanded money supply and lower interest rates.

More interesting was Roosevelt's praise for the Reconstruction Finance Corporation (RFC)—a Hoover invention following the tight-fisted lending policies of the National Credit Corporation. But Roosevelt claimed that it was "as much a Democratic measure as a Republican measure—for it was passed in the spirit of bipartisan cooperation in the Congress of the United States."[67] Moreover, the RFC, like the Federal Reserve System, was really a Wilsonian creation since it mimicked the "principles of [the] War Finance Corporation." Here was another overt clue that Roosevelt would not pursue economic policies hostile to big business, as it was the principal beneficiary of the generous loans doled out by the RFC.

The following day at Indianapolis, Roosevelt continued to court big business, but he recanted or greatly modified much of what he had stated at Pittsburgh. For example, he stated that "government must grow more national in its view, more comprehensive in its concern for every factor in the country."[68] Two days earlier, he had admonished Hoover for encouraging the federal government's centralization. Roosevelt also indicated that Hoover's "heresies" would not threaten the nation's economic foundation or structure: only "unreasoning and groundless fear and hysteria can chip away the granite foundations on which our fiscal system is based." Perhaps this statement—a corollary to his famous inaugural address aphorism—was Roosevelt's subtle revelation that hc would continue the Hoover tradition of unbalanced federal budgets.

More importantly, Roosevelt declared that only a nonmaterial reality was capable of undermining the nation's material prosperity. But that same nonmaterial reality could be shaped by presidential speech toward beneficial economic ends: "As these policies were unfolded the Nation stood by and watched the unfolding drama of political contest without fear, without trepidation and without uneasiness. As these principles came to be more widely accepted by the leaders of thought . . . the temper of the country changed. Economic and social life was stirred with the return of hope." The rhetoric of recovery was part and parcel to economic recovery: trade had actually quickened because he had articulated a policy, or so Roosevelt claimed.

He concluded his brief message by humanizing the party, the attributes of which were equally his own: "Our party stands ready to assume the responsibility that is coming to it. It is strong. It is confident. Its voice and action is quiet with the assurance of the responsibility that the election will bring." Here was a healthy, confident party headed by a healthy, confident man. Recovery would result from his words and his policies; he was the site from which the nation's economic health would be restored.

"A Delicate though Powerful Factor"

As the *Roosevelt Special* chugged further westward, the governor continued his courtship of big business, and, as in his Pittsburgh speech, he underscored the vital link between a federally balanced budget and "the foundation of the national credit."[69] Unlike his brief remarks in West Virginia, however, in which he stated that only fear and hysteria could undermine the nation's fiscal foundations, at St. Louis, Roosevelt claimed that Hoover's fiscal extravagances had "chipped away" some of the nation's "foundation stones" (823).

By the close of the speech, though, Roosevelt had changed metaphors, as if to underscore the fact that the economic foundations were far from sturdy. "The financial fabric of America is . . . a seamless web held together by the infinitely complex loyalties of men. We must protect it against men who would tear it to pieces rather than face defeat" (830). The government's duty, in conjunction with the business community, was to protect a delicate fabric; rock-hard granite, after all, did not lack for its own defense mechanism.

One powerful defense mechanism was faith—"a delicate though powerful factor in our economic life" (819). Hoover had abused this "powerful factor" by telling lies, or, in Roosevelt's vivid analogy, by throwing "economic tear bombs among the people of the country." Seeing was believing for Roosevelt, and his challenger had purposefully attempted to cloud the nation's perceptions:

> the purpose of the panic-creating tear gas which the Republican leaders are now hurling is not to open your hearts but to blind your eyes. Let me tell you from the bottom of my heart that I, for one, favor having you keep your eyes wide open, and I, for one favor keeping my own heart wide open (821).

Recovery was impossible under Herbert Hoover: he had done irreparable damage to the nation's collective economic faith. Recovery could not be expected given that the nation's economic high priest was a faithless, close-hearted deceiver. Roosevelt, though, could be believed: almost magically the tear gas had not affected him, but he was not above feeling pain or expressing sympathy. Superhuman powers and a compassionate heart, wrapped in an appeal to faith, bear some striking parallels to the Christian Savior—parallels that Roosevelt accentuated in his next major address.

Economic Apocalypse

In the span of four days, Roosevelt transformed Hoover from a close-hearted deceiver to the economic anti-Christ. Incorporating the millennial drama of

Revelations, Roosevelt likened Hoover and his henchmen to the Four Horsemen of the Apocalypse. The analogy, of course, cast Roosevelt in the role of economic savior. "I am waging a war in this campaign—a frontal attack—an onset—against the 'Four Horsemen' of the present Republican leadership: The Horsemen of Destruction, Delay, Deceit, Despair. And the time has come for us to marshal this 'Black Horse Cavalry'."[70]

The Hoover administration's evil machinations, true to Judeo-Christian form, had "brought upon us a terrible retribution" (834). The retribution, to a large extent, was manifested in the nation's collective health: the Four Horsemen had left in their wake paralysis, vertigo, blindness, soreness, and tiredness. A return to health depended on a two-fold rejection of the Hoover administration's treatment: a rejection of its "bitter medicine" (legislation) and its bedside manner. Hope was vital to economic recovery, but Hoover had resorted "to the most plaintive diagnosis of a doctor in despair that any country has ever heard from responsible statesmen" (840). Whereas Hoover "preached" despair, Roosevelt preached hope, and it was this optimistic outlook that would lead the nation to the economic millennium.

Healing and Scars

On October 30, in a radio broadcast to a nationwide audience, Roosevelt avoided the extremism and hyperbole associated with a millennial economic drama; instead, he talked about life in a post-depression United States. He cast the period in terms of which perhaps only a victim of traumatic illness could appreciate. "These surface indications [of depression] are bad enough in themselves, but the deep-seated, invisible injuries that this depression is causing are likely to bear tragic consequences for generations to come."[71]

Roosevelt had a privileged or internal view of the nation's future suffering, not because of a prophetic gift, but because of something far more profound, something he had himself experienced: "There are wounds that will heal, but there are scars that the sufferers will feel all the rest of their lives—scars that will affect not only them, but their families and their neighbors." This was the closest that Roosevelt came—at least in the 1932 campaign—to a public disclosure regarding his ongoing battle with infantile paralysis. While the polio virus had left his body, its residual damage had profoundly affected him and his relationship to those around him.[72] Thus, at an experiential level, Roosevelt, ironically, was most fit to lead: having been in a perpetual state of recovery for more than eleven years, he knew intimately and instinctually what convalescence entailed—both psychically and physically.

Constituting the Roosevelt Army

The final week of the campaign was a rhetorical microcosm of the larger whole, with one significant exception. Up to this point in the campaign, Roosevelt had avoided any talk of warfare that directly involved the people. He had indeed mentioned war, but typically in the context of a personal war that he was waging against Hoover and his administration. But in his November 4 speech to the Brooklyn Academy of Music, Roosevelt broadened the metaphor for the first time since July 2 to include the people: "In simple terms I have attempted to say to the people of this country that the way out of disaster and depression is a battle to be fought by the people."[73] Outwardly, this was the same type of war that Hoover had declared more than a year earlier.

Upon closer inspection, though, Roosevelt's battle differed from Hoover's in at least three respects: it was not a fragmented war, fought on a thousand different fronts; it was not a civil war; and, Roosevelt did not withdraw from active leadership. He would provide the "plans of action" and he also promised "to keep vividly before them the definite objectives." In a word, Roosevelt would exert the rhetorical leadership that Hoover so eagerly shirked in 1932.

Roosevelt made warfare his master metaphor in his final major campaign address—a brief speech broadcast live to the nation from New York's Madison Square Garden. The selection of the locale was not without historical irony: the site of the Democrats' darkest hours in 1924 was now home to a jubilant party and its triumphant candidate. The profound wounds opened up at that convention were symbolically healed by the only figure to emerge from it unscathed.

In many ways, the speech provided a fitting finale to Roosevelt's campaign. In other respects it appears anomalous: one typically does not declare wars and create armies at the end of a ten-month battle—electoral or otherwise. Yet Roosevelt knew that the real battle was just beginning. Nearly everyone, including Herbert and Lou Hoover, knew that Roosevelt would be the nation's next president; as such, he was rhetorically preparing the way for his inauguration-day call to arms. Part of this preparation was to create, or to "constitute," an army, one devoid of partisan and class divisions. Roosevelt skillfully constituted the ranks of his army by creating a discursive space for nearly all economic groups. He proceeded to call role:

> There is among you the man who is not bound by party lines. . . .
> There is among you the woman who knows that women's traditional
> interests—welfare, children and the home—rest on the broader basis
> of an economic system which assures her or her husband of a job. . . .
> There is among you the man in business or in trade who has heard the
> cry that change was a fearful thing but who, unafraid, has decided to
> change. . . . There is among you the man who has been brought up in
> the good American tradition to work hard and to save for a rainy
> day. . . . There is among you the man who has been brought up to believe that a livelihood could always be wrung from the soil by willing
> labor. . . . There is among you the man who has been able to save
> something from this wreck.[74]

Roosevelt's seemingly detached appeal to "the man" and "the woman" was very misleading, for he uttered the term "you" or "your" more than eighty times in just fifteen minutes. More importantly, Roosevelt's use of the second person was augmented and ultimately transcended by an inclusive rhetoric that featured more than sixty references to "we," "our" and "us." He eloquently merged the singular and the plural in his only explicit mention of war: "All of you . . . have helped shape the policies of the Democratic party in this, its war on human suffering. Your own experiences and your own fears and your own problems—all have written themselves into our program. There is something of you in all of us." Roosevelt's economic army was thus in place, ready for the leader's March 4 call to arms and for what William Leuchtenburg calls "The Hundred Days' War."[75]

Summary

The nation's electorate did not seem to mind the contradictions, ambiguities, and inconsistencies in Roosevelt's campaign rhetoric: on November 8 he received a huge majority, both in popular and electoral votes.[76] But at a time when economic "knowledge" had largely broken down and when fears for Democracy's very survival infiltrated mainstream political discourse, rigid consistency was not necessarily a prized presidential virtue. Herbert Hoover, after all, did not lack at least rhetorically for an inveterate commitment to political principle.

With the distance that more than sixty years provides, it is easy to side with the prevailing orthodoxy and conclude that Hoover and Roosevelt were very different when it came to economic policy. Precisely the opposite is true: save for reciprocal trade, the two were remarkably similar.[77] The similarities caused some contemporary commentators to argue that the election was a choice between Tweedledum and Tweedledee.[78] Marriner Eccles, a future Roosevelt appointee, trenchantly observed that, "given later developments, the campaign speeches often read like a giant misprint, in which Roosevelt and Hoover speak each other's lines."[79] But the phrase "read alike" is a crucial caveat. It is clear from anyone with eyes and ears that Hoover and Roosevelt did not *speak* alike. The Paul Y. Anderson of the *Nation* commented on what many observed: "when he [Roosevelt] is placed beside the sour and devious Hoover the contrast is almost startling."[80]

Moreover, at a strictly propositional level, Hoover and Roosevelt's policy objectives appeared to be quite similar, but the manner in which they were expressed frequently diverged. Like Hoover, Roosevelt was clearly attuned to the power of individual and collective belief to alter economic reality, yet he presented the position so that presidential rhetoric was of critical importance. Confidence, as he stated at Columbus, required external and internal sources: people needed to believe in themselves *and* in their leader. Roosevelt attempted to facilitate belief in the latter through several means, but none was more predominant than his emphasis on sickness and health—

not to mention his own ubiquitous, visible presence across the nation. The two train trips on the *Roosevelt Special* were stunning successes, perhaps best captured by Robert Barry's "9,000 Miles with Franklin Roosevelt": "I am willing to go a long way with Franklin D. Roosevelt on his political idealism," he began, but "as a traveling companion on a trans-continental campaign trip I want no more of him. You can have him. This President-to-be of ours isn't human. He is some kind of a machine. A robot, possibly. Certainly, a dynamo."[81] He continued, "If there is such a thing as 'the pace that kills' Governor Roosevelt has it copyrighted. It is all but fatal for everyone except himself. He seems actually to thrive on it. It really appears to do him good." Barry's partisan hyperbole notwithstanding, Moley received confirmation that "the showing" had its desired effects. In a letter from M. L. Wilson of Domestic Allotment fame, he wrote, "The women are also saying that he appeared in splendid physical condition and that he must be a remarkable man to have overcome his unfortunate physical disabilities in such a complete manner."[82]

The nation's economic ills and the people's individual ailments had as their symbolic healer the corporeal presence of Franklin Roosevelt, a leader not unfamiliar with both physical and mental trauma. Garry Wills, among others, notes the link between Roosevelt's illness and his response to the Great Depression:

> He knew that the soul needed healing first, and the confidence he had instilled in the patients of Warm Springs was the most measurable gift Roosevelt gave to the nation during the Depression. He understood the importance of psychology—that people have to have the courage to keep seeking a cure, no matter what the cure is. American had lost its will to recover, and Roosevelt was certain that regaining it was the first order of business.[83]

Roosevelt embodied the nation's hopes for economic recovery. This was not lost on him. "Favor comes because for a brief moment in the great space of human change and progress some general human purpose finds in him a satisfactory *embodiment.* . . . I seek to be only the *humble emblem* of this restoration of America."[84] Roosevelt fashioned himself as both the signifier and the signified, the sign or "humble emblem" of economic recovery.

Notes

1. "Mr. Roosevelt's Speech, *New York Times*, July 4, 1932, p. 10.

2. Claude G. Bowers, "The Battle Flag Unfurled," *New York Journal*, July 5, 1932, n.p.

3. Franklin D. Roosevelt, "The Governor Accepts the Nomination for the Presidency, Chicago, Ill. July 2, 1932," in *The Public Papers and Addresses of Franklin D. Roosevelt*, volume one: *The Genesis of the New Deal, 1928–1932*, ed. S. I. Rosenman, p. 658.

4. Informal extemporaneous remarks of Governor Roosevelt, Goodland, Kans., September 15, 1932, FDR Speech File, Box 10, File 500, Franklin D. Roosevelt Presidential Library, Hyde Park, N.Y. (hereafter, FRPL); emphasis added.

5. Nearly six hours later in Denver, Roosevelt was emphatic about his real motives for the train trip: "I am trying to make the people of the country understand that the real honest-to-God purpose of this swing of mine through the West . . . is primarily so that I can get in touch personally with the different sections of the country, to find out what the needs are of each section; what the thoughts of the people are" ("Informal Extemporaneous Remarks of Governor Roosevelt, Denver, Colorado, September 15, 1932," FDR Speech File, Box 10, File 502, p. 2, FRPL).

6. This is said in jest, but more than one observer believed that Hoover was personally responsible for the kidnapping; see Gene Smith, *The Shattered Dream*, p. 176.

7. Ibid., p. 177. Burns notes that the "lack of internal consistency" to Roosevelt's speeches must have been "all very confusing to the close observer" (James MacGregor Burns, *Roosevelt: The Lion and the Fox*, pp. 142–43).

8. Henry F. Pringle, "Franklin D. Roosevelt—Perched on the Bandwagon," *Nation*, April 27, 1932, p. 489.

9. "Roosevelt Steps Left and Right," *New Republic*, September 28, 1932, p. 164.

10. "Governor Roosevelt's Campaign," *Nation*, November 2, 1932, p. 414.

11. Kenneth S. Davis, *FDR: The New York Years, 1928–1933*, p. 360.

12. Raymond Moley, *After Seven Years*, p. 45.

13. Rosen claims that the speech was an "olive branch to conservative Democrats" (Eliot A. Rosen, *Hoover, Roosevelt and the Brains Trust: From Depression to New Deal*, p. 308).

14. "First draft: speech 7/30/32," FDR Speech Files, Box 10, File 488, FRPL.

15. Franklin D. Roosevelt, "The Candidate Discusses the National Democratic Platform. Radio Address, Albany, N. Y. July 30, 1932," in *The Public Papers and Addresses of Franklin D. Roosevelt, 1928–1932*, p. 661. Subsequent references are noted in the text.

16. Franklin D. Roosevelt, "The Failures of the Preceding Administration. Campaign Address at Columbus, Ohio. August 20, 1932," in *The Public Papers and Addresses of Franklin D. Roosevelt, 1928–1932*, p. 672.

17. Franklin D. Roosevelt, "Campaign Address on Prohibition, Sea Girt, N. J. August 27, 1932," in *The Public Papers and Addresses of Franklin D. Roosevelt, 1928–1932*, p. 692. Subsequent references are noted in the text.

18. Edward M. House to Franklin Roosevelt, August 30, 1932, Raymond Moley Papers, "Campaign of 1932," Box 24, File 24–73, Hoover Institution on War, Revolution, and Peace, Stanford University, Stanford, California.

19. Frank R. Kent, "How Strong is Roosevelt?" *Scribner's Magazine*, April, 1932, p. 203.

20. Hugh Gregory Gallagher, *FDR's Splendid Deception*, p. 86. Biographer John Gunther states that the motive for Roosevelt's trip was "to show himself to the people, and thus dispel any lingering rumors that he was not physically fit" (Gunther, *Roosevelt in Retrospect*, p. 272).

21. Gallagher, *FDR's Splendid Deception*, p. 85.

22. Speaker's Kit—1932, President's Subject File, Box 255, Republican National Committee, "Democratic Party, Speaker's Kit Materials, 1932," Herbert Hoover Presidential Library, West Branch, Iowa (hereafter, HHPL).

23. Lewis L. Strauss Papers, Box 15, "Campaign of 1932, Campaign Literature," HHPL.

24. Campaign Book, President's Subject File, Box 253, "Republican National Campaign Speech Data, Roosevelt, 1932," HHPL.

25. President's Subject File, Box 254, "Republican National Committee, Democratic Party, Campaign Literature, 1931–32," HHPL.

26. Article Number Two, December 15, 1932, Louis M. Howe Papers, 1928–1932, Container 54, FRPL.

27. Interview with Raymond Moley by Eliott A. Rosen, Oral History Series 1–3, 44, HHPL.

28. At Warm Springs, Roosevelt was delighted when other "polios" referred to him as "Doctor Roosevelt." According to Gallagher, Roosevelt "always saw himself as his own chief orthopedist" (Gallagher, *FDR's Splendid Deception*, p. 215).

29. For a detailed itinerary of Roosevelt's first train trip, see "I-T-I-N-E-R-A-R-Y, Honorable Franklin D. Roosevelt and Party, 1932 Campaign Western Tour," President's Personal File, File 1820, "Campaign of 1932," pp. 3–7, FRPL. For a reporter's account of the train trips, with an emphasis on Roosevelt's health, see Warner B. Ragsdale, "The Campaign Trail in 1932," in *The Making of the New Deal*, ed. Katie Louchheim, pp. 1–9.

30. "Roosevelt's Speeches," *World Tomorrow*, October 5, 1932, p. 316.

31. Quoted in "Roosevelt Reveals His Program to the Country," *Literary Digest*, October 1, 1932, p. 6.

32. "Mr. Roosevelt's Tariff Nonsense," *Nation*, September 28, 1932, p. 270.

33. Franklin D. Roosevelt, "A Restored and Rehabilitated Agriculture. Campaign Address on the Farm Problem at Topeka, Kans. September 14, 1932," in *The Public Papers and Addresses of Franklin D. Roosevelt, 1928–1932*, p. 698. Subsequent references are noted in the text.

34. The *New Republic* observed that Roosevelt's agricultural objectives "fit like a glove" with Domestic Allotment. "Roosevelt Steps Left and Right," *New Republic*, September 28, 1932, p. 165.

35. Franklin D. Roosevelt, "The Railroad Mesh Is the Warp on Which Our Economic Web is Largely Fashioned. Campaign Address on Railroads at Salt Lake City, Utah. September 17, 1932," in *The Public Papers and Addresses of Franklin D. Roosevelt, 1928–1932*, pp. 721–22. Subsequent references are noted in the text.

36. Franklin D. Roosevelt, "Campaign Address on Reciprocal Tariff Negotiations. Seattle, Wash. September 20, 1932," in *The Public Papers and Addresses of Franklin D. Roosevelt, 1928–1932*, p. 724. Subsequent references are noted in the text.

37. The following day, Roosevelt reiterated the analogy: "One of the principal things we must do is to negotiate with other nations to lower these tariff barriers. It all comes back to the old system of exchange of goods between neighbors" ("Informal Extemporaneous Remarks of Governor Roosevelt, Portland, Oregon, September 21, 1932," FDR Speech File, Container 10, File 517, FRPL).

38. "Governor Roosevelt's Campaign," p. 414.

39. "Mr. Roosevelt's Tariff Nonsense," p. 270.

40. Franklin D. Roosevelt, "A National Yardstick to Prevent Extortion against the Public and to Encourage the Wider Use of That Servant of the People–Electric Power. Campaign Address on Public Utilities and Development of Hydro-Electric Power, Portland, Ore. September 21, 1932," in *The Public Papers and Addresses of Franklin D. Roosevelt, 1928–1932*, pp. 728–29. Subsequent references are noted in the text.

41. Roosevelt elaborated the analogy in a speech in Milwaukee; see "Address of Governor Franklin D. Roosevelt, Milwaukee, Wisconsin, September 30, 1932," FDR Speech File, Box 12, File 546, 6, FRPL.

42. Adolf Berle, "Memorandum to Governor Franklin D. Roosevelt," Berle Papers, Box 15, "Memoranda from Campaign," FRPL.

43. Berle was an active supporter of Ohio's Newton Baker, even at the Democratic convention.

44. See, for example, Ronald F. Reid, ed., *American Rhetorical Discourse*, 2d. ed., pp. 706–18. Reid wrongly asserts that the speech was written principally by Robert Straus (p. 708).

45. Davis, *FDR: The New York Years*, p. 368.

46. Rexford G. Tugwell, *The Democratic Roosevelt*, p. 246. Tugwell later noted that the speech was "certainly not carefully considered by Roosevelt before it was made" (Rexford G. Tugwell, *In Search of Roosevelt*, p. 172).

47. Davis, *FDR: The New York Years*, p. 368.

48. The problem did not escape Tugwell; see Tugwell, *The Democratic Roosevelt*, p. 246.

49. Franklin D. Roosevelt, "New Conditions Impose New Requirements upon Government and Those Who Conduct Government. Campaign Address on Progressive Government at the Commonwealth Club. San Francisco, Calif. September 23, 1932," in *The Public Papers and Addresses of Franklin D. Roosevelt, 1928–1932*, p. 752. Subsequent references are noted in the text.

50. Moley interviewed by Rosen, Oral History Series 1–3, 38–39, HHPL.

51. Raymond Moley, Speech of April 15, 1965, Raymond Moley Papers, "Speeches and Writings," Box 245–46.

52. Davis, *FDR: The New York Years*, p. 370.

53. See Berle Papers, Box 18, "Draft— Progressive Govt, Commonwealth Club, 9-23-32," FRPL.

54. According to Burns, the ideas that Roosevelt expressed in the Commonwealth Club address faded away as the campaign wore on (Burns, *Roosevelt: The Lion and the Fox*, p. 143).

55. Franklin D. Roosevelt, "Campaign Address on Agriculture and Tariffs at Sioux City, Iowa. September 29, 1932," in *The Public Papers and Addresses of Franklin D. Roosevelt, 1928–1932*, p. 761. Subsequent references are noted in the text.

56. On September 24, Roosevelt began his informal remarks at the Hollywood Bowl by drawing attention to his physical and mental health: "It has been a long trip, my friends, but unlike most long trips those of us who have been making it have left behind any feeling of fatigue of the mind or body." The word "body" was pencilled in the margin by Roosevelt; see "Speech of Governor Franklin D. Roosevelt, Delivered Hollywood Bowl, September 24, 1932," FDR Speech Files, Box 12, File 526, 1, FRPL.

57. Franklin D. Roosevelt, "Address of Governor Franklin D. Roosevelt, Hotel Stevens, Chicago, Illinois, October 1, 1932," FDR Speech Files, Box 12, File 547, 1, FRPL.

58. Rosenman notes that Roosevelt thought of economic problems in terms of the people. Samuel I. Rosenman, *Working with Roosevelt* (New York: Harper & Brothers, 1952), p. 34. Scarry notes that when there is a crisis of belief in society, "the sheer factualness of the human body will be borrowed to lend that cultural construct [capitalism] the aura of 'realness' and 'certainty'" (Elaine Scarry, *The Body in Pain* [New York: Oxford University Press, 1985], p. 14).

59. Franklin D. Roosevelt, "Address of Governor Franklin D. Roosevelt, Naval Armory, Belle Isle Bridge, Detroit, Michigan, October 2, 1932," FDR Speech Files, Box 12, File 548, 4, FRPL.

60. Roosevelt gleefully confessed to being "paternalistic" (p. 11).

61. Franklin D. Roosevelt, "Radio Address on Unemployment and Social Welfare. Albany, N.Y. October 13, 1932," in *The Public Papers and Addresses of Franklin D. Roosevelt, 1928–1932*, p. 787. Subsequent references are noted in the text.

62. Davis, *FDR: The New York Years*, p. 368.

63. Moley, *After Seven Years*, p. 62.

64. Hugh S. Johnson to Raymond Moley, September 16, 1932, Raymond Moley Papers, "Campaign of 1932," Box 26–53.

65. Franklin D. Roosevelt, "Campaign Address on the Federal Budget at Pittsburgh, Pa. October 19, 1932," in *The Public Papers and Addresses of Franklin D. Roosevelt, 1928–1932*, p. 798. Subsequent references are noted in the text.

66. Franklin D. Roosevelt, "Speech, Wheeling, W.Va. Oct. 19, 1932," FDR Speech Files, Box 12, File 557, 1, FRPL.

67. By this same reasoning, of course, Democrats were proud parents of Smoot-Hawley.

68. Franklin D. Roosevelt, "Speech, Indianapolis, Oct. 20, 1932," FDR Speech Files, Box 12, File 559, 4, FRPL.

69. Franklin D. Roosevelt, "Campaign Address on the Eight Great Credit Groups of the

Nation. St. Louis. Mo. October 21, 1932," in *The Public Papers and Addresses of Franklin D. Roosevelt, 1928–1932*, p. 824. Subsequent references are noted in the text.

70. Franklin D. Roosevelt, "I Am Waging a War in This Campaign against the 'Four Horsemen' of the Present Republican Leadership—Destruction, Delay, Deceit, Despair. Campaign Address at Baltimore, Md. October 25, 1932," in *The Public Papers and Addresses of Franklin D. Roosevelt, 1928–1932*, p. 832. Subsequent references are noted in the text.

71. Franklin D. Roosevelt, "Radio Broadcast Sunday Night, October 30, 1932 at 10:56 P.M. Subject: 'Welfare & Relief Mobilization of 1932,'" FDR Speech Files, Box 12, File 559, FRPL.

72. This is the thesis cogently argued by Gallagher in his book, *FDR's Splendid Deception*. Roosevelt's labor secretary, Frances Perkins, claimed that "Franklin Roosevelt underwent a spiritual transformation during the years of his illness. I noticed when he came back that the years of pain and suffering had purged the slightly arrogant attitude he had displayed on occasion before he was stricken. The man emerged completely warmhearted, with humility of spirit and with a deeper philosophy" (Frances Perkins, *The Roosevelt I Knew*, p. 29).

73. Franklin D. Roosevelt, "Governor Roosevelt's Address, Brooklyn Academy of Music, Friday, November 4, 1932," FDR Speech File, Box 12, File 584, FRPL.

74. Franklin D. Roosevelt, "I Believe that the Best Interests of the Country Require a Change in Administration. Campaign Address at Madison Square Garden. New York City. November 5, 1932," in *The Public Papers and Addresses of Franklin D. Roosevelt, 1928–1932*, pp. 862, 863, and 864.

75. William E. Leuchtenburg, *Franklin D. Roosevelt and the New Deal, 1932–1940*, pp. 41–62.

76. Roosevelt received 22,800,000 votes to Hoover's 15,750,000. The electoral vote was more one-sided, as Roosevelt won by a margin of 472 to 59. Democratic candidates rode Roosevelt's coattails and came to rule the House of Representatives by a majority of 310 to 117 and the Senate by a majority of 60 to 35.

77. Frank Freidel, *Franklin D. Roosevelt: A Rendezvous with Destiny*, p. 78; Burns, *Roosevelt: The Lion and the Fox*, p. 143. Rowe states that "Roosevelt out-Hoovered Hoover on economics" (James L. Rowe, Jr., "Hoover, We Hardly Knew Ye," *Washington Post*, August 23, 1992, sec. C, p. 2).

78. "Roosevelt Wins!" *Nation*, July 13, 1932, p. 22.

79. Marriner Eccles, *Beckoning Frontiers*, ed. Sydney Hyman, p. 95.

80. Paul Y. Anderson, "Mourning Becomes Herbert," *Nation*, September 28, 1932, p. 280.

81. Robert Barry, "9,000 Miles with Franklin Roosevelt," *The Democratic Bulletin*, November 1932, pp. 10, 45, President's Subject File, Box 255, Republican National Committee, "Democratic Party, Printed Matter, 1932," HHPL.

82. M. L. Wilson to Raymond Moley, September 21, 1932, "Campaign of 1932," Raymond Moley Papers.

83. Garry Wills, *Certain Trumpets*, p. 32.

84. Franklin D. Roosevelt, "Address of Governor Roosevelt" [final draft], 7 November 1932, FDR Speech Files, Box 12, p. 10, FRPL; emphasis added.

Chapter Six

Rhetoric, Silence, and the "Scene" of War
The Interregnum and the First 100 Days

"You'll never be a good politician. You are too impatient."
—Franklin to Eleanor

"How do I know it's [a $10 bill] any good? Only the fact that I think it makes it so."
—FDR to Cordell Hull

Despite the eloquent visual and verbal testimony of his robust health, Roosevelt apparently had yet to convince his most discerning skeptic—himself. His skepticism was informed by the enormous weight placed squarely on his shoulders on the evening of November 8, 1932. With his victory already conceded by Herbert Hoover, Roosevelt's eldest son, James, helped put his father to bed. He remembers the solemnity and gravity that his father, perhaps for the first time, fully realized:

> "You know, Jimmy," he said, "All my life I have been afraid of only one thing—fire. Tonight I think I'm afraid of something else." "Afraid of what, Pa?" I said. "I'm just afraid," he said, "that I may not have the strength to do this job." "After you leave me tonight, Jimmy," he went on, "I am going to pray. I am going to pray that God will help me, that He will give me the strength and the guidance to do this job and to do it right. I hope that you will pray for me, too, Jimmy."[1]

Roosevelt's doubts following this moving moment with his son could not have been assuaged in the immediate aftermath of the campaign: for the next week he was largely bed-ridden with a bad cold.

Yet while Roosevelt may have harbored his own reservations, the country had clearly been persuaded of his fitness. Thus had the "whispering campaign" been rendered silent for the time being. The silence, though, also extended to the president-elect during the four-month interregnum period, a silence, I argue, that heightened the expectation and drama of his inaugural address. That speech is significant in two respects. First, Roosevelt substituted the master metaphor of war for the campaign master metaphor of sickness and health, a change that entailed an active and rapid intervention rather than a passive and slow healing. Second, the metaphor of war helps to account for both the unprecedented legislative activity of the first one hundred days and for Roosevelt's justification thereof. The administration's principal goal during this period, as Raymond Moley makes clear, was to reinvigorate public confidence, a goal engendered perhaps more by the rhetorical force of massive, concerted legislative action than by presidential rhetoric.

Before examining the events that unfolded following the inaugural address, I first examine the Hoover administration's attempts in its final days to internationalize the New Deal, principally through the channel of war debts. I move next to the national banking crisis, an event whose resolution, Hoover believed, rested squarely on rhetorical means.

The Struggle for the New Deal

The arduous campaign exacted a toll on nearly everyone in the Roosevelt circle, but perhaps none more than Ray Moley. In less than ten months, Moley went from a distant associate to Roosevelt's closest and most-relied-upon subordinate. Perhaps this should have signaled to him that Roosevelt's mercurial temperament and his propensity toward administrative change were to be closely monitored, but in the halcyon days immediately following the campaign, Moley's lack of perspicacity can be forgiven. He had, after all, lived many a college professor's dream: instead of advising and teaching uninterested undergraduates, he was formulating policy, writing speeches, and advising the day-to-day activities of the president-elect. In a letter to Louis M. Howe, just four days after the election, he waxed philosophic: "It is not given to many to know the realization of their dreams. Some of them do not live long enough; with others, the thing just stays in the dream stage."[2]

Moley's status following the November 8 realignment was initially uncertain. This mattered little to Moley, as he retreated to Barnard College and "an interlude of infinite peace."[3] The respite lasted four days. Thus began a new campaign—a campaign for Roosevelt's ideological soul and the very possibilities of a New Deal. Once again, at Roosevelt's behest, Moley was at the center of the maelstrom.

The campaign began on Sunday, November 13, with a telegram from Herbert Hoover to the president-elect. The one-year moratorium on allied war debts was to expire on December 15, 1932. Both the English and the French Ambassadors to the United States relayed to Secretary of State Henry Stimson that payment would not be forthcoming. To make matters worse, they requested that their respective country's debt obligations be renegotiated and postponed. Hoover, having presided over the international economic machinations of 1931, figured that a default on the scheduled payments would do further harm to an already precarious economic situation. With this in mind, Hoover invited Roosevelt to the White House for a November 22 meeting.[4]

Hoover made his position clear at the meeting: he wanted to renegotiate the debt agreements for fear of international economic panic. The only thing standing in his way was congressional approval, since renegotiated debt agreements could not be rendered solely by executive agreement. But congressional approval was highly unlikely given its unambiguous position the previous year: war debts would not be canceled nor adjusted downwards. This was where Roosevelt entered the picture. Hoover calculated that if he could get Roosevelt to go along with debt renegotiations, the president-elect would be able to bring Congress into line. Moley was horrified by the thought, for he realized that a protracted disagreement with Congress would greatly endanger any chance for Roosevelt's domestic recovery program. Though Hoover and Secretary of the Treasury Ogden Mills were extremely persuasive at the meeting, Roosevelt politely declined their overtures; as a private citizen he claimed to have no authority in the matter.

On December 15, England paid the $95 million it owed. France defaulted, citing inability to pay. The war-debt situation, in other words, was far from resolved. Hoover, as was his penchant, did not give up. On December 17, he sent Roosevelt another telegram, again greatly troubling Moley. The note contained a new strategy to force Roosevelt's hand, one that linked war debts with the impending London Economic Conference and the ongoing Geneva Disarmament Conference. Hoover harbored private hopes that the United States could use the debts as a pivotal bargaining chip; specifically, he wanted England and other countries to go back on the gold standard. Hoover asked for Roosevelt's cooperation in selecting a delegation for the economic conference. Again Roosevelt abstained. Not only did he want no part of the joint delegation, but he also feared the congressional backlash for what looked like a willingness to trade war debts for other economic concessions. For the moment it appeared that Moley's priorities for domestic recovery had prevailed upon the president-elect.

This conclusion proved fleeting: in late December and early January, Roosevelt flirted with the same internationalism that nearly cost him the party's nomination. Two colleagues from his days in the Wilson administration—Stimson and Norman Davis—did the courting. Stimson, according to Moley, figured that the Hoover-Roosevelt disagreement stemmed more from a clash of personalities than ideologies. Thus, the secretary of state, with the aid of Davis, appealed to the president-elect in person.

On December 26, Davis urged Roosevelt to move the date of the economic conference up to April, a date that would have likely forced Roosevelt to appoint members to the delegation prior to his inauguration. More importantly, from Moley's perspective the conference would have overlapped with the beginning of the planned special session of Congress.[5] Davis's overtures appear to have worked: on December 27, Roosevelt would not even meet with Rex Tugwell, who had hoped to counter Davis's internationalism. In Moley's eyes, Davis and Stimson held "the upper hand."[6]

His belief grew exponentially following Stimson's five-hour luncheon with Roosevelt on January 9. Though little written material survives of their conversation, Stimson apparently tried to bring Roosevelt through the back door on international economics. He did so by getting Roosevelt to agree with the administration's position on a broad range of foreign policies. Roosevelt publicly expressed such agreement on January 11 and January 17.

To make matters worse for Moley, Roosevelt agreed to meet again with

Hoover, Mills, Davis, and Stimson on January 20. "To say that I was sick at heart over what was happening would be the epitome of understatement. I was also completely baffled."[7] To Moley's relief, Roosevelt invited him to join the deliberations. Though Moley had to spar with all four internationalists, his arguments convinced Roosevelt to stay the domestic course. But Moley's perceptions of the president-elect had changed drastically: for four weeks Roosevelt had imperiled nearly nine months of arduous labor. He had seriously entertained the idea of jumping ideological ship when the going got rough—and the point was not lost on Moley. But the going would get even rougher before March 4.

The Banking Crisis, Presidential "Assurance," and Presidential Silence

In addition to debt obligations, a second, and much more grave, crisis emerged during January and February. Unlike the debt crisis, this second crisis had a decidedly more rhetorical solution, or so Hoover believed. The antecedents of the banking crisis dated to a congressional decision to publicize all Reconstruction Finance Corporation (RFC) loans. The action, precipitated by revelations and accusations of political patronage, had a dangerous consequence: it gave a ringing, public declaration of a bank's insolvency, and insolvent banks make for nervous depositors. The tenuous banking situation worsened on February 14, when Michigan's governor, William Comstock, declared an eight-day bank holiday in response to revelations that Detroit's huge Union Guardian Trust Company could not meet withdrawal demands. Comstock's declaration, coupled with the ensuing uncertainty, sparked a run on banks throughout the country.[8]

Roosevelt was oblivious to the new crisis: he was just concluding a twelve-day Bahama fishing trip aboard Vincent Astor's 263-foot yacht, the *Nourmahal.* On February 15, as the yacht reached port in Miami, Moley informed Roosevelt of the burgeoning banking crisis as well as cabinet details. That same evening, following his brief extemporaneous remarks at Miami's Bay Front Park, the New Deal nearly died for the second time in less than a month. In the large crowd that night was thirty-three-year-old Giuseppe Zangara, an unemployed bricklayer who openly despised all elected public officials. Following his brief remarks from an open car, Chicago Mayor Anton Cermak—the same man responsible for packing the 1932 convention hall with pro-Al Smith delegates—chatted with the president-elect. Their conversation was punctuated by gunfire. Roosevelt was helpless. As his car began to move forward, he ordered the driver to go back, for on the ground was a bloody, ashen Cermak. He was lifted into Roosevelt's car, where the president-elect provided comfort and reassurance to the mortally wounded mayor.[9]

Moley was amazed, not because of Roosevelt's unflinching bravery, but because of his response to the botched attempt on his life. "I confess that I have never in my life seen anything more magnificent than Roosevelt's calm that night on the *Nourmahal*."[10] Ever the rhetorician, Moley quickly went into damage-control mode: "I made it very clear in my statement to the newspapers after examining him [Zangara] that I found no political ideas. I did this not only because it was true, but because I felt it was desirable to avoid, so far as possible, any hysteria on the subject of radicalism."[11] The short-term effect of Roosevelt's response to the attempt on his life was similar to the attempted Reagan assassination forty-eight years later: it greatly bolstered his personal prestige and his effectiveness as a national leader.[12] According to Frank Freidel, the assassination attempt "brought a surge of national confidence in him as had none of his other actions since the election."[13] Roosevelt badly needed the credibility boost since he had done nothing to counter rumors of intellectual superficiality; moreover, Hoover's publication of their correspondence revealed to many a callous, uncooperative side to the president-elect.

Roosevelt's uncooperativeness extended to the mounting bank crisis—the solution to which clearly illustrates the "cash value" of presidential rhetoric. Much to Hoover's credit, he could have easily withdrawn from political activity following his public repudiation. He chose instead to battle the forces of depression to the very end—partly out of his innate humanitarianism and partly out of his own ideological stubbornness. Both were expressed in his compelling, extremely confidential letter that the Secret Service delivered to Roosevelt on the evening of February 18.

Above all else, the letter exemplifies Hoover's belief that presidential rhetoric was a vital necessity to economic recovery. The belief had evolved considerably from its different iterations following the stock market crash. Collective confidence was no longer premised on strict allegiance to the nation's historical origins or a formal fulfillment of the Christian narrative. Rather, confidence emerged from a subtle combination of presidential speech and presidential policy—a combination so subtle as to be indistinguishable. Hoover's belief, as expressed in the letter, offers an intriguing extension of Roderick Hart's thesis that presidential speech is very important presidential action.[14] As Hoover expressed it to Roosevelt, presidential rhetoric carried the status of policy, which, in turn, would lead to the confidence so crucial to economic recovery:

> The major difficulty is the state of public mind—for there is a
> steadily degenerating confidence in the future which has reached
> the height of general alarm. I am convinced that a *very early state-*
> *ment* by you upon *two or three policies* of your administration would
> serve greatly to restore confidence and cause a resumption of the
> march of recovery.[15]

Later in the hastily handwritten ten-page letter, Hoover made the connection between public confidence, presidential rhetoric and policy more explicit.

> I therefore return to my suggestion at the beginning as to the desirabil-
> ity of clarifying the public mind on certain essentials which will give
> renewed confidence. It is obvious that as you will shortly be in position
> to make whatever *policies* you wish effective you are the only one who
> can give these *assurances.* Both the nature of the cause of public alarm
> and experience give such an *action* the prospect of success in turning
> the tide. I do not refer to *action* on all the causes of alarm but it would
> steady the country greatly if there could be prompt *assurance* (empha-
> sis added).

Policy and action were indistinguishable from presidential assurances, and
Hoover was quite specific about which ones would engender confidence:
promises not to inflate the currency; promises to balance the federal budget;
and promises to cease publication of RFC loans. These resolves, not coinci-
dentally, strongly suggested a Hooverian response on Roosevelt's part.[16]

Roosevelt received the letter on February 18 at 10:00 P.M. He promptly
passed it on to Moley, who, later that same evening, roundtabled it with the
president-elect and other advisors. Roosevelt's immediate reaction was not
to respond. Only with Hoover's second frantic letter ten days later was Roosevelt compelled to acknowledge the president's entreaties.[17] His brief,
three-paragraph response outwardly downplayed the importance of presidential rhetoric, asserting that the banking crisis was "so very deep-seated
that the fire is bound to spread in spite of anything that is done by way of
mere statements."[18] One paragraph later, Roosevelt equivocated: "These
announcements [of cabinet appointments] may have some effect on the
banking situation, but frankly I doubt if anything short of a fairly general
withdrawal of deposits can be prevented now." Roosevelt likely knew otherwise. If anyone could have rallied the nation's depositors to stem the hoarding epidemic, it was the president-elect. The historical evidence indicates
that Roosevelt had no inclination to respond; he was content not to prevent
the "general withdrawal of deposits."

As all twentieth-century presidents have experienced, even an adminis-
tration's most important secrets have a way of leaking. In late February,
Tugwell inadvertently provided the leak: he mistakenly confided in James H.
Rand, Jr., the president of the Remington-Rand Company, at a luncheon.
Shortly afterwards, Rand phoned Hoover's press secretary, Ted Joslin, who
relayed the conversation in a memorandum to the president. "Professor
Tugwell, advisor to F.R., had lunch with me. He said they were fully aware
of the bank situation and that it would undoubtedly collapse in a few days,
which would thus place the responsibility in the lap of President Hoover. He
said we should worry about anything excepting rehabilitating the country
after March 4th."[19] Predictably, Hoover was furious: "I can say emphati-
cally that he breathes with infamous politics devoid of every atom of patriotism. Mr. Tugwell would project millions of people into hideous losses for a
Roman holiday."[20] Roosevelt, John T. Flynn reports, "was thinking of the

political advantage in a complete banking disaster under Hoover."[21] Though we will never likely know the full account of Roosevelt's motivations, suffice it to say that his protracted public silence reinforced, ironically, the Hooverian belief that presidential speech might radically alter economic reality.

As inauguration day neared, the banking crisis worsened. As gold withdrawals increased and many states declared bank holidays, officials at the Federal Reserve and the Treasury Department urged upon the president-elect a drastic course of action: proclaim a nationwide bank holiday. In addition, Hoover wanted Roosevelt to invoke a remnant of World War I—the Trading with the Enemy Act—in order to curtail depletion of the nation's dwindling gold reserves.

Roosevelt politely declined both requests; there was no need for action on his part—rhetorical or otherwise. His silence, though, appears not to have worked against him; in fact, it served to heighten the expectations and hopes of a nation searching desperately for a reason to believe. Secrecy, as Edwin Black notes, can function to preserve one's political and economic capital; in a word, secrecy can augment a leaderly ethos, particularly with a credulous audience.[22]

The drama that Roosevelt's pre-inaugural silence engendered was expressed by a zealous and optimistic press. Kyle D. Palmer noted, "The words and views of few men in history have been awaited as eagerly or as universally as the brief address which . . . Roosevelt will deliver."[23] The *Pittsburgh Press*, echoing Roosevelt's November 7 address at Poughkeepsie, wrote, "he has become a symbol of hope, burning in the darkness that has surrounded us and which has made so many of us afraid."[24] R. F. Paine picked up on Roosevelt's July 2 and November 5 call to arms: "We are coming, Franklin Roosevelt, a hundred million strong! . . . Close ranks and closely follow the commander whither he draws to lead, and give him cheer and the strength of united effort."[25] William Grimes was in lockstep: "Americans of all parties are pinning their hopes of a better order of things upon him and his Administration. That by itself is worth an army on his side."[26] Editors from the *New York Times*, a group not given to hyperbole, proclaimed Roosevelt's inaugural to be "the most important inaugural in the history of our country."[27] Two days later they spoke of the millions of Americans who believed that their hardships would "be mitigated or removed by the mere fact of Mr. Roosevelt's entering the White House."[28] They continued, "no President of the United States ever came to greater opportunities amid so great an outpouring of popular trust and hope. . . . Perhaps never before has the public so intensely craved a leader in the White House."

By today's standards, the public's willingness to embrace unreservedly a man they hardly even knew seems remarkable. Will Rogers spoke for many: "The whole country is with him. Even if what he does is wrong they are with him, just so he does something."[29] Through his protracted silence and his calm yet buoyant demeanor, Roosevelt paved the way for the success of his inaugural address and the soon-to-be famous-first one hundred days. Thus, the confidence that so many would express following the speech was sown, in part, from seeds that he had strategically planted during the interregnum period.

Inaugurating Warfare

As with many revered orations, no small mythology attends the composition of Roosevelt's first inaugural address. According to popular legend— one fomented largely by James MacGregor Burns—Roosevelt crafted the message on February 27 in a divinely inspired evening at Hyde Park. Two days later he added the soon-to-be-famous aphorism about fear, based on his contemplative reading of Thoreau.[30] In actuality, Roosevelt's involvement with its creation was minimal: Moley composed portions of the text in consultation with Roosevelt throughout the fall and winter. Shortly before March 4, Louis Howe added the opening paragraph.[31]

Even before his presidency began, Roosevelt was looking to the historical future and his own carefully cultivated legacy. Chronicling the construction of that legacy was Moley's personal assistant, Celeste Jedel. She documents in a diary entry of February 28, 1933, "When he [Roosevelt] had finished copying the first page, Raymond [Moley] walked over, took what he [Moley] had written and threw it in the fire—and did this again after the second page. After that F.R. threw away the pages as he wrote them."[32] Moley, though, corrected Jedel's account: "I threw the whole thing [Moley's draft] in the fire at end of copying."

Many years later, as he tried to unearth the facts of the composition of the address, biographer Frank Freidel wrote to Moley, "He [Roosevelt] refers to 'his first draft'—leaving out of his statement any allusions to your earlier drafts, as though they did not count as speech drafts but were rather the materials out of which he prepared *his* first draft."[33] Roosevelt's motives, according to Freidel, were rather transparent: "Roosevelt wanted to think of the First Inaugural as entirely his own handiwork—that he could be as adroit when he put pen to paper as Woddrow [*sic*] Wilson or Winston Churchill."

Two ironies inhere in the text. First, despite its revered place in the pantheon of great American speeches, Roosevelt expressed some antipathy for presidential rhetoric. Mere "exhortation . . . for restored confidence" had failed the bankers and financiers.[34] Moreover, "there are many ways in which it [increasing employment] can be helped, but it can never be helped merely by talking about it. We must act and act quickly" (13). On this point, the similarity between Hoover and Roosevelt is unmistakable: at the outset of their terms both deprecated presidential rhetoric and its importance for economic recovery; and both also recognized the importance of public confidence.

Second, despite being a foundational text for the modern welfare state, contemporary ideological critics would find it difficult to square with their leftist project. As Halford Ross Ryan notes, the language that Roosevelt employed was not dissimilar from the new German Chancellor, Adolf Hitler.[35] With words and phrases such as "discipline," "duty," "sacrifice," "discipline and direction under leadership," "stern performance of duty," "broad Executive power," "changes in [Constitutional] emphasis and arrangement," "common discipline," and "loyal army," only an authoritarian rightist might today find solace in the text.

Both ironies provide important critical prompts—prompts that pertain to Hoover and Roosevelt's antecedent rhetoric and the immediate historical moment. A reading of the inaugural that brackets either one overlooks many important nuances.

One of the most notable features of the speech is its emphasis on action, which, in turn, is informed by the months preceding the speech. Roosevelt had hoped to pass major reform measures—particularly agricultural reforms—during the lame-duck session of the seventy-second Congress. Yet during the "most harrowing four months of the depression," Congress failed to pass any major legislation; partisan quarrels rather than bipartisan recovery measures marked the session.[36] The public's demand for action was not lost on Moley: in a February 2 memorandum outlining the inaugural address, he wrote and underlined, "*Action needed.*"[37] Action, according to Moley, was pivotal for a public revival of confidence. "The people of the nation didn't understand what we were doing. But they were convinced that a lot of things were being done. And that alone gave them the spirit to carry on."[38]

Not surprisingly, "action" is a key term in the text. Roosevelt stated, "this Nation asks for action, and action now," and later, "We must act and act quickly." Roosevelt's emphasis on action was augmented by a "program of action" in which he foreshadowed his administration's legislative agenda during the first one hundred days. The program, moreover, would be put forward swiftly: "I shall presently urge upon a new Congress, in special session, detailed measures for their fulfillment, and I shall seek the immediate assistance of the several states" (12–13). Things were "being done" even as Roosevelt spoke.

His action, though, was not unilateral. He strategically enlisted the people in a "great army"—one that was not stationary, but would "go forward" and "move as a trained and loyal army" (14). Roosevelt was again walking, marching, and leading a great nation forward into battle. The appeal to action worked well within the framework of war. It worked poorly with the master metaphor of Roosevelt's campaign rhetoric—that of sickness and health. A sick or suffering nation could not simultaneously be an active, vigorous nation. Sickness required rest, passivity, convalescence, and time—in a word, inactivity. Perhaps because of the incongruity of key terms, nearly all references to sickness and health were excised from the final draft.[39] Roosevelt, in fact, stated bluntly that the distress "comes from no failure of substance. We are stricken by no plague of locusts" (11).

Economic warfare was not a novel theme; as Leuchtenburg notes, "Hoover resorted constantly to the imagery of war to describe the Depression."[40] But Roosevelt's economic war differed in several respects, one of which included the war's vicinity: instead of waging an international war, Roosevelt consigned the enemy to U.S. soil.[41] "Our international trade relations, though vastly important, are in point of time and necessity secondary to the establishment of a sound national economy" (14). The enemy was thus localized, and the villain was much more immediate for a people craving action. For the first time the war had clear parameters and a leader unwilling to surrender responsibility to the nation's bankers—a group whom Roosevelt collectively derided as "money changers" (12).

But Roosevelt's war differed from Hoover's in another respect. Hoover never followed through completely on the metaphor, one that stipulated active executive leadership and broad executive powers. Unlike his predecessor, Roosevelt would not be dilatory with his definitions: the situation mandated an active response, one that he would take to new heights during his administration's first one hundred days.

Roosevelt's emphasis on domestic recovery, however, departed sharply from his campaign rhetoric; more specifically, he had repeatedly claimed that national recovery depended, in large measure, on reciprocal tariff agreements. Perhaps the boycott of war debt payments by several nations had led Roosevelt to change his tune.

A second inconsistency also has antecedents in Roosevelt's campaign rhetoric—dating to his agricultural speech at Topeka and his railroad address at Salt Lake City:

> The basic thought that guides these specific means of national recovery is not narrowly nationalistic. It is the insistence . . . upon the interdependence of the various elements in and parts of the United States—a recognition of the old and permanently important manifestation of the American spirit of the pioneer. It is the way to recovery. It is the immediate way (14).

"It" is unclear; perhaps more importantly, "it" could not be reconciled by an appeal to interdependence on one hand and to individualism on the other. This is not a trifling point, especially given that "it" refers to the way to recovery.

But one area in which Roosevelt remained consistent with his campaign rhetoric was in the sphere of confidence—specifically the link between honesty and confidence. Roosevelt's famous aphorism on fear comes into sharper relief when read against the backdrop of his campaign speeches at Columbus, Ohio, and Sea Girt, New Jersey. The nation needed no longer to be afraid of fear because they had a leader who would not obscure the economic reality—however grim:

> I am certain that my fellow Americans expect that on my induction into the Presidency I will address them with a *candor* and a decision which the present situation of our nation impels. This is preeminently the time to speak the *truth,* the *whole truth,* frankly and boldly. Nor need we shirk from *honestly* facing conditions in our country today. . . . So, first of all, let me assert my firm belief that the only thing we have to fear is fear itself—nameless, unreasoning, unjustified terror which paralyzes needed efforts to convert retreat into advance (11; emphasis added).

Roosevelt's "firm belief" takes the form of a conclusion that "naturally" follows from given premises. His professed fear of fear is thus rendered unjustified; honesty and truth telling, as mentioned in the two earlier campaign speeches, would eradicate it. Perhaps words were important after all.

Yet Roosevelt's campaign rhetoric allows for a different interpretation. In his seminal work on the New Deal, Leuchtenburg states that "in declaring there was nothing to fear but fear, Roosevelt had minted no new platitude; Hoover had said the same thing repeatedly for three years."[42] Not quite. Roosevelt told the nation precisely the opposite: to fear fear. That the fear to be feared was "nameless" had important ramifications, especially in light of previous speeches. Fear that resided in the nonsymbolic realm ("nameless") implied that it could not be seen nor interrogated. Vision (hence naming) was imperative, since "when there is no vision the people perish" (12). Thus, perhaps "nameless" fear was indeed to be feared.

Talking about the effects of rhetoric is typically accompanied by several qualifiers—such are its many perils—but in the case of Roosevelt's first inaugural address, few if any are needed. The press expressed both a seemingly universal approbation for the speech and a declaration of restored confidence. Robert L. Vann, in an article titled "Confidence Has Arrived," announced that "confidence literally arose from its hiding place and is today a living actuality."[43] Roosevelt would have heartily approved of the imagery. Editors from the *Atlanta Constitution* wrote, "No more vital utterance was ever made by a president of the United States. . . . Never in the long list of presidential utterances has there ever been one more appealing in force, nor more inspiring in its power to create confidence."[44] Many, like the *Pittsburgh Press,* likened the speech to Lincoln's Gettysburg address: "His inaugural speech—one of the most dramatic speeches in American history—may well be the Gettysburg Address of the war against depression, marking the high water mark."[45] The speech itself, quite apart from any legislation, might potentially prove decisive to the war. This potentiality was expressed, perhaps wistfully, in the *Wall Street Journal,* which predicted that if the inaugural address were to restore confidence, then "emergency action might be unnecessary and conditions would be improved."[46]

Ray Moley could not have been more pleased by the nation's declaration of confidence, hope, and unflagging devotion to the new commander in chief. At one level he felt enormous pride that the words that had captivated and reinvigorated an entire nation were largely his own. More importantly, as a student of American history, he realized that an important corner had already been turned. Recalling the depression of the 1890s, Moley stated, "I had learned then that . . . the American economy had recovered because of the simple fact that a powerful nation regained its confidence in itself."[47] In 1933 the American people had confidence in their leader, and Roosevelt hoped to parlay this support into wide-ranging legislative expression. Roosevelt remained true to his campaign promises: "while the restoration of public confidence was imperative, certain remedial legislation and corrective measures were long overdue."[48] Confidence and legislation, though, were by no means separate entities; they were—as the first one hundred days indicate—symbiotic.

The Banking Crisis as Confidence Game

Moley had hoped that such "remedial and corrective measures" could begin in April so that the administration could systematically develop its legislative program. These hopes were dashed, though, by Roosevelt's noncommittal response to the banking crisis during the interregnum period. But Roosevelt's response was not symptomatic of indecision; he and his intimates knew precisely the course he wished to pursue—after he was sworn in as president. The eight-day banking crisis that ensued was a masterful rhetorical performance, one conjured up principally by Moley. He was not alone, though: he leaned heavily on Hoover's Treasury secretary and undersecretary, Mills and Arthur Ballantine, and he also enlisted Roosevelt's Treasury secretary, Will Woodin.

On Monday, March 6, Roosevelt did precisely what Hoover had urged him to do on March 2 and 3—namely, to issue a proclamation declaring a banking holiday and suspending gold and silver exports. Meanwhile, he also convened a conference of the nation's leading bankers on March 5, and he called Congress into a special session to begin on March 9. The administration assumed that the conferees would produce a temporary emergency banking bill for Congress by the week's end.

Late Monday night, after two frustrating days with the bankers, Moley and Woodin outlined the essentials for a banking bill. They were, as Moley recollected, thoroughly rhetorical: "we were facing a problem of public psychology more acutely than we were facing a problem of finance—that every step taken must be tested less on the basis of its ultimate desirability from a financial point of view than on the basis of its immediate effect in restoring confidence."[49] In order to restore confidence in the nation's banking system, the two men devised six criteria for emergency legislation: move swiftly; use conventional banking methods; reopen as many banks as possible; ignore the advice of perceived left-wing advisors; make a "tremendous gesture" in the realm of government economy; and have Roosevelt make a radio appeal for public confidence.[50] Banking solvency, as both men clearly recognized, was contingent on public perceptions of what Roosevelt said and did.

The confidence game went into effect immediately. Woodin, with the help of Mills, drafted a "profoundly conservative" banking bill.[51] The measure gave Roosevelt powers over foreign currency exchange, banking institutions, and domestic and international movements of gold and silver. It also called for the Federal Reserve to issue notes based on a bank's assets. Thus would government-backed currency be readily available to most depositors. Last, solvent banks would be reopened by the Treasury Department, while the RFC would aid banks that needed reorganization.[52] Even though most Representatives had neither seen nor read the bill, it passed the House in thirty-eight minutes. A more cautious Senate passed the bill after a few hours. Roosevelt signed the bill at 8:45 P.M.—less than nine hours after it had been introduced. The congressional gridlock characteristic of the interregnum period was shattered in one afternoon. Moley's plan, though, was just getting underway.

On the same day that he signed the emergency banking bill into law, Roosevelt extended the banking holiday until Monday morning, March 13. On Friday, March 10, he made an important rhetorical gesture to ensure that public confidence would accompany the end of the banking holiday. He announced in a brief message to Congress that his administration sought "drastic retrenchment" and "immediate economy" in the federal government's expenditures.[53] More specifically, he asked for executive authority to cut veterans' benefits and to cut the salaries of federal employees. "National recovery," Roosevelt exaggerated, "depends upon it."

The timing of the message and its call for economy were not arbitrary; it was all part of the confidence game. A balanced budget was intimately linked with the federal government's credit, and, since the federal government would be instrumental in reopening the banks, confidence in its credit was imperative.[54] Roosevelt noted that "one of the most important factors in the decreased public confidence of these early days was the continued lack of balance of the normal budget during the preceding three years."

Everything was in place for Moley's grand climax: a conservative bill had been drafted and almost unanimously endorsed by Congress, and Roosevelt had made the requisite "tremendous gesture" in the direction of government economy and fiscal orthodoxy. The president concluded a week in which "capitalism was saved" with his first fireside chat.[55] The speech was drafted, ironically, by a member of the Hoover administration, which Roosevelt had done so much to shun the previous week.[56]

The relatively short radio address is frustrating for a critic wishing to mine the text for subtle meanings and for resonances with earlier messages. The speech is clear, simple, unadorned—and therein lies much of its suasive force. The role that Roosevelt assumed was familiar—that of teacher and translator of complex economic phenomenon. His intent was simply to "talk for a few minutes with the people of the United States about banking," to explain banking "for the benefit of the average citizen."[57] He then proceeded to narrate why the banking crisis had occurred and what he and Congress had done about it. He added that, once opened, the banks would "take care of all needs" and that "it is safer to keep your money in a reopened bank than under the mattress" (64). Roosevelt concluded the eight-day crisis with a most appropriate appeal:

> There is an element in the readjustment of our financial system more important than currency, more important than gold, and that is the confidence of the people. Confidence and courage are the essentials of success in carrying out our plan. You people must have faith; you must not be stampeded by rumors or guesses. Let us unite in banishing fear. We have provided the machinery to restore our financial system; it is up to you to support and make it work. It is your problem no less than it is mine. Together we cannot fail (65).

Roosevelt was almost certain of success. Even though he made no references to warfare in the text, the army that he had constituted in November and the troops that he had mobilized for discipline and duty on March 4 were eager to follow. Employees of the May Company aptly expressed the prevailing patriotic sentiment: "Today . . . whatever our political beliefs . . . we are Americans all . . . marching shoulder to shoulder towards a brighter tomorrow."[58] Americans were "ready to accept virtually any plan he decrees as the best way out."[59] Given the public's nearly sycophantic support, the speech was an unequivocal success. As biographer Davis notes, "Of all the dozens of 'fireside chats' that would ultimately be made, none was more hugely successful, more utterly effective of its specific purpose than the first of them."[60] Unlike most speeches, the effects were quite palpable: on Monday, deposits far exceeded withdrawals; gold flowed back into Federal Reserve banks, the Federal Reserve notes were largely unused; and the New York Stock Exchange experienced its largest one-day rise in several years. "The effect of the speech," as Rexford G. Tugwell noted, was indeed "magical."[61] The confidence game had worked; in fact, it worked so well that Roosevelt, in consultation with his advisors, chose not to adjourn the special session. The decision would prove most fortuitous.

The "Scene" of War and the First 100 Days

In an article titled "The New Deal and the Analogue of War," historian William Leuchtenburg begins thus, "The metaphors a nation employs reveal much about how it perceives reality. The unconscious choice of symbols bares the bedrock of its beliefs."[62] The symbol or metaphor that animated the Roosevelt administration's first one hundred days, he argues, was that of war—specifically the nation's domestic mobilization before and during World War I. "The war was remembered as a time of movement," he notes, and Roosevelt "sought to restore national confidence by evoking the mood of wartime."[63] One could therefore expect Roosevelt to translate a national crisis such as war into the need for rapid legislative action.

Kenneth Burke's work on grammatical categories of motivation takes Leuchtenburg's observations a step further. Burke's "scene-act" ratio figures prominently in both an explanation and an understanding of the administration's actions during the first one hundred days. By labeling the situation as analogous to war (scene), swift action was imperative (act). Action, in other words, is motivated by characteristics that inhere in a scene. The scene or situation thus becomes the dominant variable in influencing an act or a series of acts. Burke states,

> The scene-act ratio can be applied in two ways. It can be applied deterministically in statements that a certain policy had to be adopted in a certain situation, or it may be applied in hortatory statements to the effect that a certain policy should be adopted in conformity with the situation.[64]

As I will attempt to illustrate, Burke's scene-act ratio aids our understanding of the first one hundred days in two ways: it helps account for both the volume of legislation and the frequently contradictory emphases thereof, and it aids our understanding of Roosevelt's rhetoric, particularly his second fireside chat, in a period during which Roosevelt was criticized by some for usurping congressional authority. Perhaps more important, though, is the extent to which the action taken during the first one hundred days transformed, in turn, the scene itself. Wars are ultimately won or lost (new scene) by the people's response, not by legislative fiat—a crucial point given that the battleground hinged so decisively on the ephemeral ground of confidence.

Roosevelt's war had a most propitious beginning with the success of the emergency banking bill, the first fireside chat, and the public's favorable response. The decision not to adjourn the special session was obvious: Roosevelt and his advisors agreed to capitalize on popular and congressional sentiment.[65] As Moley records, the successful resolution of the banking crisis "excited a vast expectancy," and, always the master of timing, Roosevelt went ahead with his administration's still inchoate legislative agenda.[66] That agenda was initially outlined by Adolf Berle in a memorandum to Moley dated November 10, 1932. Berle's memo would serve as the blueprint for the historic first one hundred days.[67] The motivating principle underlying the agenda was directly informed by a campaign theme—that of interdependence. Action was thus necessary "on many fronts at the same time."[68]

The three-and-a-half-month assault that ensued was relentless: Roosevelt sent fifteen congressional messages recommending legislation, and fifteen pieces of major legislation were signed by the close of the special session on June 16, 1933. What follows is a cursory look at the legislation that the seventy-third Congress passed and Roosevelt signed.[69]

On March 20, just ten days after his message to Congress, Roosevelt signed into law the "Act to Maintain the Credit of the United States Government." The bill gave him unilateral powers to cut nearly $500 million, all of which came from two sources: veterans' benefits and the salaries of federal employees. The former cuts were so severe that Roosevelt eventually capitulated to congressional and veteran pressure. The "Bonus Marcher" debacle of the previous summer, and the political fallout thereof, were still fresh in Roosevelt's mind. It should be remembered that this measure was part of his larger strategy to insure a successful reopening of the nation's banks. Removed from this context, the measure makes little sense, especially in light of its deflationary character and the administration's extravagant spending policies.

But emergency banking legislation and cuts in federal spending were not the sort of proactive bills that Roosevelt sought. At his third press conference on March 15, Roosevelt said that his administration had "done nothing on the constructive side."[70] This was remedied on the following day as he urged Congress to pass the Agricultural Adjustment Act (AAA). In his brief, five-paragraph message Roosevelt emphasized the scenic imperative for the bill: "I tell you frankly that it is a new and untrod path, but I tell you with equal frankness that an *unprecedented condition calls for* the trial of new means to rescue agriculture."[71]

The "new means" principally involved limiting agricultural surplus through a plan called Domestic Allotment. The plan—one that Roosevelt hinted at during his speech at Topeka—effectively paid farmers to reduce their output, which caused prices and purchasing power to rise. Less well understood and publicized was the means of payment—a $1 billion processing tax that would eventually be passed on to the consumer. The bill sailed through the House but ran into resistance in the more conservative Senate.

Given that the overriding goal of the farm bill was to increase agricultural prices, several senators wanted to expedite the inflation by monetary means—specifically by remonetizing silver. Roosevelt wanted inflation, but on his own terms. The measure he eventually accepted was an amended version of the Thomas Amendment—a measure that granted him great leeway in fixing the price of the dollar. Thus, under Title II of the farm bill, the nation effectively bid adieu to the conservatives' holy writ, the gold standard.[72] Roosevelt signed the measure into law on May 12.

Six days after his farm message, Roosevelt issued another congressional request, this time for unemployment relief. He asked specifically that a Civilian Conservation Corps (CCC) be created in order to employ 250,000 men in the areas of forestry, soil erosion, and flood control. The stated mission of the CCC was to preserve the nation's natural resources while also giving jobs to unemployed young men. But the measure also functioned to redistribute the population away from urban congestion and vice "out into healthful surroundings," a measure that Roosevelt had advocated as governor.[73] Public works projects did not lack for support at the depression's height: the bill became law in ten days.

In the same message, Roosevelt urged Congress to create the Federal Emergency Relief Administration (FERA), whose purpose would be to distribute federal grants to needy states and localities. But, like Hoover, he was reluctant to give "direct relief to individuals except through provision for work."[74] His reservations were clearly expressed upon signing FERA into law. "I want to make it very clear to citizens in every community that the Bill I have just signed . . . does not absolve States and local communities of their responsibility to see that the necessities of life are assured their citizens who are in destitute circumstances."[75] The admonition was by this time familiar: the federal government was only a reluctant participant in direct relief.

Eight days later, on March 29, Roosevelt asked Congress to adopt a measure to regulate and supervise the sale of new securities — one of the administration's first moves in the direction of permanent reform, as opposed to emergency relief measures. The bill called for the "full publicity and information" of new securities sold in interstate commerce. "Honest dealing in securities," he argued, would "bring back public confidence."[76] The appeal to honesty was attributable, in part, to the Senate Banking and Currency Committee's often-shocking investigation of banking and investing practices, an investigation that ran concurrent with the special session.[77]

On April 3, Roosevelt offered another helping hand to farmers, this time in the form of mortgage relief. The measure was designed to relieve many farmers of the mortgage obligations incurred when land values had been much higher. Given the vast agricultural surpluses, farm foreclosures would have benefitted agriculture in the long run. But Roosevelt was clearly against forced liquidation, just as he was opposed to forced migration into congested urban areas. On April 13, he asked that similar mortgage assistance be extended to all financially strapped homeowners. Both measures passed: the Emergency Farm Mortgage Act on May 12 and the Home Owners Loan Corporation Act on June 13.

Sandwiched between the mortgage relief requests was a bill whose origins dated to World War I. On April 10, Roosevelt asked Congress to pass legislation to create the Tennessee Valley Authority (TVA), a corporation to be owned and operated by the federal government. Roosevelt needed little persuasion from Nebraska Senator George Norris, whose efforts on behalf of regional planning and land development had been frustrated by both Coolidge and Hoover.

From his earliest days as governor, Roosevelt had recognized the St. Lawrence River's tremendous potential as a plentiful source of cheap public power. He sensed similar potential along the Tennessee River, particularly since much of the physical plant had been erected at Muscle Shoals, Alabama, during World War I. But there was more than just an opportunity for cheap public power: TVA would involve "the wide fields of flood control, soil erosion, afforestation, elimination from agricultural use of marginal lands, and distribution and diversification of industry."[78] One of the ironies of his brief message to Congress is the incongruous imagery: he likened the administration's most overtly socialist measure to "a return to the spirit and vision of the pioneer" (122–23). Roosevelt signed the bill into law on May 18.

The granddaddy of relief and recovery bills, like some of the legislation proposed during the first one hundred days, was accidental. What would become the National Industrial Recovery Act (NIRA) took shape as a direct response to what Roosevelt and Moley perceived as misguided attempts at industrial recovery. More specifically, on April 6, the Senate passed Hugo Black's "spread the work" bill. The measure was designed to reduce the forty-eight-hour work week to thirty hours and, thereby, to force industry to hire more workers to maintain production schedules. Roosevelt and his advisors viewed the bill in zero-sum terms: without a corresponding increase in wages, the nation's purchasing power would remain constant.

With the bill's impending passage in the House, Roosevelt needed a substitute bill quickly. He turned initially to his Labor Secretary, Frances Perkins, who proposed a shorter work week and federally supervised fair-wage boards for each industry. The industrial outcry over this proposal was vehement, and, as Moley recounts, Roosevelt was "aghast at the commotion it caused."[79] Roosevelt turned to his assistant secretary of state,[80] but Moley was overburdened with the Thomas Amendment and negotiations with the London delegation to the upcoming economic conference. So, on April 25, Moley turned over all of his files on industrial recovery to Hugh Johnson, a former Brains Truster whose close proximity to former War Industries Board Chairman Bernard Baruch proved invaluable to the administration. As Leuchtenburg notes, NIRA "rested squarely on the War Industries Board example."[81]

The administration's bill eventually emerged from a series of conflicting plans and ideas. On May 17, Roosevelt unveiled the far-reaching bill to Congress under the aegis of "a great cooperative movement throughout all industry in order to obtain wide reemployment, to shorten the working week, to pay a decent wage for the shorter week and to prevent unfair competition and disastrous overproduction."[82] Here was a mouthful, the single greatest peacetime economic reform in the nation's history.

The means to such ambitious ends were two-fold. Title I of the bill declared a national emergency, a "scenic" imperative that warranted partial suspension of the nation's anti-trust laws. Each major industry, with the federal government as supervisor, would draw up codes to regulate employment, wages, prices and production schedules. The idea of intra-industry cooperation was not altogether different from that embodied in Hoover's Trade Associations of the 1920s.[83]

Title II represented a major compromise on Roosevelt's part. The powerful senatorial triumvirate of Robert La Follette, Edward Costigan, and Robert Wagner pushed for a massive $5 billion public works program—a push that had originated in the fall of 1931. Roosevelt was averse to the idea; he wanted a public works program capitalized at no more than $1 billion. But he also realized that this was not time for fiscal scruples: the Senate would have likely rejected the bill without a large public-works provision. As was his penchant, Roosevelt compromised. Title II of NIRA called for a $3.3 billion public works program. Roosevelt, though, did exact some measure of revenge on his free-spending ideological brethren: he appointed the miserly interior head, Harold Ickes, to administer the funds.[84] Less than one month after the bill was introduced, Roosevelt concluded the historic one hundred days by signing NIRA into law on June 16.[85]

The scene of warfare that he helped to create in November and March was, legislatively speaking, most fecund. But Roosevelt's war was not fought solely with legislative armaments. Recovery or victory (new scene) had less to do with legislation than with how the public perceived the bevy of bills. The rhetorical force of rapid, legislative action was not lost on Moley or Roosevelt. As Moley recalled:

> Underneath all was a determination to achieve a psychological effect upon the country by the appearance of "action on many fronts." Roosevelt believed that the very quantity of the legislation passed would inspire wonder and confidence. Nearly everyone who participated and knew what was happening realized that these measures per se could not promote economic recovery. They would, however, create a climate in which natural forces would reassert themselves.[86]

The "natural force" was collective belief—and this collective belief, Moley stated, was enough to alter the scene. "Few could understand what Congress was doing. But their [the public's] source of news told them that a lot of things were being done that had not been done before. That, we believed, sufficed."[87] Moley elaborated on the rhetorical (hence economic) efficacy of the one hundred days in a later symposium:

> There was so much legislation in so short a time that the public, without knowing much about any of these measures, was inspirited to believe that something was happening and that that provided the stimulus to confidence which carried us through into the first phase of recovery. In other words, if you give people the idea that something good for them is happening, it doesn't matter much what it is; they'll start working, and they'll start spending, and things will start rolling.[88]

Roosevelt's skillful use, and eventual transformation, of the scene was not lost on the nation's "newspaper of record." The *New York Times* editorialized the conclusion of the one hundred days thus:

> With instant determination and great boldness he sought to render the very emergency of the nation, the wreck of business and fear for the future, the means of establishing and leading both Congress and the country into a more hopeful and resolute temper. In a true sense the public disaster was transmuted into an official triumph for him.[89]

The reaction of the *Times* was not idiosyncratic. Unlike his predecessor, Roosevelt enjoyed, at least initially, extremely favorable press relations due in part to his accessibility and informality. His press relations, in turn, only helped to foster the "wonder and confidence" vital to economic recovery. But Roosevelt would not allow the press to do all of his rhetorical bidding, as witnessed by his activities during the first one hundred days.

Presidential Rhetoric and the First 100 Days

Were we to take biographer Nathan Miller at face value, we would be seriously misled as to the quantity of Roosevelt's speechmaking during the first one hundred days. Miller, in attempting to convey the hyperbolic climate of the period, claims that Roosevelt gave ten "major speeches."[90] Only if we designated his brief greeting to the Daughters of the American Revolution and his impromptu remarks to the Future Farmers of America as "major" could we arrive at such an inflated figure. The truth of the matter is that Roosevelt delivered only three major speeches during the first one hundred days—only one of which was given after the banking crisis. But what he said in both "major" and "minor" speeches and press statements sheds further light on how Roosevelt conceptualized economic recovery and how he attempted to bring it about.

Following the banking crisis, Roosevelt gave his first speech pertaining to economics only on May 4. Roughly two weeks before he went public with NIRA, he addressed one of the citadels of economic orthodoxy, the U.S. Chamber of Commerce—an organization highly suspicious of federal economic interventions. Viewed in the shadow of NIRA, Roosevelt's almost obeisant posturing to the organization, communicated in the form of "requests," is farcical. His first two requests would have brought a smile to Hoover's otherwise frequent frown, for they were nearly identical to his requests following the stock market crash—namely, to increase wages and to maintain industrial order.[91] Little did his auditors realize that such "requests" would soon have the force of federal law. Roosevelt's third request was decidedly less material in nature—a request to "view" the national economy "in terms of the whole rather than in terms of the unit." Such a broad-based vision was essential "for a well-rounded national recovery." Roosevelt's combination of two campaign themes—vision and organicism—were well-suited to NIRA, a measure modeled on a look back to the War Industries Board and a measure that sought intra- and inter-industry interdependence.

Three days later, on May 7, Roosevelt delivered his second fireside chat. As he began signing bills into law, several of which gave him the authority "to overturn almost every basic factor in American life," some observers expressed either concern or disapproval.[92] The nation, after all, had "never seen such a display of Executive audacity and usurpation."[93] Thus, Roosevelt used this much anticipated speech not simply "to tell you about what we have been doing and what we are planning to do," but also to justify his administration's legislative actions.[94]

To no one's surprise, Roosevelt invoked the scene of warfare to substantiate his actions—a scene seemingly incongruous with Hoover's decidedly rhetorical approach:

> It was clear that mere appeals from Washington for confidence and the mere lending of more money to shaky institutions [Hoover's responses] could not stop this downward course. A prompt program applied as quickly as possible seemed to me not only justified but imperative to our *national security*. . . . The members of Congress realized that the methods of *normal times* had to be replaced in the *emergency* by measures which were suited to the serious and *pressing requirements of the moment*. There was no actual surrender of power, Congress still retained its constitutional authority and no one has the slightest desire to change the balance of these powers (161; emphasis added).

The scene called for action, not mere rhetoric. Perhaps more importantly, Roosevelt's motives derived from scenic factors and not selfish ambitions for dictatorial powers. As Burke notes, "one may deflect attention from the criticism of personal motives by deriving an act or attitude not from traits of the agent but from the nature of the situation."[95]

While the scene was the dominant factor in influencing his actions, he took the additional step of defining the consequences of such action: "It is wholly wrong to call the measures that we have taken Government control of farming, industry, and transportation. It is rather a partnership between government and farming and industry and transportation . . . a partnership in planning, and a partnership to see that the plans are carried out" (164). But Roosevelt went one step further to mollify his critics: he labeled the impending NIRA legislation a "conservative measure" (163).

The scene, in sum, justified both the measures that he had taken and the unprecedented authority such measures delegated to him. Roosevelt's emphasis on scene also helps account for why he gave so few major speeches during the first one hundred days. The situation, as he defined it in March, required immediate and far-reaching legislative action more than presidential rhetoric. "I am not going to indulge in issuing proclamations of over-enthusiastic assurance," he intoned, "we cannot ballyhoo ourselves back to prosperity" (164). The irony is again unmistakable: Roosevelt forswears presidential rhetoric while Hoover often embraces it as an instrument of policy. The scripts again appeared to be in the wrong hands.

Yet for all of Roosevelt's attempted distancing from his predecessor, his final statement of the first one hundred days brings our inquiry full-circle. Upon signing NIRA, he issued a relatively lengthy press statement. In it, he spoke of a "united drive," a "move forward promptly," "those who bravely go forward," the country's "look forward," a "great national movement back to work," a "Government-inspired movement," and "industry which now moves forward promptly in this united drive."[96] The movement forward is augmented by a movement upward: he spoke of a "step up" in jobs, laborers who "can raise their heads again," a general purpose "to lift this new threat," "rising purchasing power," "raising" consuming capacity, and "a strong, sound, upward spiral of business activity." The movement forward and upward is conditioned on "cooperation." The imagery, in sum, is identical to Hoover's inaugural address.

Yet the text's dissimilarity is also unmistakable: the message expresses precisely the opposite sentiments that Roosevelt had articulated at the Commonwealth Club. At San Francisco, recall that he castigated big business for "squeezing out" the little guy. Less than nine months later, Roosevelt expressed the "faith that we can count on our industry once more to join in our general purpose to lift this new threat and to do it without taking any advantage of the public trust which has this day been reposed without stint in the good faith and high purpose of American business." Big business, moreover, would not close off the little guy; instead "opportunities for individual initiative will *open* more amply than ever" (emphasis added). Big business would foment growth and openness, not contraction and extinction. As many others have noted, the money changers remained safely ensconced in the temple.

Summary

One of the major advantages of longitudinal treatments of rhetoric is the ability to isolate changes, and how such changes both inform and are informed by historical circumstances. Roosevelt's first inaugural address is indeed an important document in American history, but its importance has more to do with its relationship to the past and the future than with some eternally static, or bounded present.[97] Roosevelt constituted his army on November 5 and mobilized it for action on March 4. In so doing, he transformed a sick, paralyzed, and fragmented populace into a dutiful, hopeful, and active collectivity. The scene of war, moreover, demanded swift and decisive action. On this, Roosevelt and the seventy-third Congress delivered.

That some bills had contradictory purposes mattered little; things were being done. The sense of accomplishment and activity reinforced Roosevelt's principal objective of reinstilling the public's confidence—in themselves, in their economic system, and in their form of government.

That Roosevelt's use of war metaphors transcended mere tropic artifice is attested to in part by Hugh Johnson's rhetorical campaign on behalf of NIRA. In order to induce the spirit of cooperation and patriotism, Johnson employed the icon of the Blue Eagle, an image appropriated directly from World War I.[98] The symbol was potent: it "became the focus of moral and civic pressure. Parades celebrated it. Speeches praised it. Throughout the land merchants put the Blue Eagle in their windows and stamped it on their products. Over two million employers signed up."[99] Schlesinger argues further, though, that the Blue Eagle campaign achieved results far more important than economic or social reforms: it "changed the popular mood from despair to affirmation and activity. The psychological stimulus gave people new confidence in their capacity to work out their economic salvation."[100]

Both Herbert Hoover and Franklin Roosevelt recognized the economic importance of enlivening the "animal spirits." Both employed a similar rhetorical means—the metaphor of war. But Hoover attempted, at least initially, to fight a spiritual war, one largely confined to the individual in his or her physical locality. The war was thus fragmented and internal, and Hoover absconded from leading it. More pernicious was the less-decentralized war Hoover declared on March 6, 1932, one more closely resembling a civil war.

Roosevelt's war mobilized and enlisted people of all types—male and female, rich and poor, Republican and Democrat—in one mass collectivity. It also approximated a real war, as he managed to create an atmosphere in which the country was "in fact invaded by a foreign foe."[101] Roosevelt also gladly invested himself with the authority that such a situation warranted. Perhaps most importantly, the administration's war appeared to have resonated with the American people. As Moley put it, "It was the confidence of the public rather than any specific reforms that led to the recovery that followed."[102]

Notes

1. Quoted in James Roosevelt and Sidney Shalett, *Affectionately, F.D.R.*, p. 232.

2. Raymond Moley to Louis M. Howe, November 12, 1932, Raymond Moley Papers, "Indexed Correspondence," Box 24, File 30, Hoover Institution on War, Revolution, and Peace, Stanford University, Stanford, California.

3. Raymond Moley, *After Seven Years*, p. 68.

4. Much to his surprise, Roosevelt asked Moley to accompany him to the meeting.

5. The special session was originally planned to convene one month after Roosevelt's March 4 inauguration.

6. Moley, *After Seven Years*, p. 95.

7. Ibid.

8. For the standard historical account of the banking crisis, as well as events leading up to it, see Susan Estabrook Kennedy, *The Banking Crisis of 1933*. For the details surrounding the Guardian Detroit Bank complex, see pp. 77–102.

9. Zangara's bullets would have likely hit Roosevelt had it not been for the split-second reaction of a woman who apparently hit his arm just as he fired toward Roosevelt. For the only comprehensive account of the incident, see Blaise Picchi, *The Five Weeks of Giuseppe Zangara.*

10. Moley, *After Seven Years*, p. 139.

11. Letter of Raymond Moley to Fred Charles, February 24, 1933, Raymond Moley Papers, "Indexed Correspondence," Box 65, File 3.

12. Kenneth S. Davis, *FDR: The New York Years, 1928–1933*.

13. Frank Freidel, *Franklin D. Roosevelt: Launching the New Deal*, p. 174.

14. Roderick P. Hart, *The Sound of Leadership.*

15. Herbert Hoover to Franklin Roosevelt, February 18, 1933, President's Personal File, Box 820, "Herbert Hoover 1933–1944 and cross references," Franklin Roosevelt Presidential Library, Hyde Park, New York (hereafter, FRPL); emphasis added.

16. Hoover admitted as much in his "secret" memorandum of February 22 to Pennsylvania Senator David A. Reed: "I realize that if these declarations be made by the President-elect, he will have ratified the whole major program of the Republican Administration; that it means the abandonment of 90% of the so-called new deal" (Herbert Hoover, "Supplement I," in *Public Papers of the Presidents of the United States, 1932–33*, p. 1044).

17. Herbert Hoover to Franklin Roosevelt, February 28, 1933, President's Personal File, Box 820, FRPL. Roosevelt claimed that his secretary had misplaced his response to the first letter.

18. Herbert Hoover, "Supplement I," in *Public Papers of the Presidents of the United States, 1932–33*, p. 1061.

19. Quoted in Herbert Hoover to James H. Rand, Jr., February 28, 1933, President's Subject File, Box 155, "Financial Matters, Correspondence 1932–1933," Herbert Hoover Presidential Library, West Branch, Iowa (hereafter, HHPL). Tugwell's revenge came several years later, when he referred to Rand as a fascist; see Rexford G. Tugwell, *The Democratic Roosevelt*, p. 202.

20. Herbert Hoover to James H. Rand, Jr., February 28, 1933, HHPL.

21. John T. Flynn, *The Roosevelt Myth*, p. 24. Kenneth S. Davis recounts the Rand-Tugwell story in *FDR: The New Deal Years, 1933–1937*, pp. 21–22.

22. Edwin Black, "Secrecy and Disclosure as Rhetorical Forms," *Quarterly Journal of Speech* 74 (1988): 141: "From an economic standpoint, one could say that an initiation into a mystery preserves the capital; an expose expends the capital." Donald N. McCloskey makes much the same argument in "The Art of Forecasting: From Ancient to Modern Times," *Cato Journal* 12 (1992): 23–43.

23. Kyle D. Palmer, "Inaugural Hope High," *Los Angeles Times*, March 4, 1933, p. 1.

24. "The Return Of Hope," *Pittsburgh Press*, March 3, 1933, p. 1.

25. R. F. Paine, "Over the Top," *Pittsburgh Press*, March 4, 1933, p. 4.

26. William H. Grimes, "Bank Plan Ready for Roosevelt," *Wall Street Journal*, March 4, 1933, p. 1.

27. This statement appeared in an advertisement for the inaugural on March 2, 1933, p. 13.

28. "Looking for Mr. Roosevelt," *New York Times*, March 4, 1933, p. 12.

29. Will Rogers, *Los Angeles Times*, March 6, 1933, p. 1.

30. James MacGregor Burns, *Roosevelt: The Lion and the Fox*, pp. 161–62. That Roosevelt helped nurture the legend is attested to by his handwritten draft of the inaugural, a draft very similar to the one he delivered on March 4, 1933. See draft of first inaugural address, FDR Speech Files, File 610, FRPL.

31. For a genealogy of the speech, see Raymond Moley, *The First New Deal*, pp. 96–119.

32. Raymond Moley Diary, February 28, 1933, Raymond Moley Papers, Box 1. For a more detailed account, see Raymond Moley, Raymond Moley Papers, "Speeches and Writings," Box 245–46, "Draft on Writing Roosevelt's Inaugural Speech."

33. Frank Freidel to Raymond Moley, June 29, 1965, Raymond Moley Papers, "Speeches and Writings," Box 245–46.

34. Franklin D. Roosevelt, "Inaugural Address," in *The Public Papers and Addresses of Franklin D. Roosevelt, volume 2, 1933*, ed. S. I. Rosenman p. 12. Subsequent references are noted in the text.

35. Halford Ross Ryan, "Roosevelt's First Inaugural: A Study of Technique," *Quarterly Journal of Speech* 65 (1979): 147.

36. William E. Leuchtenburg, *Franklin D. Roosevelt and the New Deal, 1932–1940*, p. 18.

37. Moley, *The First New Deal*, p. 104.

38. Ibid., p. xviii.

39. Moley and Roosevelt either removed references to sickness or made them less explicit from earlier drafts; see ibid., pp. 104–105, 110.

40. William E. Leuchtenburg, "The New Deal and the Analogue of War," in *Change and Continuity in Twentieth Century America*, ed. John Braeman, Robert H. Bremner, and Everett Walters, p. 82. For a slightly revised version of this essay, see William E. Leuchtenburg, "The New Deal and the Analogue of War," in *The FDR Years*, pp. 35–75.

41. This geography is underscored in an earlier draft of the speech in which Roosevelt drew parallels with the Revolutionary War and the Civil War. "In the crisis of our War for Independence, in the poverty, the unrest and the doubts of the early days of constitutional government, in the dark days of the War between the States, a leadership of frankness and vigor has met with understanding and support of the people themselves which is essential to victory" (draft of first inaugural address, FDR Speech Files, File 610, 1, FRPL).

42. Leuchtenburg, *Franklin D. Roosevelt and the New Deal*, p. 42.

43. Robert L. Vann, "Confidence Has Arrived," *Pittsburgh Courier*, March 11, 1933, p. 1.

44. "An Epochal Message," *Atlanta Constitution*, March 5, 1933, p. 10.

45. "Roosevelt Puts Heart in America," *Pittsburgh Press*, March 5, 1933, p. 8. The *Atlanta Constitution* also likened the inaugural address to Lincoln's speech; see "An Epochal Message," p. 10.

46. Grimes, "Bank Plan Ready for Roosevelt," p. 1.

47. Moley, *The First New Deal*, p. xvii.

48. Ibid., p. xiii.

49. Moley, *After Seven Years*, p. 151.

50. Ibid.

51. Davis, *FDR: The New Deal Years, 1933–1937*, p. 47.

52. Flynn, *The Roosevelt Myth*, p. 30.

53. Franklin D. Roosevelt, "A Request to the Congress for Authority to Effect Drastic Economies in Government," in *The Public Papers and Addresses of Franklin D. Roosevelt, 1933*, p. 50. Subsequent references are noted in the text.

54. The federal budget was wildly out of balance, but Roosevelt gave the impression of a balanced budget by dividing the budget into two parts: "normal" expenditures and "ex-

traordinary relief expenditures." See Roosevelt, *The Public Papers and Addresses of Franklin D. Roosevelt, 1933*, p. 51.

55. Moley, *After Seven Years*, p. 155.

56. The speech was initially drafted by Charles Michelson and completely redrafted by Arthur Ballantine. Moley's work on the text was minimal.

57. Roosevelt, "The First 'Fireside Chat'— An Intimate Talk with the People of the United States on Banking," in *The Public Papers and Addresses of Franklin D. Roosevelt, 1933*, p. 61. Subsequent references are noted in the text.

58. The advertisement appeared in the *Los Angeles Times* on March 5, 1933; ellipses in original.

59. "Roosevelt Puts Heart in America," *Pittsburgh Press*, March 5, 1933, p. 8.

60. Davis, *FDR: The New Deal Years, 1933–1937*, p. 61.

61. Rexford G. Tugwell, *Roosevelt's Revolution: The First Year—A Personal Perspective*, p. 64.

62. Leuchtenburg, "The New Deal and the Analogue of War" (1964), p. 81.

63. Ibid., pp. 102, 105.

64. Kenneth Burke, *A Grammar of Motives*, p. 13.

65. Roosevelt's persuasiveness with Congress was facilitated by his decision to withhold political patronage until after the special session concluded.

66. Moley, *The First New Deal*, p. 224.

67. Memorandum from Adolf A. Berle to Raymond Moley, November 10, 1932, Raymond Moley Papers, "Indexed Correspondence," Box 63–65. See also Moley, Raymond Moley Papers, "Speeches and Writing," Box 245–48, "Organization of American Historians, A Review of Frank Freidel's Paper on the 1932 Interregnum," April 28, 1967.

68. Moley, *The First New Deal*, p. 228.

69. For an insider's account of the first 100 days, see Tugwell, *Roosevelt's Revolution: The First Year—A Personal Perspective*. See also Ernest K. Lindley, *The Roosevelt Revolution*. For the standard text on the Roosevelt administration's first one hundred days, see James E. Sargent, *Roosevelt and the Hundred Days: Struggle for the Early New Deal*.

70. Franklin D. Roosevelt, "The Third Press Conference," in *The Public Papers and Addresses of Franklin D. Roosevelt, 1933*, p. 67.

71. Franklin D. Roosevelt, "New Means to Rescue Agriculture" in *The Public Papers and Addresses of Franklin D. Roosevelt, 1933*, p. 74; emphasis added.

72. Upon hearing of Roosevelt's intentions to go off the gold standard, his budget director, Lewis Douglas, reportedly gasped, "this is the end of Western civilization."

73. Franklin D. Roosevelt, "Three Essentials for Unemployment Relief," in *The Public Papers and Addresses of Franklin D. Roosevelt, 1933*, p. 81.

74. Moley, *The First New Deal*, p. 265.

75. Franklin D. Roosevelt, "The President Signs the Unemployment Relief Bill and Stresses State, Local and Individual Responsibility," in *The Public Papers and Addresses of Franklin D. Roosevelt, 1933*, p. 183.

76. Franklin D. Roosevelt, "Recommendation for Federal Supervision of Investment Securities in Interstate Commerce," in *The Public Papers and Addresses of Franklin D. Roosevelt, 1933*, p. 93.

77. The hearings were popularly known as the Pecora hearings, after the lead prosecutor, Ferdinand Pecora.

78. Franklin D. Roosevelt, "A Suggestion for Legislation to Create the Tennessee Valley Authority," in *The Public Papers and Addresses of Franklin D. Roosevelt, 1933*, p. 122. Subsequent references are noted in the text.

79. Moley, *After Seven Years*, p. 187.

80. Moley was slotted in this position precisely because of its ill-defined duties.

81. Leuchtenburg, "The New Deal and the Analogue of War" (1964), p. 117.

82. Franklin D. Roosevelt, "A Recommendation to the Congress to Enact the National

Industrial Recovery Act to Put People to Work," in *The Public Papers and Addresses of Franklin D. Roosevelt, 1933*, p. 202.

83. Anthony J. Badger, *The New Deal: The Depression Years, 1933–1940*, p. 83; Stephen Skowronek, "Franklin Roosevelt and the Modern Presidency," *Studies in American Political Development* 6 (1992): 339.

84. Hugh Johnson was selected to administer Title I.

85. On the same day he also signed the Glass-Steagall banking bill, a measure that did not originate with Roosevelt. He strongly opposed the bill's provision for deposit guarantees— a provision for which he would later take credit.

86. Moley, *The First New Deal*, p. 339.

87. Ibid.

88. Raymond Moley, Rexford G. Tugwell, and Ernest K. Lindley, "Symposium: Early Days of the New Deal," in *The Thirties*, ed. Morton J. Frisch and Martin Diamond, p. 127. Similarly, in a 1967 address Moley noted, "A major factor in the depression was a crisis of confidence—in the banks, in the economic system generally, and in the capacity of the Hoover Administration to provide the means for recovery. Consequently, the major factor in the recovery that followed Roosevelt's inauguration was the igniting of confidence over the country among all sectors of the economy" (Raymond Moley, Raymond Moley Papers, "Speeches and Writing," Box 245– 46, "Organization of American Historians, A Review of Frank Freidel's Paper on the 1932– 33 Interregnum," April 28, 1967).

89. "President and Congress," *New York Times*, June 18, 1933, sec. 4, p. 4.

90. Nathan Miller, *FDR: An Intimate History*, p. 318.

91. Franklin D. Roosevelt, "Address before

United States Chamber of Commerce, Appealing for Cooperation in Recovery Program," in *The Public Papers and Addresses of Franklin D. Roosevelt, 1933*, pp. 156–57.

92. "The Long Pull," *New York Herald-Tribune*, June 18, 1933, p. 6.

93. "President and Congress," sec. 4, p. 4.

94. Franklin D. Roosevelt, "The Second 'Fireside Chat'—'What We Have Been Doing and What We Are Planning to Do,'" in *The Public Papers and Addresses of Franklin D. Roosevelt, 1933*, p. 160. Subsequent references are noted in the text.

95. Burke, *A Grammar of Motives*, p. 17.

96. Franklin D. Roosevelt, "Presidential Statement on N.I.R.A.—'To Put People Back to Work,'" in *The Public Papers and Addresses of Franklin D. Roosevelt, 1933*, pp. 251–56.

97. Suzanne Daughton's analysis of the inaugural, while incisive, carefully brackets the events prior to the message, and she withholds comment on what the speech enabled. See "Metaphoric Transcendence: Images of the Holy War in Franklin Roosevelt's First Inaugural," *Quarterly Journal of Speech* 79 (1993): 427–46.

98. David M. Kennedy, *Over Here: The First World War and American Society*, pp. 3–92.

99. Arthur M. Schlesinger, Jr., *The Coming of the New Deal*, p. 115.

100. Ibid., p. 175.

101. Roosevelt, "First Inaugural," in *The Public Papers and Addresses of Franklin D. Roosevelt, 1933*, p. 15. This pronouncement, near the close of the address, received the loudest ovation.

102. Moley, *The First New Deal*, p. xviii.

Chapter Seven

Serendip

"Roosevelt and Hoover didn't disagree. . . .
Hoover just had a lot more principles."
—Rex Tugwell, Letter to Ray Moley

"Still at the end of every hard-earned day,
people find some reason to believe."
—Bruce Springsteen, "Reason to Believe"

In attempting to retrace our steps, what have we seen? We have seen that the relationship between rhetoric and economics is fundamental to understanding economic behavior—that rhetoric, in McCloskey's words, does matter to policy. More importantly, as both Hoover and Roosevelt clearly recognized and practiced, presidential economic rhetoric could function as *the* policy. It could move millions of people to positive (or negative) economic action, quite divorced from the coercive designs of legislation. Moreover, both men understood that the concept of an "economic reality" was a very malleable construct, shaped, in part, by the public's confidence and belief rather than an externally real, objective reality. Confidence levels, in turn, could be modified by presidential speech and presidential action. Both recognized, in sum, that "the behavior of the economy is determined by human beings who learn from experience and who shape their economic activity in accordance with their expectations."[1]

Macroeconomics does not redound solely to some point of equilibrium on an IS/LM graph. In addition to the money supply and government spending, presidential rhetoric can affect the economy in the aggregate. Similarly, microeconomics is not strictly about consumption choices prefigured by a person's ability to maximize his or her utility. Numerous factors influence individual economic behavior, one of which is presidential rhetoric.

The person on the street who occupies a world estranged from models and theories might not be surprised with our findings. Abstract economics has little if any cash value for the average citizen. Clear and compelling rhetoric, not mystification, influences his or her "consumption function." Felix Frankfurter offered such advice to the Roosevelt administration: "neither abstract or abstruse economic explanations can enlist the interest of the general public."[2]

John Maynard Keynes and his Post Keynesian colleagues were attuned to "man-on-the-street economics." Specifically, he rejected classical economic theory because it "did not portray [economic] reality correctly."[3] More specifically, he argued that "the major fault of the classical theory of economics was that it had failed to understand the implications of uncertainty."[4] Economic behavior in the present was contingent on expectations about the future—a future, Keynes argued, that was largely unknowable. Economic expectations, moreover, had less to do with quantitative probabilities than with "utter irrationality," confidence, and faith—in other words, the "animal spirits."[5]

Expectations about the economic future could thus affect the economy of the present. Such expectations have several potential sources, one of the most important of which is presidential rhetoric. A president, through a mass communication medium such as radio, could provide the crucial source for influencing aggregate expectations. Indeed, presidential rhetoric could function as Keynes's "multiplier."

But presidential rhetoric could also have deflationary results if expectations were negative or pessimistic. Jimmy Carter learned this lesson the hard way. He created such expectations in his infamous July 15, 1979, televised address to the nation. At issue was a familiar issue—confidence:

> I want to speak to you first tonight about a subject even more serious than energy or inflation. I want to talk to you right now about a fundamental threat to American democracy. . . . The threat is nearly invisible in ordinary ways. It is a crisis of confidence. It is a crisis that strikes at the very heart and soul and spirit of our national will. We can see this crisis in the growing doubt about the meaning of our own lives and the loss of a unity of purpose for our nation. The erosion of our confidence in the future is threatening to destroy the social and the political fabric of America. The confidence that we have always had as a people is not simply some romantic dream or a proverb in a dusty book that we read just on the Fourth of July. It is the idea which founded our nation and has guided our development as a people. Confidence in the future has supported everything else—public institutions and private enterprise, our own families and the very Constitution of the United States. Confidence has defined our course and has served as a link between generations.[6]

The diagnosis may have been accurate, but Carter's prescription was reminiscent of Hoover's: turn inward for confidence, not to Washington. Carter would suffer a similar fate: he was thoroughly trounced by an optimistic, smiling actor who loved the spotlight. His message: government was to blame, not the people.

To conclude, however, that persuasive presidential rhetoric is all in the complex fields of macro-and microeconomics misses the point. The Hoover presidency, particularly the years 1930 and 1931, is a powerful testament to the limits of presidential rhetoric. It is hard for a president to engender mass optimism under circumstances of grumbling bellies, creditors knocking on doors, and no jobs. Hoover attempted to create optimism with his promises of prosperity, but the countercyclical forces loosed by World War I and its aftermath and the stock market crash—along with the expectations engendered by such events—were simply too powerful to counteract through rhetorical means alone.

Roosevelt clearly learned from his predecessor's rhetorical panaceas. The scene of war called for concerted action, and Roosevelt capitalized on the sentiment he strategically fostered from November through March. Collective confidence and belief were imperative to economic recovery, but the means were both legislative and rhetorical.

Hoover and Roosevelt: A New View?

Beyond the relationship between presidential rhetoric and economic recovery, what pictures emerge of our two protagonists? The plural is purposive: no single portrait does justice to either president. I would like to believe that our inquiry has dispelled a few "certainties"—that it constitutes what Martin J. Medhurst respectfully terms "historical revisionism" and David Lehman irreverently calls "Archie Debunking."[7]

Not only does history repeat itself; historiography does, too. From the 1960s into the early 1970s, a resurgence of Hoover scholarship confirmed much of what had been written about him in the 1940s—namely, that Hoover was not a laissez-faire pessimist, but an active, progressive leader in the fight against the Great Depression.[8] By 1973, Murray N. Rothbard, perhaps more out of hope than anything else, pronounced that the laissez-faire myth associated with Herbert Hoover "has been buried forever, so that historians may now examine Hoover without being forced to wrestle with [his] ghost."[9] Unfortunately this "ghost" is still very much with us; Rothbard and others only managed to inter it for a few years. This ghost recently re-surfaced in a four-hour, 1994 documentary aired by the Public Broadcasting Station (PBS) on Franklin Roosevelt. Here is what the narrator concludes about Hoover and the Great Depression: "Since the start of the Depression, the Republican president, Herbert Hoover, had settled into a dismal pessimism. . . . Hoover believed there was nothing he could do to turn the economy around. The crisis would have to resolve itself without the aid of government."[10] The Hoover historiographical version of *Groundhog Day* continues.

Hoover was not a dour pessimist, as many believe. If anything, he was an eternal optimist, and this optimism appeared in nearly every presidential speech he delivered. He did not combat the Great Depression with silence, as many believe. He battled it frequently with presidential rhetoric broadcast to the entire nation. Only during the first seven months of 1932 did he grow increasingly silent, as a result of his ideological compromises with Congress. Hoover did not stick to one and only one response to the depression, as many believe. He changed rhetorical strategy throughout his four-year term. He did not believe that economic markets were impersonal things governed by the laws of nature, as many believe. Fifty years before McCloskey and his colleagues, Hoover recognized that market behavior was fundamentally human behavior, that today's collective beliefs could alter tomorrow's economic realities. Had the term been in circulation Hoover might have identified himself as a social constructionist, a belief that economic realities are collectively created, in part, through discursive channels.

Importantly, these sketches are just that—sketches, or perhaps even crude stick figures. There remains much filling out and redrawing to be done. I hold no grand illusions, though, about future research in this area, primarily because of a selection bias among public address scholars. The "great speeches" approach to the study of rhetoric occludes Herbert Hoover. Based on the standard criteria—stylistic nuance, argumentative force, situational drama, novelty, and a speaker's reputation—Hoover never delivered a "great speech." As I have shown throughout, he was not very adroit with words. But there is hope. Medhurst has successfully resurrected the rhetorical ghost of Dwight Eisenhower, and David Zarefsky has offered important insights into Lyndon Johnson. In addition, recent conference panels have explored speeches that failed, thus giving neglected or forgotten texts new life. Whether Hoover remains a rhetorical footnote remains to be seen.

The "great speeches" approach to public address also holds important ramifications for Roosevelt studies. Scholars have repeatedly plucked out "great speeches" from his oeuvre and offered their close readings. Yet such an approach seems anathema to the man. One of the few areas of agreement among Roosevelt scholars is that he was not committed to a rigid set of beliefs; change and experimentation, not consistency, were the hallmarks of his presidency. Such characteristics suggest an approach to his rhetoric—one that shuns "snap shot" or "freeze frame" criticism and embraces rhetoric as it unfurls. Only in this manner do we begin to glimpse Roosevelt in his full complexity—warts and all. A great deal of work remains, during both his pre-presidential and presidential years. I have only drawn a very rough composite, one constrained by the brief span of time covered.

The traces that emerge share a common characteristic—difference. Hoover was right: based on his public statements, Roosevelt was a chameleon on scotch plaid. By present-day standards he makes Bill Clinton look remarkably consistent and principled. But consistency counts for little when people are hungry and tomorrow is uncertain. Almost to a person, the country wanted action and results—not ideological consistency and partisan debate. This he delivered.

Roosevelt had something for everyone: to the farmer he promised higher prices; to the railroads he promised consolidation and efficiency; to the progressives he promised enlightened administration; to the utility companies he promised regulation; to the conservatives he promised balanced budgets and protective tariffs; and to the unemployed he promised jobs. All could, therefore, find a place in the Roosevelt army. Although his army, like all movements, eventually splintered and rebelled against its commander in chief, it initially followed Roosevelt's inauguration day call for collective sacrifice and duty. The legacy of that fleeting army remains with us today.

Like Hoover, Roosevelt recognized the force of collective confidence on economic recovery. Keynes's "animal spirits" were not lost on him or those advising him. He simply went about moving them in a different manner— one that relied less on presidential speech than on cooperative legislative action. The war could not be fought lying down, nor could the enemy be localized. Each measure passed was a blow to the enemy—an enemy both structural and personal.

In Brief

As Kenneth Burke is fond of saying, "so, what does all this mean?" Although the reader might find other meanings, I would highlight four. First, and perhaps most importantly, we have established the crucial relationship between rhetoric and economics. Specifically, economic recovery is premised, in part, on collective confidence, which, in turn, is influenced by both presidential speech and cooperative legislative action.

Second, through our case study approach, we have found Herbert Hoover to be a complex rhetorical figure, a man whose aims for economic recovery deeply implicated presidential rhetorical leadership. That he was not eloquent or occasionally shirked his rhetorical responsibilities does not change the fact that he saw recovery principally as a matter of collective belief. The rhetorical presidency need no longer be a stranger to the Hoover administration.

Third, we have seen that Franklin Roosevelt's rhetorical and legislative response to the Great Depression owed much to the successes and failures of the Hoover administration. Thus, we have further advanced the continuity thesis proposed by Lippmann, Moley, Tugwell, Degler, and Hoff Wilson. But, apart from Hoover, we have shown Roosevelt to be a complex, often contradictory, figure, someone more attuned to daily exigencies than to abstract principles. We have also seen how Roosevelt skillfully transformed a physical liability into a rhetorical strength. He further transformed the "scene" of health and sickness into one of warfare, a redefinition that greatly facilitated his legislative agenda during his administration's first one hundred days.

Fourth, and related to the previous two, our study suggests the many benefits of studying rhetoric longitudinally and within its unique historical moment. Rhetorical criticism does not have to be a zero-sum game in which many close readings are at constant loggerheads. Reading both horizontally and vertically enable us to isolate transformations and to see speakers in their full complexity.

Future Travels

Economists and rhetoricians, as this study suggests, have a lot to say to each other. Yet despite the efforts of McCloskey and many others, rhetoric remains largely ensconced in the cloistered "blackboard" world, far-removed from Burke's "Scramble, the Wrangle of the Market Place, the flurries and flare-ups of the Human Barnyard."[11] Perhaps to get the conversants talking, we would do well to consult the earliest surviving rhetoric of economics text—Aristophanes's *The Clouds.* The comedy revolves around a farmer, Strepsiades, and the many debts he has incurred by his free-spending wife and slackard son, Pheidippides. Rather than pay off his creditors, Strepsiades consults Socrates at his Thinkery. Strepsiades's wish is for Socrates to make him an orator, so that he might learn "that Argument of yours—you know, that one that always pays off and never pays up?"[12] While the play functions as a morality tale of the twin evils of base rhetoric and rampant consumerism, rhetoricians and economists might well spend some time together in the Thinkery rather than segregating themselves from each other.

One possible productive conversation might begin from a set of disciplinary "sore spots," what some economists have more alarmingly labeled a crisis.[13] For many academic economists the crisis stems from the vast gulf separating economic theory from economic policy and its effects in the "real world." Robert E. Lucas captures the conflict: "progress in economic thinking means getting better and better abstract, analogue economic models, not better verbal observations about the world."[14] The problem of effects in the real world is also no stranger to rhetoricians. While no longer deemed a crisis, the problem still pervades much contemporary scholarship, as a recent review by George C. Edwards III makes painfully clear.[15] Rhetoric's effects on an audience are often assumed without tangible evidence. The problem is one of "proving" effects—and the attendant dangers of making a causal claim.

But how might such weaknesses be transformed into strengths? One possibility is suggested by a recent story in *USA Today.* Under the headline of "Stocks Retreat on Fed Speech," James Kim reports that "stocks, bonds and the dollar staggered Wednesday after Federal Reserve head Alan Greenspan said optimism on Wall Street might be excessive."[16] Here is rhetoric in the real economic world with very real monetary consequences—rhetoric as currency. The research possibilities are suggestive: why Greenspan rather than Bill Clinton, Robert Rubin, or Louis Rukeyser? What are the institutional relationships that give more or less "currency" to economic rhetoric? What are the knowledge/power/ethics relations at work in making clinical diagnoses of a nation's collective optimism (or pessimism)? Who is authorized to speak about macroeconomic expectations and their creation? And what of the New York Stock Exchange as some sort of synechdochic arbiter of the economy? This is just one set of possibilities that arises by situating human economic activity where it occurs—in the barnyard of the symbol-using animal.

There are many others. The somewhat far-flung notion that thoughts and beliefs function to shape our external realities is not novel. For decades medical researchers have studied the placebo effect, whereby belief, not drugs, results in healing. Similarly, quantum physicists like David Bohm have argued that thoughts and perceptions influence our collective realities.[17] Within economics, Elisabeth Noelle-Neumann has developed statistical evidence for the claim that "the hopes of the population represent a kind of prognosis of coming developments." Even more interesting, such hopes, she discovered, do "not have anything to do with concrete knowledge of the economy or expectations about how certain important elements of the economy will develop."[18] If not "concrete knowledge" of the economy, on what are these economic hopes premised? Like Noelle-Neumann, Harold M. Zullow found that consumer pessimism (and optimism) was not a reaction to "the economy," but it was influenced by "culturally transmitted fantasies of hope and despair."[19] More specifically, Zullow found that pessimism expressed in popular songs and news magazines actually predicted a decline in economic growth with a one- to two-year lead time.

As for rhetoricians, the possibilities are many, but I'll mention only those that bear fairly directly on this study. First, more work needs to be done with regard to "economic confidence." Specifically, the term's origin needs to be tracked down: when did presidents first associate economic recovery and economic performance with "confidence?" This leads to related questions: when did presidents assume responsibility for leading the nation's economy? How did presidents respond during previous depressions? When did presidents assume a managerial function for the nation's economy? How did they legitimate such a role to the public?

Aside from origins, what about "economic confidence" in the present? Clearly the federal government deems it important; after all, we get monthly reports on "consumer confidence" levels. What factors comprise the index? Is there a link between levels of consumer confidence and economic performance? Is there a correspondence between presidential approval ratings and levels of consumer confidence?

Such questions lead us logically into the sphere of government-sponsored economic statistics and the politics of naming. William Alonso and Paul Starr have called our attention to the politics of government statistics, but their anthology stands alone.[20] Much important work remains. Today for example, we collectively define two consecutive contractions of Gross National Product as a "recession." Yet official government economic statistics did not exist until 1938—nearly nine years into what we collectively term "the Great Depression." Thus the term "depression" had no basis in statistical fact. Was the term, then, associated with a purely psychological or clinical condition? Or have we retroactively imposed the term on the period?

Government statistics, moreover, "do not merely hold a mirror to reality. They reflect presuppositions and theories about the nature of society. They are products of social, political, and economic interests that are often in conflict with each other."[21] Government economic statistics are interested: they function to constitute economic "reality," to influence public policy, and to guide private economic behavior.[22] In a word, they function rhetorically; as such, government economic statistics could be productively read from a rhetorical perspective.

Finally, much more work needs to be done on John Maynard Keynes and his seemingly rhetorical approach to government fiscal policy. To date, academic economists have largely worked around the rhetorical implications of his emphasis on human expectations and uncertainty. In order to preserve the precision and predictability of their models, they have fashioned an entirely new approach to macroeconomics, designated by the oxymoronic term "rational expectations."[23] The Keynesians and Post Keynesians have fought back, but rhetoric's relationship to the Keynesian calculus remains largely unexplored.[24]

In sum, much work remains for the rhetorical critic interested in "the dismal science." As a field we've only just begun to explore the "great opportunities" that inhere in America's "economic heritage."[25] Here's to hoping for many more happy travels.

Notes

1. Helmut Arndt, *Economic Theory Vs Economic Reality*, trans. William A. Kirby, p. 112.

2. Felix Frankfurter to Adolf Berle, September 23, 1932, "Felix Frankfurter, 1932–April 1933," President's Personal File, 148, Franklin D. Roosevelt Presidential Library, Hyde Park, N.Y. (hereafter, FRPL).

3. M. Stohs, " 'Uncertainty' in Keynes' General Theory," in *John Maynard Keynes: Critical Assessments*, volume 2, ed. John Cunningham Wood, p. 400.

4. Athol Fitzgibbons, *Keynes's Vision*, p. 80.

5. Ibid., p. 82.

6. Jimmy Carter, "Energy Crisis (Malaise) Speech," in *Great Speeches for Criticism & Analysis*, 2d. ed., ed. Lloyd Rohler and Roger Cook, pp. 132–33.

7. Martin J. Medhurst, "Public Address and Significant Scholarship: Four Challenges to the Rhetorical Renaissance," in *Texts in Context: Critical Dialogues on Significant Episodes in American Political Rhetoric*, ed. Michael C. Leff and Fred J. Kauffeld, pp. 32–35; David Lehman, *Signs of the Times: Deconstruction and the Fall of Paul de Man*, pp. 65–92.

8. See, for example, Eugene Lyons, *Our Unknown Ex-President: A Portrait of Herbert Hoover*; Broadus Mitchell, *Depression Decade* (New York: Rinehart, 1947).

9. Murray N. Rothbard, in *Herbert Hoover and the Crisis of American Capitalism*, ed. J. Joseph Huthmacher and Warren I. Susman, p. 121.

10. *FDR: A Documentary*, PBS, 1994, written and directed by David Grubin.

11. Kenneth Burke, *A Rhetoric of Motives*, p. 23.

12. Aristophanes, *Lysistrata/The Acharnians/The Clouds*, trans. Alan H. Sommerstein, p. 122.

13. Daniel Bell and Irving Kristol, eds. *The Crisis in Economic Theory*; Robert L. Heilbroner and William S. Milberg, *The Crisis of Vision in Modern Economic Thought*; Sheila Dow, "Keynes' Epistemology and Economic Methodology," in *Keynes as Philosopher-Economist*, ed. R. M. O'Donnell, pp. 144–67.

14. Quoted in Tony Lawson, "Economics and Expectations," in *Keynes, Knowledge and Uncertainty*, ed. Sheila Dow and John Hillard (Brookfield, Vt.: Edward Elgar, 1995), p. 78.

15. George C. Edwards III, "Presidential Rhetoric: What Difference Does It Make?" in *Beyond the Rhetorical Presidency*, ed. Martin J. Medhurst, pp. 199–217.

16. James Kim, "Stocks Retreat on Fed Speech," *USA Today*, October 9, 1997, sec. B, p. 1.

17. David Bohm, *Wholeness and the Implicate Order*.

18. Elisabeth Noelle-Neumann, "The Public as Prophet: Findings From Continuous Survey Research and Their Importance for Early Diagnosis of Economic Growth," *International Journal of Public Opinion Research* 1 (1989): 137, 145.

19. Harold M. Zullow, "Pessimistic Rumination in Popular Songs and Newsmagazines Predict Economic Recession via Decreased Optimism and Spending," *Journal of Economic Psychology* 12 (1991): 502.

20. William Alonso and Paul Starr, eds., *The Politics of Numbers*.

21. Ibid., p. 1.

22. The "interest" was not lost on the ninety-ninth Congress. See Congress, House and Senate, Joint Economic Committee, *The Quality of the Nation's Economic Statistics: Hearings Before the Joint Economic Committee*, 99th Cong., 2d sess., 1986.

23. For a helpful discussion of rational expectations, see Arjo Klamer, *Conversations with Economists*.

24. In addition to this study, I have explored the relationship in an essay titled "Rhetoric, Science, and Economic Prophecy: John Maynard Keynes's Correspon-

dence with Franklin D. Roosevelt," in *New Economics Criticism*, eds. Martha Woodmansee and Mark Osteen, pp. 352–64. See also Alessandra Marzola and Francesco Silva, eds., *John Maynard* *Keynes: Language and Method*, trans. Richard Davies.

25. Medhurst, "Public Address and Significant Scholarship," p. 38.

Bibliography

Manuscript Collections

Adolf Berle Papers, Franklin D. Roosevelt Presidential Library, Hyde Park, New York.

Herbert Hoover Papers, Herbert Hoover Presidential Library, West Branch, Iowa.

Louis M. Howe Papers, Franklin D. Roosevelt Presidential Library.

Theodore G. Joslin Papers, Herbert Hoover Presidential Library.

Raymond Moley Papers, Hoover Institution on War, Revolution, and Peace, Stanford University, Stanford, California.

Edgar Rickard Diaries, Herbert Hoover Presidential Library.

Franklin D. Roosevelt Papers, Franklin D. Roosevelt Presidential Library.

Paul Shoup Papers, Stanford University, Stanford, California.

Lewis T. Strauss Papers, Herbert Hoover Presidential Library.

Books and Articles

Adams, Henry Carter. "Economics and Jurisprudence." *Science* 8 (1886): 14–19.

Adams, James Truslow. "Presidential Prosperity." *Harper's Magazine,* August, 1930, p. 266.

Adelstein, Richard P. " 'The Nation as an Economic Unit': Keynes, Roosevelt, and the Managerial Ideal." *Journal of American History* 78 (1991): 160–87.

Allen, Frederick Lewis. *The Big Change.* New York: Harper & Row, 1952.

———. *Since Yesterday.* New York: Bantam, 1961.

Alonso, William, and Paul Starr, eds. *The Politics of Numbers.* New York: Russell Sage Foundation, 1987.

Anderson, Paul Y. "Herbert Hoover and the Press." *Nation,* October 14, 1931, pp. 382–84.

———. "Mourning Becomes Herbert." *Nation,* September 28, 1932, p. 280.

Arestis, Philip. *The Post-Keynesian Approach to Economics.* Aldershot, U.K.: Edward Elgar, 1992.

Aristophanes. *Lysistrata/The Acharnians/The Clouds.* Trans. by Alan H. Sommerstein. New York: Penguin, 1973.

Arndt, Helmut. *Economic Theory Vs Economic Reality.* Trans. by William A. Kirby. East Lansing: Michigan State University Press, 1984.

Arnold, Peri Ethan. "Herbert Hoover and the Continuity of American Public Policy." *Public Policy* 20 (1972): 525–44

Babson, Roger. "Everybody Has a Job." *World's Work,* February, 1931, pp. 67–69.

———. "How to Cure the Blues." *Collier's,* March 28, 1931, pp. 12–13, 60.

Badger, Anthony J. *The New Deal: The Depression Years, 1933–1940.* New York: Noonday, 1989.

Barber, James D. "Classifying and Predicting Presidential Styles: Two 'Weak' Presidents." *Journal of Social Issues* 24 (1969): 55–80.

Barber, William J. *From New Era to New Deal.* Cambridge: Cambridge University Press, 1985.

Bell, Daniel, and Irving Kristol, eds. *The Crisis in Economic Theory.* New York: Basic, 1981.

Bellah, Robert N. "Civil Religion in America." *Daedalus* 96 (1967): 1–21.

Benson, Thomas W. "Inaugurating Peace: Franklin D. Roosevelt's Last Speech." *Speech Monographs* 36 (1969): 138–47.

———, ed. *Landmark Essays in Rhetorical Criticism.* Davis, Calif.: Hermagoras, 1993.

Berle, Adolf A. "Reshaping the American Economy." *Centennial Review* 9 (1965): 209–21.

Bernheim, Alfred L. "Prosperity by Proclamation." *Nation,* December 25, 1929, p. 772.

Black, Edwin. "Secrecy and Disclosure as Rhetorical Forms." *Quarterly Journal of Speech* 74 (1988): 133–50.

———. *Rhetorical Criticism: A Study in Method.* New York: MacMillan, 1965.

Bohm, David. *Wholeness and the Implicate Order.* London: Routledge & Kegan Paul, 1980.

Bonadei, Rossana. "John Maynard Keynes: Contexts and Methods." In *John Maynard Keynes: Language and Method,* edited by Alessandra Marzola and Francesco Silva, translated by Richard Davies, 13–75. Aldershot, U.K.: Edward Elgar, 1994.

Braden, Walso W., and Earnest Brandenburg. "Roosevelt's Fireside Chats." *Speech Monographs* 22 (1955): 290–302.

Braeman, John, Robert H. Bremner, and Everett Walters, eds. *Change and Continuity in Twentieth Century America.* Columbus: Ohio State University Press, 1964.

Braeman, John, Robert H. Bremner, and David Brody, eds. *The New Deal.* Columbus: Ohio State University Press, 1975.

Brandenburg, Earnest. "Franklin D. Roosevelt's International Speeches, 1939–41." *Speech Monographs* 16 (1949): 21–40.

———. "The Preparation of Franklin D. Roosevelt's Speeches." *Quarterly Journal of Speech* 35 (1949): 214–21.

Brandenburg, Earnest, and Waldo W. Braden. "Franklin D. Roosevelt's Voice and Pronunciation." *Quarterly Journal of Speech* 38 (1952): 23–30.

Burgchardt, Carl R. "Herbert C. Hoover." In *U.S. Presidents as Orators: A Bio-Critical Sourcebook,* edited by Halford Ryan, 134–45. Westport, Conn.: Greenwood, 1995.

———. "President Herbert Hoover's Inaugural Address, 1929." In *The Inaugural Addresses of Twentieth-Century American Presidents,* edited by Halford Ryan, 81–92. Westport, Conn.: Praeger, 1993.

Burke, Kenneth. *A Grammar of Motives.* Berkeley: University of California Press, 1969.

———. *The Philosophy of Literary Form.* 3d ed. Berkeley: University of California Press, 1973.

———. *A Rhetoric of Motives.* Berkeley: University of California Press, 1969.

Burner, David. "Before the Crash: Hoover's First Eight Months in the Presidency." In *The Hoover Presidency: A Reappraisal,* edited by Martin L. Fausold and George T. Mazuzan, 50–65. Albany: SUNY Press, 1974.

———. *Herbert Hoover: A Public Life.* New York: Knopf, 1979.

Burns, James MacGregor. *Roosevelt: The Lion and the Fox.* New York: Harcourt, Brace, 1956.

Carson, Herbert L. "War Requested: Wilson and Roosevelt." *Central States Speech Journal* 10 (1958): 28–32.

"The Castor-Oil School of Economics." *Business Week,* July 9, 1930, p. 40.

"Christian Science Economics." *Nation,* February 17, 1932, p. 185.

Clark, James Bayard. "A Doctor Looks at Economics." *Review of Reviews,* June, 1932, pp. 29–31.

"Confidence." *National Auditgram,* January, 1932, n.p.

Cowperthwaite, L. Leroy. "Franklin D. Roosevelt at Harvard." *Quarterly Journal of Speech* 38 (1952): 37–41.

Crispell, Kenneth R., and Carlos F. Gomez. *Hidden Illness in the White House.* Durham, N.C.: Duke University Press, 1988.

Crowell, Laura. "Franklin D. Roosevelt's Audience Persuasion in the 1936 Campaign." *Speech Monographs* 17 (1950): 48–64.

———. "Roosevelt the Grotonian." *Quarterly Journal of Speech* 38 (1952): 31–36.

———. "Word Changes Introduced *Ad Libitum* in Five Speeches by Franklin Delano Roosevelt." *Speech Monographs* 25 (1958): 229–42.

Cruikshank, Nelson H. "Prosperity by Suggestion." *World Tomorrow,* March, 1931, pp. 85–87.

Cuff, Robert D. *The War Industries Board: Business-Government Relations During World War I.* Baltimore: Johns Hopkins University Press, 1973.

Daughton, Suzanne M. "FDR as Family Doctor: Medical Metaphors and the Role of Physician in the Domestic Fireside Chats." Paper presented at the Speech Communication Association convention, New Orleans, La., November, 1994.

———. "Metaphorical Transcendence: Images of the Holy War in Franklin Roosevelt's First Inaugural." *Quarterly Journal of Speech* 79 (1993): 427–46.

Davidson, Paul. *Post Keynesian Macroeconomic Theory.* Aldershot, U.K.: Edward Elgar, 1994.

———. "Reality and Economic Theory." *Journal of Post Keynesian Economics* 18 (1996): 470–508.

———. "Uncertainty in Economics." In *Keynes, Knowledge and Uncertainty*, edited by Sheila Dow and John Hillard, 107–16. Brookfield, Vt.: Edward Elgar, 1995.

Davis, Elmer. "Confidence in Whom?" *Forum and Century*, January, 1933, pp. 31–33.

———. "Hoover the Medicine Man." *Forum*, October, 1930, pp. 195–99.

Davis, Joseph S. "Herbert Hoover, 1874–1964: Another Appraisal." *South Atlantic Quarterly* 68 (1969): 295–318.

Davis, Kenneth S. *FDR: The New Deal Years, 1933–1937.* New York: Random House, 1986.

———. *FDR: The New York Years, 1928–1933.* New York: Random House, 1985.

———. *Invincible Summer.* New York: Atheneum, 1974.

Dawley, Alan. *Struggles for Justice.* Cambridge: Harvard University Press, 1991.

De Carvalho, Fernando J. Cardim. "Keynes on Probability, Uncertainty, and Decision Making." *Journal of Post Keynesian Economics* 11 (1988): 66–81.

Degler, Carl N. "The Ordeal of Herbert Hoover." *Yale Review* 52 (1963): 563–83.

"Demagogues and Plutogogues." *New Republic*, April 27, 1932, pp. 285–87.

Doriot, Georges F. "Our Sick Industries." *Yale Review*, March, 1931, pp. 442–55.

Dow, Alexander, and Sheila Dow. "Animal Spirits and Rationality." In *Keynes' Economics*, edited by Tony Lawson and Hashan Pesaran, 46–65. Armonk, N.Y.: Sharpe, 1985.

Dow, Sheila. "Keynes' Epistemology and Economic Methodology." In *Keynes as Philosopher-Economist*, edited by Rod M. O'Donnell, 144–67.

Duffy, John. "Franklin Roosevelt: Ambiguous Symbol for Disabled Americans." *Midwest Quarterly* 29 (1987): 113–35.

Eccles, Marriner. *Beckoning Frontiers.* Edited by Sydney Hyman. New York: Alfred A. Knopf, 1951.

Eckes, Alfred E. "Revisiting Smoot Hawley." *Journal of Policy History* 7 (1995): 295–310.

Eckley, Wilton. *Herbert Hoover.* Boston: Twayne, 1980.

Edelman, Murray. *The Symbolic Uses of Politics.* Urbana: University of Illinois Press, 1964.

Edwards, George C. III. "Presidential Rhetoric: What Difference Does It Make?" In *Beyond the Rhetorical Presidency*, edited by Martin J. Medhurst, 199–217. College Station: Texas A&M University Press, 1996.

Ely, Richard T. "Ethics and Economics." *Science* 7 (1886): 529–33.

"An Epochal Message." *Atlanta Constitution*, March 5, 1933, p. 10.

Farley, James A. *Behind the Ballots: The Personal History of a Politician.* New York: Harcourt, Brace, 1938.

Farr, Finis. *FDR.* New Rochelle, N.Y.: Arlington House, 1972.

Farrell, Thomas B. *Norms of Rhetorical Culture.* New Haven, Conn.: Yale University Press, 1993.

Fausold, Martin L. *The Presidency of Herbert C. Hoover.* Lawrence: University Press of Kansas, 1985.

Fausold, Martin L., and George T. Mazuzan. "Introduction." In *The Hoover Presidency: A Reappraisal,* edited by Martin J. Fausold and George T. Mazuzan, 3–25. Albany: SUNY Press, 1974.

Ferderer, J. Peter, and David A. Zalewski. "Uncertainty as a Propagating Force in The Great Depression." *Journal of Economic History* 54 (1994): 825–49.

Fitzgibbons, Athol. *Keynes's Vision.* Oxford: Clarendon, 1988.

Flacco, Paul R., and Randall E. Parker. "Income Uncertainty and the Onset of the Great Depression." *Economic Inquiry* 30 (1992): 154–71.

"A 'Flattering' Campaign." *New York Times,* October 17, 1928, p. 28.

Flynn, John T. *The Roosevelt Myth.* Garden City, N.Y.: Garden City Publishing, 1948.

Foster, William Trufant. "When a Horse Balks." *North American Review,* July, 1932, pp. 4–10.

"Franklin D. Roosevelt Better." *New York Times,* August 29, 1921, p. 11.

"Franklin D. Roosevelt Ill." *New York Times,* August 27, 1921, p. 9.

"Franklin D. Roosevelt Improving." *New York Times,* September 10, 1921, p. 4.

Freidel, Frank. *Franklin D. Roosevelt: A Rendezvous with Destiny.* Boston: Little, Brown, 1990.

———. *Franklin D. Roosevelt: Launching the New Deal.* Boston: Little, Brown, 1973.

———. *Franklin D. Roosevelt: The Triumph.* Boston: Little, Brown, 1956.

———. *Franklin D. Roosevelt: The Ordeal.* Boston: Little, Brown, 1954.

———. "The Interregnum Struggle Between Hoover and Roosevelt." In *The Hoover Presidency: A Reappraisal,* edited by Martin J. Fausold and George T. Mazuzan, 135–49.

Galbraith, John Kenneth. *Economics, Peace and Laughter.* Edited by Andrea D. Williams. Boston: Houghton Mifflin, 1971.

———. *The Great Crash.* Boston: Houghton Mifflin, 1961.

Gallagher, Hugh Gregory. *FDR's Splendid Deception.* New York: Dodd, Mead, 1985.

Gilbert, Robert E. "Disability, Illness, and the Presidency: The Case of Franklin D. Roosevelt." *Politics and the Life Sciences* 7 (1988): 33–49.

Goldberg, Robert T. *The Making of Franklin D. Roosevelt.* Cambridge, Mass.: Abt, 1981.

Gould, Jean. *A Good Fight.* New York: Dodd, Mead, 1961.

Gould, Tony. *A Summer Plague: Polio and Its Survivors.* New Haven, Conn.: Yale University Press, 1995.

"Governor Roosevelt's Campaign." *Nation,* November 2, 1932, p. 414.

"The Governor's Campaign." *New York Times,* October 20, 1930, p. 20.

Gravlee, G. Jack. "Franklin D. Roosevelt's Speech Preparation During His First National Campaign." *Speech Monographs* 31 (1964): 437–60.

Greenstein, Fred I., ed. *Leadership in the Modern Presidency.* Cambridge: Harvard University Press, 1988.

Grimes, William H. "Bank Plan Ready for Roosevelt." *Wall Street Journal,* March 4, 1933, p. 1.

Gunther, John. *Roosevelt in Retrospect.* New York: Harper & Brothers, 1950.

Hart, Roderick P. *The Sound of Leadership.* Chicago: University of Chicago Press, 1987.

Hawley, Ellis W. "Herbert Hoover and Modern American History: Sixty Years After." In *Herbert Hoover and the Historians,* edited by Mark M. Dodge, 1–38. West Branch, Iowa: Herbert Hoover Presidential Library Association, 1989.

———, ed. *Herbert Hoover as Secretary of Commerce 1921–1928: Studies in New Era Thought and Practice.* Iowa City: University of Iowa Press, 1981.

———. In *Herbert Hoover and the Crisis of American Capitalism,* ed. J. Joseph Huthmacher and Warren I. Susman, 3–33. Cambridge: Schenkman, 1973.

"Hazard in the Bull Market." *Kansas City Star,* September 6, 1929, n.p.

Heilbroner, Robert L. "Reflections: Economic Predictions." *New Yorker,* July 8, 1991, pp. 70–78.

———. *The Worldly Philosophers.* 6th ed. New York: Simon & Schuster, 1986.

Heilbroner, Robert L., and William S. Milberg. *The Crisis of Vision in Modern Economic Thought.* New York: Cambridge University Press, 1995.

Henderson, Willie, Tony Dudley-Evans, and Roger Backhouse, eds. *Economics and Language.* London: Routledge, 1993.

Himmelberg, Robert F. In *Herbert Hoover and the Crisis of American Capitalism,* edited by J. Joseph Huthmacher and Warren I. Susman, 59–85.

———. In *Herbert Hoover and the Crisis of American Capitalism,* edited by Huthmacher and Susman, 128–32.

Hodgson, Geoff. "Persuasion, Expectations and the Limits to Keynes." *In Keynes' Economics,* edited by Tony Lawson and Hashem Pesaran, 10–45. Armonk, N.Y.: Sharpe, 1985.

Hofstadter, Richard. *The American Political Tradition.* New York: Vintage, 1974.

Hoover, Herbert. *The Memoirs of Herbert Hoover: The Cabinet and the Presidency 1920–1933.* New York: MacMillan, 1951.

———. *Public Papers of the Presidents of the United States.* 4 volumes. Washington, D.C.: Government Printing Office, 1974, 1975, 1976, 1977.

"The Hoover Atmosphere." *New York Times,* April 28, 1929, sec. 3, p. 4

"Hoover Looks Forward." *New Republic,* October 15, 1930, p. 220.

"The Hoover Method." *New York Times,* December 6, 1929, p. 26.

"Hoover Plays His Part." *New Republic,* December 11, 1929, p. 55.

Houck, Davis W. "Rhetoric, Science and Economic Prophecy: John Maynard Keynes's Correspondence with Franklin D. Roosevelt." In *New Economics Criticism,* edited by Martha Woodmansee and Mark Osteen, 352–64. New York: Routledge, 1999.

"Humpty Dumpty Hoover." *New Republic,* June 25, 1930, pp. 137–39.

"In Brown-Derbyland." *Time,* October 15, 1928, p. 12.

James, E. J. "The State as an Economic Factor." *Science* 7 (1886): 485–91.

Johnson, Walter. *1600 Pennsylvania Avenue: Presidents and The People, 1929–1959*. Boston: Little, Brown, 1960.

Joslin, Theodore G. *Hoover Off the Record*. Garden City, N.Y.: Doubleday, Doran, 1934.

Katona, George. *Essays on Behavioral Economics*. Ann Arbor, Mich.: Survey Research Center, 1980.

———. *The Powerful Consumer*. New York: McGraw-Hill, 1960.

———. *Psychological Analysis of Economic Behavior*. New York: McGraw-Hill, 1951.

Kennedy, David. *Over Here: The First World War and American Society*. New York: Oxford University Press, 1980.

Kennedy, Susan Estabrook. *The Banking Crisis of 1933*. Lexington: University Press of Kentucky, 1973.

Kent, Frank R. "How Strong is Roosevelt?" *Scribner's Magazine*, April, 1932, pp. 199–203.

Kernell, Samuel. *Going Public: New Strategies of Presidential Leadership*. Washington, D.C.: Congressional Quarterly Inc., 1986.

Keynes, John Maynard. *The Economic Consequences of the Peace*. New York: Harcourt, Brace, and Howe, 1920.

———. "The General Theory of Employment." *Quarterly Journal of Economics* 48 (1937): 209–23.

———. *A General Theory of Employment, Interest, and Money*. San Diego: Harcourt, Brace, Jovanovich, 1953.

———. *The Means to Prosperity*. London: MacMillan, 1933.

Kiewe, Amos. "The Body as Proof: Franklin D. Roosevelt's Preparations for the 1932 Presidential Race." *Argumentation & Advocacy* 36 (1999): 88–100.

———. "A Dress Rehearsal for a Presidential Campaign: FDR's Embodied 'Run' for the 1928 New York Governorship." *Southern Communication Journal* 64 (1999): 155–67.

———. "Introduction." In *The Modern Presidency and Crisis Rhetoric*, edited by Amos Kiewe, xv–xxxvii. New York: Praeger, 1994.

Kim, James. "Stocks Retreat on Fed Speech." *USA Today*, October 9, 1997, sec. B, p.1.

King, Robert D. "Franklin D. Roosevelt's Second Inaugural Address." *Quarterly Journal of Speech* 23 (1937): 439–44.

Kingsbury, H. D. "Roosevelt to be Freed of Heavy Campaign Work." *New York Herald-Tribune*, October 3, 1928, p. 16.

Klamer, Arjo. *Conversations with Economists*. Totowa, N.J.: Rowman & Allanheld, 1983.

Krock, Arthur. *Memoirs*. New York: Funk and Wagnalls, 1968.

Lachmann, L. M. "G. L. S. Shackle's Place in the History of Subjectivist Thought." In *Unknowledge and Choice in Economics*, edited by Stephen F. Frowen, 1–8. New York: St. Martin's 1990.

Lash, Joseph P. *Eleanor and Franklin.* New York: W. W. Norton, 1971.

Lee, Robert M. "Nothing But Smith as Gentlemen from Bowery Pack Gallery." *Los Angeles Times,* June 27, 1924, p. 3.

Lehman, David. *Signs of the Times: Deconstruction and the Fall of Paul de Man.* New York: Poseidon, 1991.

Leuchtenburg, William E. *The FDR Years.* New York: Columbia University Press, 1995.

———. *Franklin D. Roosevelt and the New Deal, 1932–1940.* New York: Harper & Row, 1963.

———. *The Perils of Prosperity 1914–1932.* Chicago: University of Chicago Press, 1958.

Liebovich, Louis W. *Bylines in Despair: Herbert Hoover, the Great Depression, and the U.S. News Media.* New York: Praeger, 1994.

Lindley, Ernest K. *The Roosevelt Revolution.* New York: Viking, 1933.

Lippman, Theo, Jr. *The Squire of Warm Springs.* Chicago: Playboy, 1977.

Lippmann, Walter. "The Peculiar Weakness of Mr. Hoover." *Harper's Magazine,* June, 1930, pp. 1–7.

———. "The Permanent New Deal." *Yale Review* 24 (1935): 649–67.

———. *Public Philosopher: Selected Letters of Walter Lippmann,* edited by John Morton Blum. New York: Ticknor & Fields, 1985.

———. *Public Opinion.* New York: Macmillan, 1956.

———. "Today and Tomorrow." *New York Herald-Tribune,* March 1, 1933, p. 15.

Lisio, Donald J. *The President and Protest: Hoover, MacArthur, and the Bonus March.* Rev. ed. New York: Fordham University Press, 1994.

Lloyd, Craig. *Aggressive Introvert: Herbert Hoover and Public Relations Management 1912–1932.* Columbus: Ohio State University Press, 1972.

"The Long Pull." *New York Herald-Tribune,* June 18, 1933, p. 6.

Looker, Earle. *The American Way: Franklin Roosevelt in Action.* New York: John Day, 1933.

"Looking for Mr. Roosevelt." *New York Times,* March 4, 1933, p. 12.

Love, Adelaide. "Go Forth." *Chicago Tribune,* March 3, 1933, p. 12.

Lowitt, Richard. *George W. Norris: The Persistence of a Progressive.* Urbana: University of Illinois Press, 1971.

Lyons, Eugene. *Our Unknown Ex-President: A Portrait of Herbert Hoover.* Garden City, N.Y.: Doubleday, 1948.

Lyotard, Jean-Francois. *The Postmodern Condition: A Report on Knowledge.* Trans. Geoff Bennington and Brian Massumi. Minneapolis: University of Minnesota Press, 1984.

McCloskey, Donald N. "The Art of Forecasting: From Ancient to Modern Times." *Cato Journal* 12 (1992): 23–43.

———. *If You're So Smart: The Narrative of Economic Expertise.* Chicago: University of Chicago Press, 1990.

———. *Knowledge and Persuasion in Economics.* Cambridge: Cambridge University Press, 1994.

McCormick, Anne O'Hare. "A Year of the Hoover Method," *New York Times,* March 2, 1930, sec. 5, p. 1.

McFadden, Louis T. "Convalescent Finance." *Saturday Evening Post,* February 15, 1930, pp. 5, 145–46, 149.

"Major Surgery for the Depression." *New Republic,* November 2, 1932, pp. 314–15.

Marshall, Alfred. *Principles of Economics.* London: Macmillan, 1890.

Medhurst, Martin J. "The Academic Study of Public Address: A Tradition in Transition." In *Landmark Essays in American Public Address,* edited by Martin J. Medhurst, iii–xliii. Davis, Calif.: Hermagoras, 1993.

———. "Public Address and Significant Scholarship: Four Challenges to the Rhetorical Renaissance." In *Texts in Context: Critical Dialogues on Significant Episodes in American Political Rhetoric,* edited by Michael C. Leff and Fred J. Kauffeld, 29–42. Davis, Calif.: Hermagoras, 1989.

Miller, Nathan. *FDR: An Intimate History.* Garden City, N.Y.: Doubleday, 1983.

Mirowski, Philip. *More Heat Than Light.* Cambridge: Cambridge University Press, 1989.

———, ed. *Natural Images in Economic Thought.* Cambridge: Cambridge University Press, 1994.

Moley, Raymond. *After Seven Years.* New York: Harper & Brothers, 1939.

———. *The First New Deal.* New York: Harcourt, Brace & World, 1966.

———. "Reappraising Hoover." *Newsweek,* June 14, 1948, p. 100.

Moley, Raymond, Rexford G. Tugwell, and Ernest K. Lindley. "Symposium: Early Days of the New Deal." In *The Thirties,* edited by Morton J. Frisch and Martin Diamond, 124–43. De Kalb: Northern Illinois University Press, 1968.

"Mr. Hoover Bids Us Hope." *New York Times,* May 3, 1930, p. 18

"Mr. Hoover on Peace and Panic." *New York Evening Post,* November 12, 1929, p. 12.

"Mr. Roosevelt's Tariff Nonsense." *Nation,* September 28, 1932, p. 270.

Muth, John F. "Rational Expectations and the Theory of Price Movements." *Econometrica* 29 (1961): 315–35.

Myers, William Starr, and Walter H. Newton, eds. *The Hoover Administration: A Documented Narrative.* New York: Charles Scribner's Sons, 1936.

Nash, George H. "'An American Epic': Herbert Hoover and Belgian Relief in World War I." *Prologue* 21 (1989): 75–86.

———. *The Life of Herbert Hoover: The Humanitarian, 1914–1917.* New York: Norton, 1988.

Nash, Lee, ed. *Understanding Herbert Hoover.* Stanford, Calif.: Hoover Institution Press, 1987.

"Nature's Course." *Saturday Evening Post,* October 1, 1932, p. 20.

Newcomb, Simon. "Can Economists Agree Upon the Basis of their Teachings." *Science* 8 (1886): 25–26.

Nichols, Marie Hochmuth, ed. *A History and Criticism of American Public Address.*
New York: Russell and Russell, 1965.

Noelle-Neumann, Elisabeth. "The Public as Prophet: Findings From Continuous
Survey Research and Their Implications for Early Diagnosis of Economic
Growth." *International Journal of Public Opinion Research* 1 (1989):
136–50.

O'Donnell, Rod M. "Keynes on Probability, Expectations and Uncertainty." In
Keynes as Philosopher-Economist, edited by O'Donnell, 3–60. New York:
St. Martin's, 1991.

Oliver, Robert T. "The Speech that Established Roosevelt's Reputation." *Quarterly
Journal of Speech* 31 (1945): 274–82.

Olson, James S. "The End of Voluntarism: Herbert Hoover and the National Credit
Corporation." *Annals of Iowa* 41 (1972): 1104–13.

———. "Herbert Clark Hoover." In *American Orators of the Twentieth Century:
Critical Studies and Sources,* edited by Bernard K. Duffy and Halford R. Ryan,
203–208. Westport, Conn.: Greenwood, 1987.

———. *Herbert Hoover and the Reconstruction Finance Corporation.* Ames: Iowa
State University Press, 1977.

———. "Herbert Hoover and the 'War' on the Depression." *Palimpsest* 54 (1973):
26–31.

———. *Saving Capitalism: The Reconstruction Finance Corporation and the New
Deal, 1933–1940.* Princeton, N.J.: Princeton University Press, 1988.

"One Hundred Doses, One Dollar." *Saturday Evening Post,* September 26, 1931,
p. 22.

Oulahan, Richard. *The Man Who . . . : The Story of the Democratic National
Convention of 1932.* New York: The Dial Press, 1971.

Paine, R. F. "Over the Top." *Pittsburgh Press,* March 4, 1933, p. 4.

Palmer, Kyle D. "Inaugural Hope High." *Los Angeles Times,* March 4, 1933, p. 1.

———. "Ku Klux Hood and Gown Foil Democratic Craft." *Los Angeles Times,*
June 27, 1924, sec. 1, p. 5.

Parrish, Michael E. *Anxious Decades.* New York: Norton, 1992.

Parsons, Stephen D. "Time, Expectations and Subjectivism: Prolegomena to a
Dynamic Economics." *Cambridge Economic Journal* 15 (1991): 405–23.

Peel, Roy V., and Thomas C. Donnelly. *The 1932 Campaign: An Analysis.* New
York: Farrar & Rinehart, 1935.

Perkins, Frances. *The Roosevelt I Knew.* New York: Viking, 1946.

Picchi, Blaise. *The Five Weeks of Giuseppe Zangara.* Chicago: Academy Chicago,
1998.

Pirsig, Robert M. *Zen and the Art of Motorcycle Maintenance.* New York: Morrow,
1974.

"A Plea for Convalescence." *Commonweal,* April 27, 1932, p. 705–706.

"Political Notes." *Time,* June 15, 1931, pp. 16–17.

Post, Jerrold M., and Robert S. Robins. *When Illness Strikes the Leader.* New
Haven, Conn.: Yale University Press, 1993.

"President and Congress." *New York Times*, June 18, 1933, p. 4.

"Presidential Leadership." *New York Times*, March 9, 1930, sec. 3, p. 4.

Pringle, Henry F. "Franklin D. Roosevelt—Perched on the Bandwagon." *Nation*, April 27, 1932, pp. 487–89.

"Prohibition." *Time*, April 27, 1931, p. 18.

Pusey, Merlo J. *Eugene Meyer.* New York: Knopf, 1974.

Putnam, George E. "The Hardened Arteries of Business." *Atlantic Monthly*, October, 1931, pp. 504–13.

Ragsdale, Warner B. "The Campaign Trail in 1932." In *The Making of the New Deal*, edited by Katie Louchheim, 1–9. Cambridge: Harvard University Press, 1983.

Reid, Ronald F., ed. *American Rhetorical Discourse*. 2d ed. Prospect Heights, Ill.: Waveland, 1995.

Reinsdorf, Walter D. "'This Nation Will Remain Neutral': Franklin D. Roosevelt Uses Inclusive and Exclusive Terms to Justify a Policy." *Today's Speech* 22 (1974): 17–21.

Renaud, Ralph E. "Mac Slips on Sidewalks of N.Y.; Bang! Away Goes His Majority." *New York Herald-Tribune*, June 27, 1924, p. 5.

"The Return of Hope." *Pittsburgh Press*, March 3, 1933, p. 1.

Richards, I. A. "An Experiment in Criticism." In *Richards on Rhetoric*, edited by Ann E. Berthoff, 25–37. New York: Oxford University Press, 1991.

Rogers, Naomi. *Dirt and Disease: Polio Before FDR*. New Brunswick, N.J.: Rutgers University Press, 1992.

Rogers, Will. *Los Angeles Times*, March 6, 1933, p. 1.

Rohler, Lloyd, and Roger Cook, eds. *Great Speeches for Criticism & Analysis*. 2d ed. Greenwood, Ind.: Alistair Press, 1993.

Rollins, Alfred B., Jr. *Roosevelt and Howe*. New York: Knopf, 1962.

———. "The View from the State House: FDR." In *The Hoover Presidency: A Reappraisal*, edited by Martin J. Fausold and George T. Mazuzan, 123–33.

Romasco, Albert U. "Hoover-Roosevelt and the Great Depression: A Historiographical Inquiry Into a Perennial Comparison." In *The New Deal*, edited by John Braeman, Robert H. Bremner and David Brody, 3–26. Columbus: Ohio State University Press, 1975.

———. *The Poverty of Abundance*. New York: Oxford University Press, 1965.

Romer, Christina D. "The Great Crash and the Onset of the Great Depression." *Quarterly Journal of Economics* 105 (1990): 597–624.

Roosevelt, Elliott, ed. *F.D.R.: His Personal Letters, 1905–1928, Volume One*. New York: Duell, Sloan, and Pearce, 1950.

———, ed. *F.D.R.: His Personal Letters, 1928–1945, Volume Two*. New York: Duell, Sloan, and Pearce, 1950.

Roosevelt, Franklin D. *The Public Papers and Addresses of Franklin D. Roosevelt*. Vols. 1 and 2. Edited by Samuel I. Rosenman. New York: Random House, 1937, 1938.

————. *Public Papers of Franklin D. Roosevelt: Forty-Eighth Governor of the State of New York.* 3 vols. Albany: J. B. Lyon Company, 1931, 1932, 1933.

Roosevelt, James, and Sidney Shalett, *Affectionately, F.D.R.* New York: Harcourt, Brace, 1959.

"Roosevelt Boom Grows Despite His Reticence." *New York Herald-Tribune,* June 28, 1924, p. 6.

"Roosevelt Puts Heart in America." *Pittsburgh Press,* March 5, 1933, p. 8.

"Roosevelt Reveals His Program to the Country." *Literary Digest,* October 1, 1932, pp. 5–7.

"Roosevelt Steps Left and Right." *New Republic,* September 28, 1932, pp. 164–65.

"Roosevelt Wins." *Nation,* July 13, 1932, p. 22.

"Roosevelt's Life Insured for $500,000 by Warm Springs." *New York Times,* October 18, 1930, p. 1.

"Roosevelt's Speeches." *World Tomorrow,* October 5, 1932, pp. 316–17.

Rosen, Eliot A. *Hoover, Roosevelt and the Brains Trust: From Depression to New Deal.* New York: Columbia University Press, 1977.

Rosenman, Samuel I. *Working with Roosevelt.* New York: Harper & Brothers, 1952.

Rothbard, Murray N. In *Herbert Hoover and the Crisis of American Capitalism,* edited by J. Joseph Huthmacher and Warren I. Susman, 35–58, 121–27. Cambridge, Mass.: Schenkman, 1973.

Rotheim, Roy J. "Keynes and the Language of Probability and Uncertainty." *Journal of Post Keynesian Economics* 11 (1988): 82–99.

Rowe, James L., Jr. "Hoover, We Hardly Knew Ye." *Washington Post,* August 23, 1992, sec. C, p. 2.

Ryan, Halford Ross. *Franklin D. Roosevelt's Rhetorical Presidency.* New York: Greenwood, 1988.

————. "Roosevelt's First Inaugural: A Study of Technique." *Quarterly Journal of Speech* 65 (1979): 137–49.

————, ed. *The Inaugural Addresses of Twentieth-Century American Presidents.* Westport, Conn.: Praeger, 1993.

Samuels, Warren J. "'Truth' and 'Discourse' in the Social Construction of Reality: An Essay on the Relation of Knowledge to Socioeconomic Policy." *Journal of Post Keynesian Economics* 13 (1991): 511–24.

Sargent, James E. *Roosevelt and the Hundred Days: Struggle for the Early New Deal.* New York: Garland, 1981.

Scarry, Elaine. *The Body in Pain.* New York: Oxford University Press, 1985.

Schiffman, Joseph. "Observations on Roosevelt's Literary Style." *Quarterly Journal of Speech* 35 (1949): 222–26.

Schlesinger, Arthur M., Jr. *The Coming of the New Deal.* Boston: Houghton Mifflin, 1958.

Schwarz, Jordan. *The Interregnum of Despair.* Urbana: University of Illinois Press, 1970.

Scott, Robert L. "Against Rhetorical Theory: Tripping to Serendip." In *Texts In Context: Critical Dialogues on Significant Episodes in American Political Rhetoric,* edited by Michael C. Leff and Fred J. Kauffeld, 1–9.

Seligman, Edwin R. A. "Change in the Tenets of Political Economy with Time." *Science* 7 (1886): 375–82.

Simons, Herbert W., and Aram A. Aghazarian, eds. *Form, Genre, and the Study of Political Discourse.* Columbia: University of South Carolina Press, 1986.

Skidelsky, Robert. "Keynes' Philosophy of Practice and Economic Policy." In *Keynes as Philosopher-Economist,* edited by Rod M. O'Donnell, 104–23.

Skowronek, Stephen. "Franklin Roosevelt and the Modern Presidency." *Studies in American Political Development* 6 (1992): 322–58.

———. *The Politics Presidents Make: Leadership from John Adams to George Bush.* Cambridge: Harvard University Press, 1993.

Smith, Adam. *Essays on Philosophical Subjects.* Edited by W. P. D. Wightman and J. C. Bryce. Oxford: Clarendon, 1980.

Smith, Gene. *The Shattered Dream.* New York: Morrow, 1970.

Smith, Richard Mayo. "Methods of Investigation in Political Economy." *Science* 8 (1886): 81–87.

Smith, Richard Norton. *An Uncommon Man.* New York: Simon & Schuster, 1984.

Snyder, J. Richard. "Hoover and the Hawley-Smoot Tariff: A View of Executive Leadership." *Annals of Iowa* 41 (1973): 1173–89.

The Statistical History of the United States. Compiled by Ben J. Wattenberg. New York: Basic Books, 1976.

Steel, Ronald. *Walter Lippmann and the American Century.* Boston: Little, Brown, 1980.

Stein, Herbert. *The Fiscal Revolution in America.* Chicago: University of Chicago Press, 1969.

———. "The Washington Economist." *American Enterprise* 5 (1994): 6–10.

Stelzner, Herman. "'War Message,' December 8, 1941: An Approach to Language." *Speech Monographs* 33 (1966): 419–37.

Stiles, Lela. *The Man Behind Roosevelt: The Story of Louis McHenry Howe.* Cleveland: World, 1954.

"Still To Be Done." *Business Week,* October 14, 1931, n.p.

Stimson, Henry L., and McGeorge Bundy. *On Active Service in Peace and War.* New York: Harper, 1947.

Sumner, W. G. *Science* 7 (1886): 221–28.

Taussig, F. W. "Doctors, Economists and the Depression." *Harper's Magazine,* August, 1932, pp. 355–65.

Thiemann, William. "President Hoover's Efforts on Behalf of FDR's 1932 Nomination." *Presidential Studies Quarterly* 24 (1994): 87–91.

Tugwell, Rexford G. *The Brains Trust.* New York: Viking, 1968.

———. *The Democratic Roosevelt.* Garden City, N.Y.: Doubleday, 1957.

———. *In Search of Roosevelt.* Cambridge: Harvard University Press, 1972.

———. *Roosevelt's Revolution: The First Year—A Personal Perspective.* New York: Macmillan, 1977.

Tulis, Jeffrey K. *The Rhetorical Presidency.* Princeton: Princeton University Press, 1987.

Turner, Kathleen J., ed. *Doing Rhetorical History.* Tuscaloosa: University of Alabama Press, 1998.

"An Unfair Sacrifice." *New York Herald-Tribune,* October 3, 1928, p. 26.

U.S. Congress, House and Senate, Joint Economic Committee. *The Quality of the Nation's Economic Statistics, 99th Cong., 2d sess., 1986.* Washington, D.C.: Government Printing Office, 1986.

Vann, Robert L. "Confidence Has Arrived." *Pittsburgh Courier,* March 11, 1933, p. 1.

Villard, Oswald G. "The Roosevelt Candidacy." *Nation,* June 1, 1932, p. 612.

———. "An Unconventional Convention." *Nation,* July 9, 1924, pp. 35–36.

Ward, Geoffrey C. *A First-Class Temperament.* New York: Harper & Row, 1989.

Warn, W. A. "Roosevelt in Line for 1932 After Trip." *New York Times,* July 6, 1930, sec. 2, p.1.

Warren, Harris Gaylord. *Herbert Hoover and the Great Depression.* New York: Oxford University Press, 1959.

Waters, W. W., and William C. White. *B.E.F.: The Whole Story of the Bonus Army.* New York: Arno, 1969.

"The West and the Bull Market." *Kansas City Star,* September 18, 1929, n.p.

White, William Allen. *The Autobiography of William Allen White.* New York: MacMillan, 1946.

———. *The Selected Letters of William Allen White 1899–1943.* Edited by Walter Johnson. New York: Greenwood, 1968.

Wiegele, Thomas C. "Presidential Physicians and Presidential Health Care: Some Theoretical and Operational Considerations Related to Political Decision Making." *Presidential Studies Quarterly* 20 (1990): 71–89.

Williams, William Appleman. *Some Presidents: From Wilson to Nixon.* New York: Vintage, 1972.

Wills, Garry. *Certain Trumpets.* New York: Simon & Schuster, 1994.

Wilson, Joan Hoff. *Herbert Hoover: Forgotten Progressive.* Boston: Little, Brown, 1975.

Wilson, John Frederick. *Public Religion in American Culture.* Philadelphia: Temple University Press, 1979.

Wolfe, W. Beram. "Psycho-analyzing the Depression," *Forum,* April, 1932, pp. 209–14.

Wood, John Cunningham, ed. *John Maynard Keynes: Critical Assessments.* Volume 2. London: Croom Helm, 1983.

"The Wrong Medicine." *Business Week,* January 21, 1931, p. 44.

Zarefsky, David. *President Johnson's War on Poverty: Rhetoric and History.* Tuscaloosa: University of Alabama Press, 1986.

Zernicke, Paul Haskell. *Pitching the Presidency: How Presidents Depict the Office.* New York: Praeger, 1994.

Zieger, Robert H. *Republicans and Labor, 1919–1929.* Lexington: University of Kentucky Press, 1969.

Zullow, Harold M. "Pessimistic Rumination in Popular Songs and Newsmagazines Predict Economic Recession via Decreased Optimism and Spending." *Journal of Economic Psychology* 12 (1991): 501–26.

Presidential Rhetoric Series
Martin J. Medhurst, General Editor

Medhurst, Martin J., ed. *Beyond the Rhetorical Presidency.* 1996

Medhurst, Martin J. and H. W. Brands, eds. *Critical Reflections on the Cold War: Linking Rhetoric and History.* 2000.

Pauley, Garth E. *The Modern Presidency and Civil Rights: Rhetoric on Race from Roosevelt to Nixon.* 2001.

Index

ISBN 1-58544-109-0

90000